EVERY EMPLOYEE
A MANAGER
Third Edition

M. Scott Myers, Ph.D.

San Diego • Toronto • Amsterdam • Sydney

Library of Congress Cataloging-in-Publication Data
Myers, M. Scott (Marvin Scott), 1922-
    Every employee a manager / M. Scott Myers.
        p.   cm.
    Includes bibliographical references and index.
    ISBN 0-88390-259-1 (hard : alk. paper)
    1. Personnel management.   2. Psychology, Industrial. 3. Job
enrichment.   I. Title.
HF5549.M93   1990   90-21040
658.3—dc20   CIP

Pfeiffer & Company
8517 Production Avenue
San Diego, California 92121
Telephone (619) 578-5900
FAX (619) 578-2042

Editing: Ann Bertram
Cover and Design: Paul Bond
Page Composition: Judy Whalen

This book is printed on acid-free, recycled stock that meets the
minimum GPO and EPA specifications for recycled paper.

Contents

Foreword

Scott Myers is a pioneer in the empowerment process, having formulated the theory of *every employee a manager* in the early '60s while employed by Texas Instruments. The concept, which few could comfortably embrace at the time and which was even derided by some, is no longer novel but, rather, has become the norm for vanguard organizations.

Except for the first three chapters, the book is an update of previous editions, presenting a wide-ranging analysis of leadership practices and management systems that shape organizational cultures. Chapter 1 describes an old problem under the new label *functional silo syndrome*. The characteristics of cultures are presented along with processes for overcoming functional silos and other barriers to change.

Chapter 2 introduces an innovative three-dimensional prescription for reward systems, which shows the importance of having a balance of individual monetary, group monetary, and nonmonetary reward systems. Company examples in this chapter make a strong case for nonmonetary rewards as the key ingredients for enhancing commitment and teamwork. Moreover, nonmonetary reward systems are free (except for the priceless ingredient of facilitative leadership, which is often more scarce than money).

Chapter 3 presents a succinct analysis of the Toyota organizational system, which is widely emulated in Western companies. An analysis of Normandale South's large disk-drive manufacturing plant near Minneapolis (Normandale South is a division of Seagate) illustrates the empowerment of employees in a flattened organization and the role changes essential to success.

This edition places more emphasis on application than on theory. The theoretical foundation that was highlighted in the first chapter of previous editions has been moved to Appendix A as optional reading for those who wish to review the theoretical underpinnings of principles presented throughout the book. As before, theories presented here are examined to show their common purpose in enhancing human effectiveness and that presumed differences are more often semantic than substantive.

This update will be useful to readers who already accept the notion of empowerment, because the book contains specific guidelines and procedures to help leaders reinvent their organizations to meet the challenge of global competition and the changing values and expectations of an increasingly enlightened populace. It will also be a useful reference for students of organizational psychology and industrial engineering and is written in simple language that makes it a useful reference for worker-manager teams in the workplace.

October, 1990

> Warren Bennis
> Distinguished Professor
>   of Business Administration
> University of Southern California

Preface

When the first edition of *Every Employee a Manager* was published in 1970, I was admonished that I was ahead of my time—that people were not ready to accept the degree of empowerment recommended in the book. In fact, the publisher suggested that I retitle it.

Today the first edition is behind the times, and this third edition contains concepts that exceed the fondest fantasies I had in 1970. Of course, some ideas will never become obsolete, such as Allan Mogensen's Work Simplification theory (Uris, 1965). However, Shigeo Shingo (1985) has amplified on Work Simplification in ways not anticipated by Mogensen. New sections in this edition include an update on reward systems, on just-in-time principles (JIT) and value-adding management (VAM), and on the functional silo syndrome.

A few managers still cannot accept the first edition, but they are being replaced by leaders who can. The new leaders are reading exciting books such as *Re-inventing the Corporation* (Naisbitt & Aburdene, 1985), *Thriving on Chaos* (Peters, 1988), *Japanese Manufacturing Techniques* and *Building a Chain of Customers* (Schonberger, 1982, 1990), and *On Becoming a Leader* (Bennis, 1989). This update of *Every Employee a Manager* in part reflects my proprietary feelings about the concept. More importantly, I hope to show that innovation never ends.

The first edition cited Texas Instruments (TI) as an exemplary model of innovative management. Texas Instruments is still innovating but is being surpassed by organizations that have more successfully incorporated the management of change into their leadership styles. Relevant references to TI remain in this update, but further examples are drawn from organizations recognized as leaders in the management of innovation.

New leaders are learning to learn from each other, to overcome the not-invented-here syndrome, and to abandon outmoded success formulas. They are benefiting from professional associations, foremost of which is AME (Association for Manufacturing Excellence), a new and rapidly expanding membership guided by Robert W. Hall, author and professor of operations management at Indiana University. AME coordinates workshop-tours of leading-edge organizations and publishes hands-on descriptions of success stories in *Target*, its quarterly journal.

Management of change is the key function of a leader, in regard to both human effort and technology. The responsibility is not new, of course, but is becoming increasingly complicated as world cultures interact more with one another.

Warren Bennis[*] (1989, pp. 44, 45) draws a sharp distinction between the leader, who masters the context of his mission, and the manager, who surrenders to it:

- The manager administers; the leader innovates.

- The manager is a copy; the leader is an original.

- The manager maintains; the leader develops.

- The manager focuses on systems and structure; the leader focuses on people.

- The manager relies on control; the leader inspires trust.

- The manager has a short-range view; the leader has a long-range perspective.

- The manager asks how and when; the leader asks what and why.

- The manager has his eye always on the bottom line; the leader . . . on the horizon.

- The manager imitates; the leader originates.

- The manager accepts the status quo; the leader challenges it.

- The manager is the classic good soldier; the leader is his own person.

- The manager does things right; the leader does the right thing.

This is not to say that managers cannot be good leaders, nor is this list intended to place a stigma on anyone who has the word

---

[*] Adapted from W. Bennis, *On Becoming a Leader*, 1989, Reading, MA: Addison-Wesley. Used with permission of the author.

manager in his or her job title. Rather, the Bennis book offers guidelines for those who wish to become better leaders.

In reality people do not fall neatly into one category or the other, as there are leadership and managerial traits in all of us. We have frequently heard allegations that the Japanese are copycats who imitate the managerial techniques and technology developed elsewhere. These allegations would seem to put Japan in the managerial category. However, the Japanese have exhibited unsurpassed leadership in the management of both technology and human resources. Akio Morita, as representative of post-World War II Japanese entrepreneurs, has demonstrated a creative amalgamation of imitation and originality in creating and developing the world-famous Sony corporation. Will success spoil Japanese companies as it has some American organizations? Only time will tell.

The Bennis model serves a useful purpose in defining the philosophy and techniques necessary for managing change and has been useful to me in describing the qualities that enable the downtrodden, subservient, and rebellious to exercise responsible leadership in managing their jobs.

September 1990

M. Scott Myers
Fort Walton Beach, Florida

REFERENCES

Bennis, W. (1989). *On becoming a leader*. Reading, MA: Addison- Wesley.
Morita, A. (1988). *Made in Japan*. New York: E.P. Dutton.
Naisbitt, J., & Aburdene, P. (1985). *Re-inventing the corporation*. New York: Warner Books.
Peters, T. (1988). *Thriving on chaos*. New York: Alfred A. Knopf.
Schonberger, R.J. (1982). *Japanese manufacturing techniques*. New York: Free Press.
Schonberger, R.J. (1990). *Building a Chain of Customers*. New York: Free Press.
Shingo, S. (1985). *A revolution in manufacturing: The SMED system*. Cambridge, MA: Productivity Press.
Uris, A. (1965, September). Mogy's Work Simplification is working new miracles. *Factory*, p. 112.

A master in the art of living
draws no sharp distinction
between his work and his play,
his labor and his leisure,
his mind and his body,
his education and his recreation.
He hardly knows which is which.
He simply pursues his vision
of excellence through whatever
he is doing and leaves
others to determine
whether he is working or playing.
To himself he always seems
to be doing both.

Author unknown; quoted by Peter T. McKinney, Exxon Chemical Company, U.S.A., Houston, Texas, August 11, 1977.

1

Barriers to Change

Walt Kelly's Pogo could have been talking about business leaders when he said, "We have met the enemy and they is us!" His comment applies to the leaders of many good old American institutions—people caught up in the struggle to change their bureaucratic, reactive organizations into nimble and proactive enterprises.

Several cases in point might be General Motors, Kodak, and Goodyear. Although they have strong earning records and have served their customers and shareholders well in the past, they are finding it difficult to keep up with the changing times. These grand old companies had always been industry leaders. Because they had been told for so long that they were "the best in the business," they had trouble acknowledging new competitors who could produce high-quality products at costs lower than their own. At first, their managers refused to recognize the powerful new realities, and the transition was traumatic; however, senior executives realized that to survive and succeed, their proud old businesses would have to reinvent themselves.

THE ERA OF COMMAND AND CONTROL

The bosses of these tottering giants have a long history of imposing command-and-control tactics on their underlings. Their management styles were strongly top-down and authoritarian; organizational structures were deeply layered on both the vertical and horizontal planes; and the jobs of subordinates were narrow in scope, boring, and easy to control. Labor relations in the unionized companies were legalistic, confrontational, and colored by mistrust; performance expectations, which were usually at the heart of the adversarial work environment, were imposed by top management, resented by middle management, and contested by the union. In nonunion companies the damage was done with paternalism and bureaucratic controls. Organizations thus spent more energy on internal issues and conflicts than on serving customers.

Their managers eventually learned that if they wanted to form nimble and proactive organizations, they would have to redesign their total corporate cultures. Of the many barriers faced when trying to change time-honored traditions, interfunctional conflicts are among the most pervasive and inhibiting. All organizations are vulnerable to this corporate malady; but the worst cases are usually found in large, mature bureaucracies. Over the decades, command-and-control efforts to cope with mushrooming growth and complexity have led to what former Goodyear executive Phil Ensor refers to as the gradual formation of a forest of towering *functional silos* across the corporate landscape.

THE FUNCTIONAL SILO SYNDROME

Corporations and government bureaucracies have sets of silos just like those that dot America's rural landscape. Although not physically visible, they make their presence known through the structure of management systems and the behavior of employees. In fact, corporate silos generally outnumber farm silos.

The silos of the various corporate functions (engineering, manufacturing, purchasing, personnel, sales, unions, and so on) create formidable barriers that frustrate attempts to carry out corporate-wide changes.

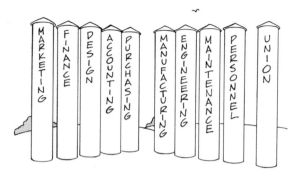

Each silo gradually develops its unique culture, which is reflected in buzzwords and terminology not easily understood by members of other silos. Because a culture is circumscribed by its language, intersilo communication is difficult.

Although the silos are separated functionally, each one tries to keep tabs on any other silo whose function might influence its own.

Manufacturing tries to second-guess engineering, personnel snoops into union strategy, and marketing tries to anticipate finance's edicts.

Some silos develop an early-detection-and-warning system so they can be the first to learn what is going on in corporate headquarters or to identify the business strategy of competing silos.

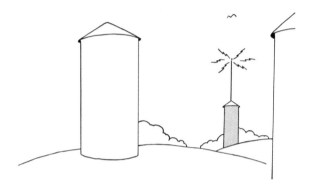

Others protect their autonomy with organizational armor plate to prevent intervention and penetration by hostile silos. This insulation also prevents silo residents from escaping or fraternizing with the enemy.

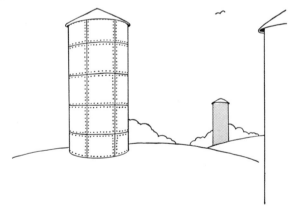

Some silos have selective intercourse with other silos, employing a moat-and-drawbridge system to control who shall enter and who shall leave. This approach also prevents the serfs from coming and going except during official shift changes when the bridge is down.

Other silos seem to be governed by a more aggressive policy of divide and conquer; they equip themselves with the clout to intimi-

date would-be predators. Although these silos are armed ostensibly for self-protection, if a competing silo makes an unfriendly overture, the warring mentality of the commanding general often leads him to strike a fatal blow.

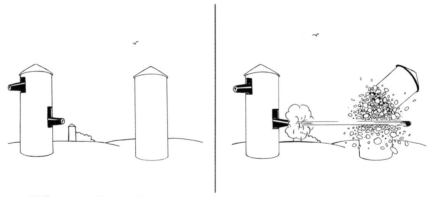

When a silo is destroyed, some functions are left untended. Before the corporation discovers that it can function well (perhaps better) without the services provided by the stricken silo, the aggressor declares, "I am in charge!" and hastens to confiscate the duties of the vanquished silo, thereby adding prestige and clout to its empire. The successful maneuver of the conquering silo does not go unnoticed by competing silos, who then begin adopting similar aggressive strategies.

Meanwhile, the presiding chief executive officers (CEO) survey their domains with equanimity and pride from their executive suites. They think that they know what is going on in the silos because their silo chiefs recite their own achievements during weekly staff meet-

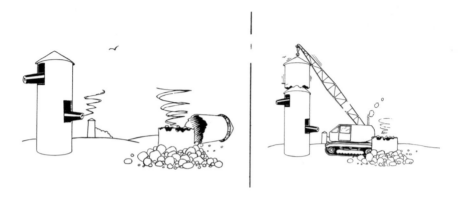

ings and quarterly reviews. They bring the CEO encouraging numbers on cash flow, profitability, cost reductions, and productivity improvement. The CEO is protected from information about insurrections or impending disasters within the silos because the silo bosses, having witnessed the hapless fate of messengers, remain mute on developments that might furrow their tribal chieftain's brow.

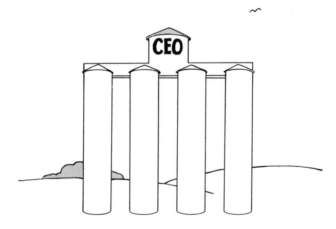

The view from within the silos is quite different. The natives are restless and frustrated by their circumscribed jobs. Wherever they turn, they are confronted by legalistic and bureaucratic constraints, unclear goals, lack of information, and the multilayered status symbols that accompany a caste system. Their bosses have a procedure-manual mentality and are reactive fire fighters rather than problem-solving leaders. Management seems more interested in exacting obedience and preventing contamination from other silos than in developing a chain of customers (Schonberger, 1990).

The elements of the functional silo syndrome may be summarized as follows:

Separate identities. Each silo has its own separate identity. Its members are employed by the silo and are loyal to it first, to the company second, and only incidentally to their customers. Moreover, the members of the corporate finance committee, who dominate most command-and-control organizations, seem to be primarily interested in receiving a proper monthly balance sheet from each department. The committee is less interested in hearing that a department has made a contribution to the long-term success of the company.

Closed cultures. Silos do not communicate with one another. Each department generates so many occupational specialties and accompanying buzzwords that the members of any given silo can no longer clearly describe their ideas and concerns to outsiders. When problems occur and functional representatives meet to discuss causes, effects, and remedies, the dialog is often lengthy, defensive, and stressful to all concerned. Soon, a vital exchange of information is seen as an unproductive diversion rather than as an opportunity for collaborative effort.

Competitors. Members of each silo view their counterparts as competitors. In a corporate world where everyone wants to look good, get credit for successes, and avoid blame for failures, a climate of suspicion and jealousy emerges. Members of the organization are confined by a lack of mutual caring and trust. Maneuvering for the inside track to top jobs, employees and managers engage in political game playing that undermines the long-term interests of the company.

Stymied learning. When the representative of a silo or function withdraws from serious problems in order to avoid blame, he or she creates an environment that discourages learning. Although big problems offer big learning opportunities, managers tend to opt for short-term solutions that merely detect and correct errors. Because they have not discovered how to learn together, these officers treat symptoms rather than causes. Each division has its own explanation for every problem, and the blame is generally placed at the door of a competitor silo.

Protected sovereignty. Internal measurement-and-reward systems tend to perpetuate the structure and style of silo groups until eventually these patterns become a way of life. Horizontal integration is seen as a threat to their autonomous empires, and they compete to increase the size and importance of their fiefdoms. A silo chieftain is willing to integrate horizontally only if he remains on top of the resultant combination.

CONDITIONS FOR CHANGE

Seminars and staff meetings are not likely to bring about the massive culture changes necessary to overcome the functional silo syndrome. Psychiatrists know that people seek help only when the pain of maladjustment exceeds the pain of the therapy. The same is true for company CEOs and their silo managers.

When leaders in pain learn that culture change is the key to escaping their dilemma, they are willing to pursue a transformation even if they do not know what they are pursuing. Before managers undertake a culture change, however, they should understand and accept certain guiding principles.

1. *Cultures should be changed for the right reason.* The right reason for changing a culture is to make money (in the public sector the purpose is to keep the taxpayer solvent). Changes should be made in order to attain the short- and long-term goals of the organization by serving customers, shareholders (or taxpayers), and members. When modifications are made for the wrong reasons, such as mimicking the latest fad, following a corporate edict, or trying to create a happy work force, the changes usually exacerbate existing problems.

2. *A company culture is not monolithic.* Companies are usually split into two camps, one made up of managers and the other of workers. In addition, there are subcultures related to factors such as functional responsibility, geographic location, ethnic composition, political orientation, and vocational and gender groupings. Sometimes the cultures of specific silos conflict with one another.

3. *An organization's culture reflects its leadership.* The signals given by CEOs and their lieutenants through words, behavior, and systems are amplified as they spread through the organization. Effective leadership is essential for creating a harmonious culture and a productive work force.

4. *Culture change cannot be delegated.* No silo can do the job alone. Culture change is a mainstream responsibility requiring the continual, active participation of the CEO. However, the expertise of human resource workers and the engineering staff can facilitate the concerted line effort.

5. *Culture change requires total involvement.* Changes are accomplished and institutionalized when a large percentage of the work force is actively involved in the change. The rate of success is directly related to the percentage of workers who have ownership of the change process.

6. *Culture change is a long-term process.* The time required to change a culture is a function of the permanence and stability of its membership. If members of the culture are committed to change, it will be achieved more quickly. Although temporary changes can be observed immediately, permanent changes require at least three to five years.

7. *Cultures are always changing.* Whether planned or not, changes constantly bombard cultures because of countless external and internal factors. Active leaders can deliberately alter the structure of a culture in order to steer the changes in the right direction.

OWNERSHIP

It is clear that ownership is the key ingredient for changing a culture. Though top management may have initial ownership of the decision to change the culture, ownership of the vision of the new culture and the change mechanisms and resultant conditions must be shared by all members of the organization. That is, every employee must be a managing partner in the change process.

Changing a culture requires active leadership and organization-wide involvement in a three-step process:

1. Assembling a vision of the desired culture;

2. Mobilizing the work force to develop this vision and to organize change strategies;

3. Institutionalizing the new culture by putting practices and
systems in place to assure its continuity.

The first hurdle to overcome when assembling a vision is to
convince top management that all three steps require the full involvement of the entire work force. Command-and-control managers customarily mastermind a corporate vision and then send their
underlings out to sell it to the great mass of the dirty unwashed.
Although top-down changes are easy to bring about, they are the
least likely to succeed. Mandates generally result in overt compliance and covert opposition. Participatory approaches are more difficult and time-consuming but are more likely to result in changes
that last. These strategies bring about both outward commitment
and inner acceptance.

One may wonder how a vision can be assembled. It is not difficult
to find paradigms for desired cultures. Some of these models have
been around for many years and have been proliferating at an
increasing rate. An article by Jay Forrester (1965) advocated with
amazing foresight the conditions now being implemented in today's
most successful organizations. During the last decade countless
books and articles were published that can serve as resources for
planning new cultures. Several of these books are mentioned in the
preface.

Peter Drucker[1] (1988) offers a vision that would eliminate corporate silos and prevent their formation:

The typical large business 20 years hence will have fewer than half
the levels of management of its counterpart today, and no more
than a third the managers. In its structure, and in its management
problems and concerns, it will bear little resemblance to the typical
manufacturing company, circa 1950, which our textbooks still
consider the norm. Instead it is far more likely to resemble organizations that neither the practicing manager nor the management
scholar pays much attention to today: the hospital, the university,
the symphony orchestra. For like them, the typical business will be

[1] From P. Drucker, "The Coming of the New Organization," *Harvard Business Review*, January-February, 1988, p. 45. Used by permission.

knowledge-based, an organization composed largely of specialists who direct and discipline their own performance through organized feedback from colleagues, customers, and headquarters. For this reason, it will be what I call an information based organization. (p. 45)

When the members of an organization are forming a vision and redesigning their culture, they may find it helpful to review the options presented in journals and books. However, few employees have access to ideas detailed in scholarly works and often do not have the perspective necessary to assimilate and implement those ideas. Moreover, many published concepts are rejected if they upset the comfortable status quo.

Fortunately, we are not restricted to the printed word when designing a vision for a culture change. Because of the great ground swell of response to foreign competition, many North American organizations have introduced effective plans similar to the model described by Peter Drucker. American adaptations of the successful Toyota manufacturing techniques, commonly referred to as JIT or just-in-time principles, are renewing American competitiveness in the world markets. For further information on JIT principles see Chapter 3.

In addition to textbooks and articles describing these various models of excellence, examples of information-based JIT/VAM applications are now available to all members of the work force through movies, videotapes, field trips, seminars, and training programs.

Culture changes that bridge functional boundaries and integrate silos require leadership initiative at the top to make the whole procedure possible. Failure to follow through with supportive leadership is the most common cause of breakdowns in the change process.

Signals that top managers send through the organization through their behavior toward one another are perhaps the most important factor in effecting a culture change. The executive suite is a goldfish bowl. Teamwork or backbiting at the top becomes the role model that permeates the entire organization. Although the language of words and the language of the systems activated by the culture change are very important, the language of behavior, when it differs from the other languages, is the only one that is heard.

If an organization is to reinvent itself, every member must participate, and many role changes are required. Managers become facilitators, advisors, and coaches and develop new supervisory skills in Adult-Adult positive reinforcement. Operator skills are broadened through training in work simplification, statistical process control (SPC), work sampling, cause-and-effect diagnosis, workplace layout, measurement techniques, materials-handling analysis, and setup-time reduction. Trainees learn to think like managers by analyzing constraints (environmental, logistical, behavioral, and leadership) and resources (machines, labor, materials, methods, and environment). They systematically attack eight kinds of waste (those relating to processing, overproduction, waiting, defects, motion, inventory, transportation, and talent) and use process flow charts to discover improvement opportunities and to arrive at cost estimates and target dates. Command-and-control managers discover the futility of threats, bribery, or manipulation and embrace new principles of motivation:

1. People are motivated to achieve their own personal goals—not someone else's.

2. People are supportive of someone else's goals if they believe they will lead to the achievement of their own goals.

3. People will pursue unattractive goals if their attainment leads to the achievement of more attractive goals.

4. Most people are already motivated to pursue their goals (although the motivation is not always apparent).

5. People have a greater proprietary interest in goals that they help to establish than in goals they are forced to accept.

6. Creativity that cannot be directed toward the attainment of constructive goals is usually directed toward diversionary or counterproductive goals.

7. People get more excited about goals that are understandable, attractive, challenging, and measurable.

8. The goal-setting process itself has potential for satisfying both achievement and affiliation needs.

Although training may be initiated by corporate or outside experts, the training functions should then be taken over by the line people who will have to make the new system work. Not only does this procedure reduce training costs, but—more importantly—it increases the relevance of the training and installs local experts in the workplace who can respond to changing needs. When line people carry out the training functions, the processes are institutionalized, consolidating operator ownership of the system.

In the context of information-based management, ownership is not a function of position and authority but, rather, of knowledge and control of the production process (whether in shop or office). Operators, managers, and staff people share a common data base regarding the mission of the organization and are involved jointly in planning, measuring, evaluating, and correcting the production processes. Operators must also establish networking relationships with peers, staff, suppliers, and users (all of whom are recognized as customers). Because ownership cannot thrive in strait jackets, employees become versatile in changing roles and locations. Finally, shared ownership justifies shared rewards, which are described in Chapter 2.[2]

REFERENCES

Drucker, P. (1988, January-February). The coming of the new organizations. *Harvard Business Review*, pp. 45-53.

Ensor, P. (1988, Spring). The functional silo syndrome. *Target*, p. 16.

Forrester, J. (1965). The new corporate design. *Industrial Management Review*, 7.

Schonberger, R.J. (1990). *Building a chain of customers.* New York: Free Press.

---

[2] Conditions of ownership are described further in Chapter 3.

2

Reward Systems

Reward systems have been the great blind spot of modern management. This major resource could spark the energy to meet the global competitive challenge. However, the traditions and practices governing pay are so deeply entrenched that adjusting to a new concept of reward systems is like adjusting to a round world after centuries of seeing it flat. Traditional reward systems are not doing what they are intended to do: attract, motivate, and retain competent people. In most organizations these systems represent a wasteful use of money. Worse, they often contribute to adversarial and counterproductive behavior, as witnessed for decades in the automotive industry and in the late 1980s in Boeing, Eastern Airlines, and the Pittston coal mines. Traditional reward systems are punitive and yield a negative return on investment. [1]

Problems arise both from narrowly conceived reward systems and from mismanagement of otherwise acceptable systems. The traditional, narrow view has been that reward systems encompass only pay and benefits. This outlook reflects an assumption that money is the driving force behind motivation and commitment—that people will put up with hateful jobs to get enough money to pay for necessities and discretionary needs. However, employees are better informed now and want information about their jobs; they want an opportunity to solve problems and to participate in decisions and need assurance that their contributions to productivity will be rewarded.

Money is important, of course, and always will be. Pay to the wage earner is like cash flow to the organization; if cash flow

---

[1] I am indebted to Carla O'Dell and Jerry McAdams for their survey report entitled *People, Performance, and Pay*, published in 1987 by the American Productivity and Quality Center in Houston, Texas.

disappears, nothing else matters. For people at the subsistence level, money is all-important. However, complementary reward systems not only relieve poverty but can also enliven the spirit of those with discretionary income. Moreover, these adjunct systems are highly cost effective; and most of them are free.

Figure 2-1 offers a broader view of reward systems, defining them as individual monetary, group monetary, and nonmonetary. The thesis here is that an organization's reward system can be truly effective only if it is three-dimensional; that is, the system must contain one component or more from each of the three categories listed.

A reward system cannot be fully evaluated when considered alone. Its effectiveness depends on how it is combined with other reward systems and on the culture in which they are implemented. Still, a look at each system individually will help to define its function.

HOW REWARD SYSTEMS WORK

1. Level Automatic

When pay levels are assigned automatically, employees in each job grade are paid the same salary and receive uniform across-the-board periodic increases and cost-of-living adjustments (COLAs). This system is commonly found in unionized organizations in which employees oppose attempts to recognize individual differences. Some nonunion organizations also follow this practice on the mistaken assumption that mimicking union patterns will foil unionization attempts. Paying all people alike is also a choice made by managers who do not like to face up to the responsibility of recognizing merit. However, people at all levels are coming to expect a relationship between performance and pay, and the trend is moving away from the old system.

Effectiveness. If level automatic is to be effective, it must be used in conjunction with other reward systems that inspire teamwork and initiative. When the automatic method is used alone, employees should all be doing the same task, an arrangement that places no

INDIVIDUAL MONETARY	GROUP MONETARY

1. Level automatic
   Flat
   Percentage
 	
2. Benefits
   Maintenance
   Motivational
 	
3. Piecework
   Methods limited
   Performance based
 	
4. Merit pay
   Productivity based
   Judgmentally determined
 	
5. Pay for knowledge
   Vertical job enlargement
   Horizontal job enlargement
   Learning pursuits
 	
6. Lump-sum bonuses
   Flat
   Percentage
   Discretionary
 	
7. Two-tier systems
   Temporary/permanent
   Hourly/salaried
   Dual ladder
 	
8. Premium pay
   Overtime
   Hardship
   System adjustment
 	
9. Paid suggestions
   Individual
   Group
	10. Gain sharing
	   Scanlon
	   Rucker
	   Improshare
	   Customized
	
	11. Profit sharing
	   Deferred
	   Cash
	
	12. Stock ownership
	   ESOP, participative
	   ESOP, passive
	   Options
	
	NONMONETARY
	
	13. Discretionary time
	   Earned time off
	   Recognition
	   Flextime
	
	14. Career enhancements
	   Promotions
	   Growth opportunities
	
	15. Empowerment
	   Egalitarianism
	   Process ownership
	   Recognition

Figure 2-1. Reward Systems

premium on individual differences or on the expression of initiative or creativity. Such tasks are rarely found in effective organizations.

Advantages. Level automatic is easily administered and minimizes allegations of favoritism.

Disadvantages. This reward system indulges freeloaders and low achievers but displeases high achievers, whose frustrations find expression in counterproductive activities such as job hunting, horseplay, and collective adversarial activities.

2. Benefits

This category includes legally or contractually required benefits, such as workmen's compensation, vacation pay, and paid sick leave, and optional plans such as free coffee, company picnics, and recreational facilities. The nature of the benefits and the manner in which they are administered have a significant influence in shaping an organization's culture. Benefits include programs and plans funded separately from other monetary compensation systems and usually make up one-third or more of the cost of employment.

Effectiveness. To be effective, benefits should emphasize growth and achievement through programs such as tuition refunds, employee-edited newspapers, professional-society memberships, credit unions, and employee-managed recreational facilities and pursuits. Employers should place less emphasis on unearned rewards that are dispensed equally to high and low achievers. Dissatisfactions are fewer if benefits are competitive in the community and in industry.

Advantages. A balanced mix of benefits satisfies the needs of employees for growth, achievement, responsibility, recognition, status, security, and information. A successful benefit program also helps satisfy the economic, social, and physical requirements of employees and can be instrumental in shaping a cohesive work culture.

Disadvantages. Nondiscriminatory benefits, such as Christmas turkeys and free coffee, which apply equally to low and high achievers, have no motivational value and are more potent as dissatisfiers.

They simply exist as one of the fixed costs of doing business and offer employers little return on investment.

3. Piecework

When rewards are offered for piecework, an individual's pay is tied to productivity and is usually based on imposed performance quotas and standardized methods. However, some piecework systems encourage and reward individual initiative. Employers usually measure productivity in terms of quantity but may also include quality and other factors.

Effectiveness. To be successful, the piecework plan must permit and reward individual creativity and must be used in conjunction with other reward systems that encourage teamwork and inspire the operator to use initiative in improving methods. When used alone, the plan is most acceptable for single-task temporary jobs such as picking strawberries or machine-paced mass assembly. Most progressive organizations replace piecework with reward systems keyed to initiative and teamwork.

Advantages. Less skill is required on the part of supervisors, and productivity is easily measured.

Disadvantages. The threat of adjusting standards upwards tends to put a ceiling on productivity. Piecework employees are reluctant to improve work methods or to engage in teamwork activities that might reduce individual differences. Adversarial relationships often exist between employees and the staff people who set standards. The company loses a competitive advantage through its inability to harness the creative talent of employees.

4. Merit Pay

When the merit-pay system is used, an employee's pay level and increase rate are related to his or her contribution to the success of the organization. Merit is determined by objectively measurable production data and/or by the judgments of others (e.g., supervisors, peers, staff, and customers).

Effectiveness. Employees must understand the basis for determining merit and trust and accept the system by which they are judged.

Merit-pay requires objective and evenhanded treatment on the part of evaluators and should be used in conjunction with reward systems that encourage teamwork and initiative.

Advantages. High achievers are rewarded for their performance and are more likely to remain; low achievers are motivated to improve or to leave the organization.

Disadvantages. Merit-pay requires a high level of supervisory competence. Productivity criteria are not always comparable, and in a climate of low trust the system precipitates allegations of favoritism and unfairness.

5. Pay for Knowledge

In a pay-for-knowledge system (also known as skill-based pay) the pay level rises with the number of tasks employees can handle at their own levels or at levels above and below their current classifications. Some organizations reward learning itself, regardless of task relevance.

Effectiveness. Learning opportunities are available, and employees are free to learn new skills and to rotate through mastered tasks. The plan works best in conjunction with nonmonetary or group monetary systems.

Advantages. Work is more challenging and career development is enhanced. People have a broader perspective, making them more resourceful in solving problems. Employee versatility and operational flexibility enhance customer responsiveness and enable the organization to operate with a leaner staff. People are more likely to stay with this kind of organization.

Disadvantages. Training costs are higher; and not all employees have the incentive, the aptitude, or the opportunity to acquire a broad range of skills.

6. Lump-Sum Bonus

Instead of a pay increase, employees get a one-time cash payment based on performance or the terms of a union contract. The lump-sum bonus is sometimes used as an incentive for early retirement.

Bonuses may be a flat amount for all employees, a percentage of existing pay scales, or a reward tied to individual merit. The bonus does not become part of the base pay.

Effectiveness. For this reward system to be effective, employees must understand and accept the company-employee joint-stake need to hold the line on fixed costs and must appreciate the role of discretionary merit bonuses. The plan is more acceptable when used with nonmonetary or group monetary reward systems.

Advantages. The company is able to control fixed costs by limiting pay raises and benefit increases. Discretionary bonuses reinforce high achievers.

Disadvantages. In a climate of adversarial relationships, employees may not trust a bonus formula and may feel that their career progress is being held in check. Discretionary bonuses may evoke allegations of partiality.

7. Two-Tier Systems

In a two-tier plan newly hired employees are paid at a lower rate than previously hired workers. The arrangement may be either temporary or permanent. A de facto two-tier system exists in America because the Fair Labor Standards Act creates a two-class system of hourly-paid and salaried employees governed by different work rules.

Effectiveness. Two-tier systems are seldom effective but are more acceptable when lines of demarcation between the two levels are obliterated to avoid the development of a caste system. As a condition of employment, employees hired on a lower tier must have a clear understanding and acceptance of the arrangement and must see the scheme as a necessary strategy for the economic viability of the organization. Dual-ladder pay scales are sometimes used to avoid a two-tier relationship between managers and technical/professional employees.

Advantages. Two-tier pay scales reduce the firm's compensation costs without disturbing the status quo of existing employees.

Disadvantages. Two-class pay scales are divisive. They raise questions of equity when peers with equal responsibilities receive unequal pay, and they place undue emphasis on seniority.

8. Premium Pay

A premium-pay system provides higher rates for overtime work, for night shifts, and for work done under undesirable conditions. Sometimes premium or red-circle rates are used temporarily to bridge the buyout of a piecework incentive system or to facilitate the merger of two or more work forces.

Effectiveness. The system must be administered within the framework of relevant labor laws. To be effective, it should be used primarily as an administrative expedient.

Advantages. Premium pay is an economical and fair means of staffing undesirable jobs, converting pay schemes, or maintaining a lean work force.

Disadvantages. Sometimes premium pay increases labor costs and encourages malingering to create overtime.

9. Paid Suggestions

Individuals or groups receive financial rewards for cost-saving suggestions. Rewards are based on evaluations by industrial engineers or by an ad hoc review staff. The plan is often restricted to hourly paid workers.

Effectiveness. To be effective, the system should be group oriented to reward teamwork and should provide prompt and equitable feedback to suggesters. It works best when supported by nonmonetary and group monetary reward systems.

Advantages. Reimbursing employees for good suggestions promotes initiative and encourages workers to introduce productivity improvements that benefit both the organization and its members.

Disadvantages. If not monitored carefully, paid suggestion plans discourage teamwork. Innovative employees become dissatisfied if feedback is inadequate or delayed or if implementation and reward procedures seem capricious.

10. Gain Sharing

All members of a unit, usually a plant site, get bonuses for beating a predetermined performance target. In addition to standard Scanlon, Rucker, and Improshare plans, numerous hybrid designs are used to calculate bonuses. Objectives often include improved productivity, quality, cost effectiveness, and customer satisfaction. Periodic (usually monthly or quarterly) bonus checks are issued separately from regular pay checks.

Effectiveness. Gain sharing requires organizational teamwork, operator control, a climate of mutual trust, and other conditions fostered by nonmonetary reward systems. The plan is more effective when supplemented with an appropriate system of individual rewards, such as merit pay or pay for knowledge. Objectives must be clearly understood and measurable by all participants.

Advantages. Gain sharing fosters a joint-stake concern that enhances teamwork and productivity. Employees learn more about the business, focus on objectives, and increase commitment.

Disadvantages. Bonus checks during prosperous times may lead to unrealistic expectations and disappointments in lean times.

11. Profit Sharing

Employees receive a bonus (usually annually) based on corporate profits. Payments can be made in cash or deferred into a retirement fund.

Effectiveness. Employees must have realistic opportunities to influence company profits through individual initiative and collective participation. Profit sharing works best with pay-for-knowledge and nonmonetary reward systems. The profit-sharing formula should be simple and easy to communicate.

Advantages. Profit sharing unites the financial interests of all employees. The plan is guaranteed to be affordable because it pays off only when the company shows a profit.

Disadvantages. Factors influencing profitability are often seen by employees as beyond their control. Annual payouts and deferred benefits are not effective reinforcement for day-to-day productivity improvements. The plan also forces private companies to open their books.

12. Stock Ownership

Employees acquire stock through employee stock-ownership plans (ESOPs) or by exercising purchase options or as a reward for performance.

Effectiveness. For this system to be effective, employees must own a significant amount of stock and must be permitted to have an active role in managing improvements. (See Figure 2-4 and the related discussion of ESOPs.)

Advantages. Employees are more productive and more interested in protecting company resources. An ESOP offers tax advantages to the company and the employees and provides protection against hostile takeovers.

Disadvantages. Under an ESOP the value of stock ownership fluctuates with stock price and, in the case of company failure, jeopardizes the value of stock-based retirement funds. Because payout is usually not available until retirement or termination, some employees opt for premature termination.

13. Discretionary Time

Employees work under self- and group-discretionary flextime schedules and may receive paid time off as a reward for good performance or in place of overtime pay for long hours.

Effectiveness. A discretionary-time plan must be administered within the guidelines of labor laws and union contracts. To be effective, it must also be understood and accepted by members of the work force. It is most effective when accompanied by appropriate individual and group monetary reward systems.

Advantages. Discretionary time provides positive reinforcement for responsible behavior and offers a more economical means of administering overtime. It also helps prevent stress and counterproductive behavior.

Disadvantages. The plan requires competent supervision and is vulnerable to abuse by vocational misfits.

14. Career Enhancements

When career enhancements are offered, high achievers are allowed to assume greater responsibilities and are rotated through a variety of challenging tasks, usually without a change in compensation.

Effectiveness. For career enhancements to be effective, employees must have a genuine sense of process ownership and must experience opportunities for growth, achievement, responsibility, and recognition. The plan is more effective if used in conjunction with empowerment and monetary reward systems. The absence of monetary increases must be understood and accepted by employees as a joint-stake strategy to promote long-term company success and career-opportunity enhancements.

Advantages. The system provides growth opportunities for employees and enhances company flexibility and competitiveness.

Disadvantages. When provided without monetary reinforcement over a sustained period of time, particularly in a climate of mistrust, it may increase moonlighting and collective adversarial behavior.

15. Empowerment

Empowered employees own the processes of productivity through the self-reliant manner in which they operate, maintain, adjust, and organize their workplace facilities and equipment. They are directly involved in production schedules and quality surveillance and usually function as self-managed work teams to form a chain of customers from supplier to user.

Effectiveness. The system is most effective in flat organizations when operators are treated like customers by supervisors and staff support personnel. Empowerment is facilitated by an egalitarian culture (see Figure 2-3) and by support from appropriate monetary and nonmonetary systems.

Advantages. Empowerment reduces delays by putting process management in the hands of the people who are closest to the problems. It improves morale and motivation and brings out the best in people, encouraging versatile individuals and self-managed work teams at no added cost to the organization.

Disadvantages. The system requires extensive reorientation of managers and operators, as well as the transfer or termination of individuals who are not able to adapt to the change from authority to knowledge as the source of influence.

The Impact of Reward Systems

Although these reward systems cannot be fully assessed when considered singly, certain generalizations can be made about each. Every employee has basic maintenance needs, satisfied through financial, physical, status, and social requirements and assurance of job security and access to information about his or her organization. Most employees are motivated through opportunities for growth, responsibility, recognition, and achievement. Figure 2-2 shows the potential of each of the fifteen systems for encouraging teamwork and for satisfying these maintenance and motivation requirements. (Maintenance and motivation needs are discussed further in Appendix A.)

Limitations of Individual Rewards

The exclusive use of individual reward systems is a holdover from the era when employees were hired to be individual performers. Today's world-class organizations are hiring team players. Individual reward systems fail to inspire teamwork and in some cases undermine initiative. Piecework employees conspire against engineered performance standards and harass high achievers, in effect putting a cap on productivity. Level-automatic pay kills the incentive of high achievers and ratifies low performance. Such systems foster peer pressure, featherbedding, strikes, slowdowns, and walkouts, which further limit production. Though merit pay, piecework,

++ = strong	+ = moderate	0 = neutral	- = negative	- - = adversarial

SYSTEM	MAINTENANCE	MOTIVATION	TEAMWORK
1. Level Automatic			
Flat	+	0	-
Percent	+	0	-
2. Benefits			
Maintenance	+	0	-
Motivational	+	++	0
3. Piecework			
Method limited	+	+	- -
Performance based	++	++	0
4. Merit Pay			
Productivity based	++	++	0
Performance based	++	++	0
5. Pay for Knowledge			
Vertical job enlargement	++	++	+
Horizontal job enlargement	++	++	+
Learning pursuits	+	++	0
6. Lump-Sum Bonus			
Flat	+	0	0
Percentage	+	0	0
Discretionary	+	++	0
7. Two-Tier Systems			
Temporary/permanent	+	0	-
Hourly/salaried	+	0	-
Dual ladder	+	+	0
8. Premium Pay			
Overtime	++	0	0
Hardship	+	0	0
System adjustment	+	0	0

Figure 2-2. Impact of Reward Systems

++ = strong	+ = moderate	0 = neutral	- = negative	- - = adversarial

SYSTEM	MAINTENANCE	MOTIVATION	TEAMWORK
9. Paid Suggestions			
Individual	++	++	- -
Group	++	++	++
10. Gain Sharing			
Scanlon	++	++	++
Rucker	++	++	++
Improshare	++	++	+
Customized	++	++	++
11. Profit Sharing			
Deferred	+	0	+
Cash	++	++	++
12. Stock Ownership			
ESOP, participative	++	++	++
ESOP, passive	+	0	+
Options	+	0	+
13. Discretionary Time			
Earned time off	+	0	0
Recognition	++	+	0
Flextime	+	++	+
14. Career Enhancements			
Promotions	+	++	0
Growth opportunity	+	++	0
15. Empowerment			
Egalitarianism	++	++	++
Process ownership	++	++	0
Recognition	++	++	0

Figure 2-2. Impact of Reward Systems (continued)

pay for knowledge, and discretionary bonuses do reward high achievers, they do not inspire teamwork.

Although the era of rugged individualism is past, individual reward systems are not. Because they help to override the socialistic and bureaucratic mentality that quashes creativity and initiative, they still have an important role. Individual rewards inspire an entrepreneurial and competitive spirit. High achievers can influence their own pay through piecework, merit pay, pay for knowledge, discretionary bonuses, and paid suggestion systems without being held back by the norms. However, individual reward systems cannot stand alone.

Group Monetary Systems

Group monetary systems pay off to groups and encourage individuals to pull together in order to achieve mutual goals. As witnessed in the communes and collective farms of collapsed Eastern European economies, the plan does not work well unless workers also have an opportunity to be rewarded for individual initiative. However, when group monetary systems are combined with individual and nonmonetary systems, the three dimensions encourage teamwork in spite of any deficiencies that might exist in the individual monetary system. As a case in point, Donnelly Corporation (discussed later) has a level-automatic pay plan that alone could not sustain the high degree of commitment and productivity demonstrated by Donnelly employees. Nor would its gain-sharing plan stand alone as an adequate reward system. But the combination of group, individual, and nonmonetary systems creates a synergy that one system alone could not inspire. Perhaps Donnelly's combination could be enhanced further by substituting pay for knowledge or merit pay for a level-automatic system.

Some managers and union leaders scoff at the notion that employees would be willing to share in anything but gain. They say that employees are fair-weather friends who turn against the company or the union when profits disappear. Such an assumption is valid only when pay practices discourage employees from identifying with the welfare of the organization.

Nonmonetary Systems

Nonmonetary reward systems are the richest source of job satisfaction and give a company its greatest return on investment. They place a high premium on leaders who can unite people in the joint pursuit of common goals. Starting a nonmonetary reward system is difficult if management is traditional in its orientation. However, except for the initial training and facilitation costs, these plans are virtually free and self-perpetuating.

Functional dress code	Common dining facilities
Informal first-name relationships	First-come, first-served parking
Unifying titles and terminology	Common entrances to site/building
Single-class timekeeping	
Uniform reward system	Names, not titles, at all work stations
Shared recreational activities/facilities	Open-door/open-floor practices
Uniform ID badges—prominent first name	Common coffee bars, rest areas
Operator control of work systems	Common restrooms, locker rooms
Self-managed work teams	Functional office size/location
Operators diagnose/solve problems	Functional office furnishings
Joint worker/manager training	Peer-group disciplinary processes
Operators/managers co-trainers	Cross-function/level networking
Operator-customer interaction	Reprisal-free whistle blowing
	Right of appeal

Figure 2-3. Conditions for an Egalitarian Work Culture

Egalitarianism is perhaps one of the most widely misunderstood, underrated, and underutilized conditions of empowerment. Even when understood, it is often not implemented because it violates the traditional command-and-control orientation of managers. Many companies make token gestures in the form of common parking areas, shared lunchrooms, and first-name relationships. Important as these are, they are not sufficient to permeate the culture of the workplace. Figure 2-3 lists examples of the wide-ranging media conducive to empowerment.

Nonmonetary systems are important adjuncts to monetary systems, but care must be taken to avoid contaminating them with money. Achievement is its own reward. Although monetary rewards should reinforce desired behavior, they should not be handed out at the expense of teamwork. Paying individuals for improving methods is like paying children for high grades. The risk here is that the focus will be changed from the joy of achievement to a competition for money. Of course, individuals should be recognized and rewarded through merit pay and discretionary bonuses; but the rewards should never overwhelm the pleasure of the work itself.

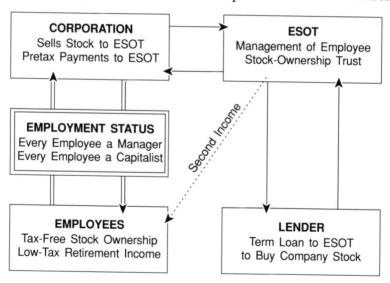

Figure 2-4. Employee Stock-Ownership Plan

Employee stock-ownership plans deserve special mention because of their unique potential for combining monetary and nonmonetary reward systems for individuals and groups. An individual's stock-ownership account is a function of his or her tenure and cumulative gross income, and the collective efforts of teams enhance every employee's stock value. Administered as shown in Figure 2-4, ESOPs also provide nonmonetary rewards. They help to reverse the socialistic drift by making every employee a capitalist.

Figure 2-5 represents a three-dimensional "smorgasbord" of eighty-one systems from which an organization can assemble its own most workable combinations. Using more blocks is not necessarily better; it is the complementary combination of at least one from each of the three categories that counts.

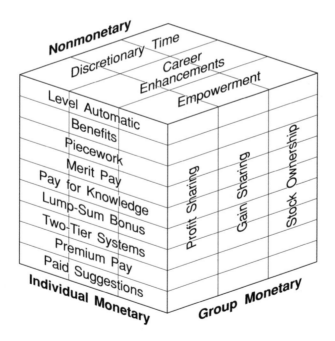

Figure 2-5. Three-Dimensional Reward Systems

The Major Role of Benefits

Although benefits are listed under the heading "individual monetary," they are so diverse that many of them can also be classed as group monetary and nonmonetary. For instance, coffee bars and company picnics can be classed as both group oriented and nonmonetary. However, most benefits can be assessed in terms of their cost to the company per individual by measuring the cost per employee per year or the percentage of total payroll. Figure 2-6 lists examples of the diverse benefits offered in modern organizations at costs ranging from 30 to 40 percent of the payroll.

Little can be done to reduce the costs of the benefit package. However, more selective use of motivation-oriented programs such as tuition refunds, society memberships, and performance-recognition plans yield a better return on investment to the organization and its members than do gifts distributed to high and low achievers alike or benefits that pay for time not worked.

Case Studies

The three-dimensional systems of five successful companies are described and shown graphically below. In each case it will be shown that the individual components are not unique; it is the combination of all three components that makes the difference.

Donnelly Corporation

Donnelly Corporation is a privately held company of approximately two thousand employees headquartered in Holland, Michigan. It manufactures more than 90 percent of the rearview mirrors used by the U.S. automobile industry, plus other automotive products, with annual sales exceeding a hundred million dollars. Named in *The 100 Best Companies to Work for in America* (Levering, Moskowitz, & Katz, 1984), Donnelly has earned numerous quality awards and continues to excel in cost effectiveness and innovation. It has been in business since 1905; but its present unique form of participative management was initiated in 1952 by the late John Donnelly, its previous CEO. Donnelly Corporation is managed through two separate organizational structures: the executive committee and the Donnelly

SECURITY AND HEALTH

1. Workmen's Compensation*
2. Social Security*
3. Unemployment insurance*
4. Supplemental unemployment benefits

5. Life, health, & accident insurance
6. Pension plans
7. Health & fitness services
8. Severance pay

*Legally required in U.S.A

TIME NOT WORKED

1. Vacations
2. Holidays
3. Lunch & rest breaks
4. Personal excused absence
5. Sick leave
6. Grievances & negotiations
7. Business meetings

8. Educational leave
9. Community services
10. Perfect attendance
11. Reporting time
12. Socializing
13. Waiting & delays**
14. Work rules**

**Not benefits, but part of the cost of employment

EMPLOYEE SERVICES

1. Thrift savings plans
2. Stock-purchase plans
3. Counseling
4. Credit unions
5. Service/seniority awards
6. Performance recognition
7. Merchandise-purchase plans
8. Social/recreational activities
9. Tuition refunds
10. Skills training
11. Professional-society memberships

12. Christmas (or other) gifts
13. Moving/transfer allowances
14. Legal services
15. Auto insurance
16. Umbrella liability coverage
17. Transportation & parking
18. Company car
19. Child Adoption
20. Day care
21. Food Services
22. Career clothing

Figure 2-6. Employee Benefits

committee. The executive committee consists of the total work force formed into interlinking work teams, which are in charge of the mainstream creation, production, and marketing activities of the company. The Donnelly committee is composed of nominees from the executive committee and handles issues of equity concerning policies, pay, and grievances. All decisions made in the Donnelly committee must be unanimous, which means that any one of the fifteen voting members of the committee has veto power over the entire process.

As illustrated in Figure 2-7, individual monetary rewards at Donnelly are limited to level automatic (plus benefits), which provides equal pay and pay increases to all people in each job classification. Gain sharing is a group monetary system that fosters teamwork. Each month employees share a distribution composed of 44 percent of net profits above 5.25 percent of net worth divided by twelve. If the company runs a deficit, a negative bonus is accumulated, which must be paid off with positive bonuses before a standard monthly bonus is paid. Nonmonetary systems are the key

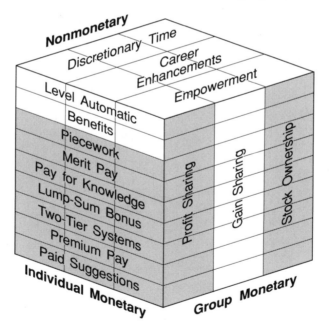

Figure 2-7. The Donnelly Corporation's Reward System

driving force at Donnelly. Through membership in the executive committee, which blankets the organization, every employee is directly empowered to influence business matters. And through representatives on the Donnelly committee, employees help to shape company reward systems and other policies. Rotation through a variety of assignments offers further opportunities for career enhancement, and flextime work schedules provide discretionary time.

Tellabs

Located in Lisle, Illinois, Tellabs is a rapidly growing company of eighteen hundred employees that was spawned by deregulation in 1984. It designs, manufactures, and services equipment for voice and data transmission for international telephone companies and related businesses and records annual sales of $180 million. Within only nine months beginning in 1986, Tellabs eliminated the "not-my-job" syndrome, converted to an all-salaried work force, and formed cells of

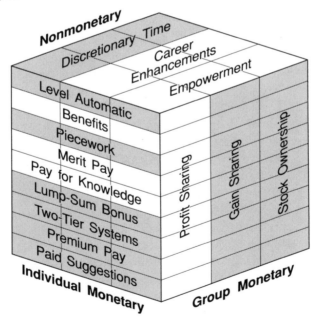

Figure 2-8. Tellabs' Reward System

work teams. Job titles and restrictive job descriptions were eliminated; all employees are referred to as *associates*. The associates are taught skills in joint problem solving, have the opportunity to learn new job skills, and receive pay increases for improved performance and versatility. Successful JIT applications increased product quality while reducing work in process by 95 percent, lot sizes by 65 percent, engineering design-revision time by 90 percent, space requirements by 65 percent, labor costs by 54 percent, and lead time from six weeks to two days.

The pay-for-knowledge plan and the merit-pay plan (plus benefits) are the individual monetary systems used at Tellabs (see Figure 2-8). Each employee's rate range is keyed to the number of tasks mastered. More than 90 percent of employees learn additional skills by taking advantage of the training opportunities provided on company time. Each person's performance is evaluated semiannually, and pay levels in the rate range are based on merit. Tellabs' group monetary system consists of profit sharing. The system resembles gain sharing in that more than half the employees are located in Lisle and cash bonuses are received quarterly. Empowerment and career enhancements are the nonmonetary reward systems in Tellabs that enable employees to rotate through a wide variety of assignments and to participate in problem-solving and goal-setting sessions.

Lincoln Electric

Headquartered in Cleveland, Ohio, Lincoln Electric is famed for productivity 250 percent above the industry norm and for paying its employees in excess of forty thousand dollars per year. A manufacturer of welding equipment, electric motors, and related equipment, Lincoln outperforms competitors worldwide and guarantees employment to its work force of 2,700 employees. The company was founded in 1895 by John C. Lincoln and was developed with the help of his brother, James F. Lincoln. Both were sons of a Congregationalist minister and operated under disciplined and frugal principles that demanded much from employees and paid them well in return.

Each production employee is judged on the basis of piecework performance and the ratings of his or her supervisor. Bonuses have averaged about 70 percent during the last ten years. Despite the high pay, the tightly disciplined workplace is not for everyone; and Don Hastings, president since 1987, is taking steps to modify the culture to adapt to changing values. An effort is being made to solicit employees' ideas, listen to their concerns, and empower them to have more control over their work environment. Employees own more than 40 percent of the company stock and can now influence the way the company is run.

Lincoln Electric has long been recognized for its powerful individual monetary system, composed of piecework and lump-sum bonus plans plus a group monetary ESOP (see Figure 2-9). The company recently included nonmonetary empowerment processes, which made its reward system three dimensional. Individual paychecks reflect piecework performance during the week, and each person's annual bonus is determined by company profits and individual achievement. Hence, both personal performance and teamwork are rewarded. The new practice of soliciting and acting on employee suggestions has made an effective work force even better, forestalling a growing mood of disenchantment that had been noted in recent years.

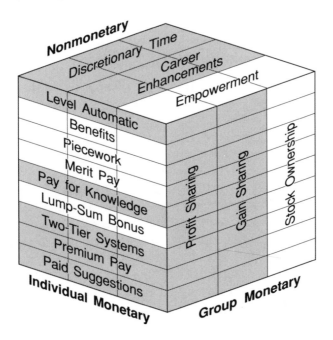

Figure 2-9. Lincoln Electric's Reward System

Johnsonville Foods

Headquartered in Sheboygan Falls, Wisconsin, Johnsonville Foods has grown in ten years from a small family sausage business to an organization that handles food operations in forty states. It has continued to prosper and expand in a business fraught with labor and production problems and is committed to a policy of continuous improvement. Three hundred permanent and one hundred temporary employees work in the Sheboygan Falls plant. Employees, called *members,* have a joint stake in the business and participate in all aspects of decision making (see Figure 2-10). There is no formal organizational structure or chain of command, and autonomous work teams decide how best to apply their resources. "Anybody can talk to anybody," says Ralph Stayer, president and CEO. The company is led by a five-member resource team made up of representatives of major functional divisions. The goal of the team is to push decision making to the lowest possible organizational level.

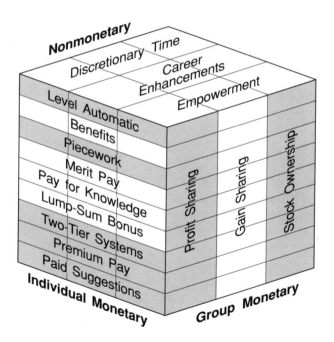

Figure 2-10. Johnsonville Foods' Reward System

Johnsonville has no personnel department, and hiring and firing occurs on the production line by members of work teams. Each member writes his or her own job description beginning with the words "I make customers for Johnsonville by..."

A great deal of emphasis is placed on personal development, and each year a certain amount of money is allocated for each member to pursue mentally stimulating activities—not necessarily related to job skills. Pay is competitive in the industry and is awarded on the basis of merit and personal development, without regard to seniority. Individual monetary rewards in Johnsonville Foods include merit pay, pay for knowledge, and the lump-sum bonus. Merit pay and bonuses are specifically tied to the acquisition of new knowledge and skills, whether or not those educational pursuits are related to job requirements. If an employee is not learning something new, pay increases are withheld. The group monetary system is a Scanlon-type gain-sharing plan that pays off quarterly in cash. Nonmonetary rewards, which are boundless and constantly evolving, include empowerment, career enhancements, and discretionary time. Organizational boundaries and chains of command are nonexistent, and autonomous work teams decide how best to apply their resources.

Normandale South

Normandale South, situated on the outskirts of Minneapolis, was formerly owned by Control Data and is now a subsidiary of Seagate Corporation. Through the application of JIT principles (discussed more fully in Chapter 3) it has become a leader in the highly competitive production of large disk drives. The work force of eight hundred employees is managed through a three-tier hierarchy: (1) manufacturing manager, (2) unit managers and support staff, and (3) operators and technicians. Communication among the three organizational levels is shortened further by informal and spontaneous networking across levels and functions, in apparent disregard for traditional chain-of-command reporting relationships. Class distinctions are further blurred by the blue smocks and clean-room coveralls worn by employees at all levels and by the absence of traditional rank-oriented status symbols. Few companies can match the versatility and teamwork of Normandale South employees. Autonomous units may be either natural work groups or ad hoc task teams. Employees participate in widely diverse activities: manufacturing, scheduling, calibrating their own tools, evaluating suggestions, maintaining equipment, controlling statistical processes, planning the layout of work stations, attending meetings with buyers and planners, and visiting suppliers. Normandale South began to use JIT principles in the mid-1980s when managers attended seminars on world-class manufacturing and began sharing this information with all members of the work force, mostly through on-the-job applications and internal training programs.

Individual monetary systems at Normandale South include the merit-pay plan and the paid-suggestion plan, both of which reward individuals for job skills, performance, creativity, and teamwork (see Figure 2-11). Performance reviews are conducted semiannually, and individual pay adjustments are made within a common rate range. Feedback is given continuously to both individuals and teams. Teamwork is further enhanced through two group monetary systems consisting of a profit-sharing plan (corporate) and a gain-sharing plan. Nonmonetary plans are the driving force behind the

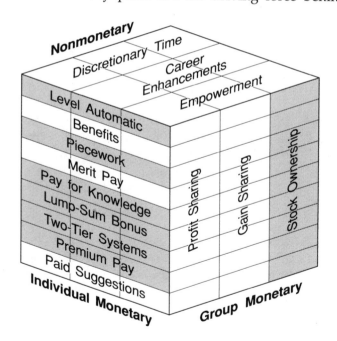

Figure 2-11. Normandale South's Reward System

Normandale reward system and include empowerment, career enhancement, and discretionary time.

The U.S. Automotive Industry

The U.S. automotive industry is notorious for its high pay and alienated work force. Despite its huge expenditures on automation, it has not achieved world-class status in terms of quality, innovation, elimination of waste, cost reduction, lead times, flexibility, and customer and supplier relations. And for good reason: the auto industry has emphasized individual monetary compensation as its primary reward system. The blame for this narrow view must be shared with labor unions, which make wages and benefits the focal point of collective bargaining. Even when gain sharing is added, as was the case with the defunct Studebaker Corporation, the system will fail if adversarial conditions prevent the implementation of nonmonetary systems (see Figures 2-12 and 2-13).

OLD LESSONS RELEARNED

The late Allan Mogensen spent a lifetime teaching people the principles of work simplification that he learned in the 1930s. A man ahead of his time, he encouraged empowerment by teaching operators how to take charge of and improve their jobs. He departed from tradition by making the operators, rather than the engineers, the masters of change. Modern literature is replete with examples of Mogensen-type empowerment in the form of self-managed work teams, quality circles, problem-solving groups, project teams, and task forces.

One difficult lesson is that managerial authority is the major obstacle to the implementation of change. However, many managers have reached the awareness stage and would change if they knew how. In the words of Rosabeth Moss Kanter (1989, p. 85), "Managerial work is undergoing such enormous and rapid change that many managers are reinventing their profession as they go. With little precedent to guide them, they are watching hierarchy fade away and the clear distinction of title, task, department, and even corporation blur. Faced with extraordinary levels of complexity and inter-

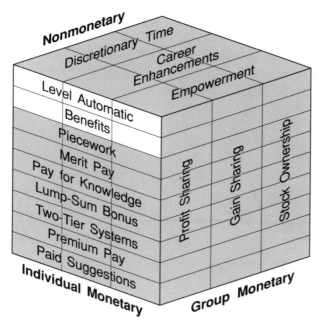

Figure 2-12. Automotive Industry's Reward System

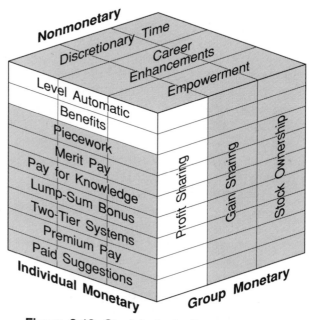

Figure 2-13. Studebaker's Reward System

dependency, they watch traditional sources of power erode and the old motivational tools lose their magic."

As the nature of work is re-examined and changed, it becomes apparent that reward systems are the framework around which jobs are designed. However, unrelated administrators often handle the separate components of the reward system—sometimes as adversaries. Wage and salary administrators are often numbers oriented—preoccupied with job evaluation, wage and salary surveys, head counts, and annual budgets—while other human resource specialists focus on job enrichment, attitude surveys, training programs, team building, conflict resolution, and improving the quality of work life. These specialists seldom get together to build an integrated reward system.

During economic downturns it has been customary to reduce overhead by eliminating training programs and other indirect costs. A large timber company in the Northwest abolished its work-simplification training program during a budget squeeze and in doing so destroyed the richest part of its reward system. Not only did they disenchant their work force but they eliminated a process that was netting them seven dollars for every dollar spent on the program. However, the returns would not have shown up during the next quarter.

Cash flow, return on investment, and profits are among the short-term gauges of organizational success. Among the long-term gauges are factors that contribute to organizational renewal and its impact on society. All these considerations are related to the role of employees. Self-actualized people take home a happy face to foster optimism and success in home and community. Underutilized people go home frustrated and angry to precipitate dissension, failure, and despair, which infiltrate society and return to haunt organizations in later generations.

Sometimes companies add nonmonetary reward systems for the wrong reason: as a cheap way to satisfy people without increasing wages. However, a company with a well-balanced three-dimensional reward system is usually able to afford pay increases. The five companies discussed in this chapter can afford higher-than-average pay because of the impact of three-dimensional reward systems on productivity. The origin of the Scanlon Plan itself is a case in point. In 1935 the Empire Steel and Tinplate Company in Mansfield, Ohio, reduced wages to avoid closing the mill. Joseph Scanlon, local president of the United Steel Workers, negotiated an agreement with the mill owner to enlist the help of workers in reducing costs. According to the terms of the agreement, the workers would share in any gains that resulted. The strategy, which added group monetary and nonmonetary rewards, saved the company, restored full wages, and ultimately provided gain-sharing bonuses.

High pay alone will not buy productivity, and by itself it jeopardizes job security. The pay levels of some unionized steelworkers almost match the wages at Lincoln Electric. However, inflated wage costs without productivity gains can price a company out of the market. Even Lincoln Electric, which for years successfully bribed employees with high wages, became aware that good pay alone is not enough and has adapted to changing values by adding nonmonetary systems to its reward package.

Reward systems are amplified by the JIT/VAM principles described in Chapter 3. These principles encourage operator control and versatility, standardize techniques for regulating quality, shorten setup time, reduce inventory, and eliminate waste. In 1986 employees in the Eaton manufacturing plant in Watertown, Wisconsin, were faced with layoffs and agreed to a pay cut. In a last-gasp effort to forestall plant closure, plant manager John Brooks enlisted the help of the entire work force in implementing JIT processes. Within a year employees were back to full pay under conditions that gave them greater influence on operations. Eaton replaced a stifling piecework incentive system with merit pay and gainsharing, but empowerment was the magic ingredient. He gave operators control of JIT/VAM processes that restored previous pay levels and improved the quality of their work lives.

A three-dimensional reward system cannot be orchestrated through a command-and-control top-down strategy; the process must involve all the team players. Wage earners and managers must share a common data base and be bona fide partners in the design of the reward system. If a deeply entrenched adversarial relationship exists between company and union, the first step is a joint educational process leading to the development of a vision that neither party can afford to abandon.

Enhancing a reward system is not easy but is facilitated by modifying the compensation system that is already in place. Moreover, adding new dimensions to an existing pay scheme can sometimes bring about culture changes that were attempted unsuccess-fully through other employee-involvement programs.

One- and two-dimensional reward systems risk the fate of quality circles. Mistakenly perceived as the secret of Japanese manufacturing success, quality circles were launched across American corporate landscapes. Most failed because they represented a one-dimensional process injected into an unreceptive culture; alone they could not make fundamental changes in the organization. Similarly, the new fascination with gain sharing and pay for knowledge can bring about quick-fix failures if they are not combined with complementary systems.

Organizations have two incentives for updating their reward systems. One is the need to survive and prosper; if the company fails, jobs disappear. The other is a taste of dignity, worth, and freedom. Once employees have achieved this kind of fulfillment in the workplace, the survival incentive is no longer necessary; and there is no limit to what the organization can accomplish. As when the Berlin Wall was breached, or when apartheid and totalitarianism weaken, once freedom is tasted, there is no turning back.

REFERENCES

Kanter, R.M. (1989, November-December). The new managerial work. *Harvard Business Review*, pp. 85-92.

Levering, R., Moskowitz, M., & Katz, M. (1984). *The 100 best companies to work for in America*. Reading, MA: Addison-Wesley.

O'Dell, C., & McAdams, J. (1987). *Survey Report*. Houston, Texas: American Productivity and Quality Center.

3

JIT/VAM—A Revolution in Management

In the 1970s and '80s advanced manufacturing technology in Western companies began evolving along the lines developed by Toyota in Japan. The most common term used for this process in the manufacturing industry is JIT (just in time), which has become a generic reference to a combination of factors: TPI (total people involvement), TQC (total quality control), and TPM (total preventive maintenance). Because JIT principles also apply to nonmanufacturing organizations, the term VAM (value-adding management) is sometimes preferred. Hence, VAM and JIT—as used in this text—are synonymous and interchangeable.

Toyota borrowed many of its ideas from Western sources but was the first to standardize those ideas into a holistic concept that could be widely emulated. Many variations of JIT/VAM have evolved to fit different work cultures, but most of them contain the elements portrayed in the JIT/VAM circle (Figure 3-1).

The heart and soul of JIT/VAM is elimination of waste: processing, overproduction, delays, defects, motion, inventory, transportation, and talent. Of these eight kinds of waste, the most damaging and the most often overlooked is the waste of talent. Freeing talent is the key to eliminating the other seven kinds of waste.

Of the remaining seven, the most costly form of waste is delays—delays in the support and management system and in the production operations themselves. Delays add cost but not value. Worse, they disconnect the provider from the customer, making it impossible for the organization to respond quickly to the customer's real needs and desires. There are numerous reasons for delays, but many of these causes can be traced to the functional silos discussed in Chapter 1. Organizations are chopped up into production specialties and sup-

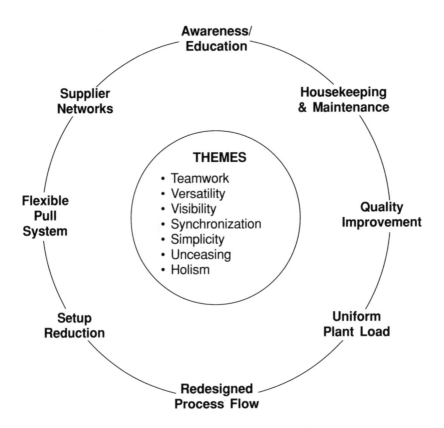

Figure 3-1. JIT/VAM Circle

port specialties. The antidote is cementing groups back together into cross-functional teams, or what Dick Schonberger has termed a chain of customers. In the broad sense JIT/VAM requires teamwork—a level of teamwork that few could have imagined a few years ago. The job of the teams is to get work done and to serve customers fully without delays.

HOW WE ARE DOING

There have been dozens of spectacular and well-publicized JIT/VAM successes in North America. Delays have been reduced fivefold, tenfold, twentyfold, and more. In other words, throughput time, the transition from raw material to finished goods, or from order entry to shipment, has been spectacularly reduced. Those successes have raised expectations of similar breakthroughs in thousands of other companies. Such success seems easy. It would be easy, too, if it were not for one forbidding obstacle that is all too common in industry: an entrenched culture that views managers as thinkers and production employees as doers.

The same problem is found in Japan where JIT was perfected. It took top Japanese companies decades to learn how to shift the locus of quick action for process control and improvement to the factory floor. The rest of the world can profit from the lessons learned in Japan and now replicated by JIT/VAM leaders in the West. The JIT/VAM principles can be implemented much more quickly in the West than they were in Japan, partly because Western countries have models to emulate. More importantly, the free-wheeling, nonconformist spirit of Westerners is in harmony with the JIT/VAM requirement for innovative, delay-free problem solving on the factory floor. JIT/VAM provides guidelines for harnessing that spirit.

CASE STUDY IN JIT/VAM

The following case study (Myers & Schonberger, 1988) provides examples of JIT/VAM as implemented at Seagate's Normandale-South manufacturing plant on the outskirts of Minneapolis. (Normandale-South was purchased by Seagate from Control Data.) The study reports observations of plant operations and the results of personal interviews.

In 1989 Ray Flygare was manufacturing manager of the Normandale-South plant, which produces large disk drives. He was in charge of one product group within the operation and reported to Dale Hooper, who was responsible for managing two plant sites. Flygare likes having Hooper as his boss because Hooper lets him run the plant as he sees fit. As mentioned in Chapter 2, only three organizational layers exist within Ray's group: (1) the manufacturing manager (Flygare), (2) the unit managers and staff support personnel, and (3) the operators and technicians. Communications are simplified by informal and spontaneous networking across levels and functions.

Flygare's switch to the informal JIT style of managing was probably facilitated by his earlier hands-on experience in crop and livestock farming. He has an easy rapport with local employees from similar backgrounds. He still performs as a professional rodeo cowboy on weekends and wears cowboy boots in the factory.

In 1986 Flygare and other Normandale-South managers attended a two-day seminar on world-class manufacturing. When Flygare came to Normandale-South from Control Data's Burnsville plant in early 1987, he and others began applying JIT concepts in the new location. Normandale-South people were exposed to study groups, publications, and video tapes by widely recognized JIT authorities and began blanketing the factory with JIT applications.

As a result of the free hand given him by Hooper, Flygare sees himself as a catalyst who "takes a lot of risks." He also credits people like Judy Hein and Dianne Oney, first-line supervisors who also transferred from Burnsville, as key movers in introducing JIT concepts to work groups in the plant. Hein and Oney have brought JIT to Normandale South through on-the-job applications and training programs. Flygare found that most people supported the concepts, but he had to terminate some employees who could not adapt.

Flygare spends a lot of time on the floor networking with work groups and encouraging them to apply their newly learned concepts. For instance, on the subject of visibility he told a work team, "Nothing should be higher than my shoulders or lower than the top of my boots." (Flygare is about five feet, seven inches tall.) Employees asked him, "Can we do anything we want?" and he answered, "Do whatever you want as long as it doesn't cost any money." A few days later he returned to the area to find everything moved to between boot-high level and shoulder height. The changes implemented by employees reduced stooping, facilitated cleaning, improved lighting, and enabled them to see one another, making possible the quick and easy visual work-flow concepts that are a hallmark of JIT/VAM.

Role of the Unit Manager

Judy Hein began as an operator with Control Data twenty years ago when that company still owned Normandale-South. She obtained a high school equivalency certificate and a two-year college degree in business management through the company educational assistance program. Hein was promoted into first-line supervision ten years ago and began reading books by JIT experts Deming and Ishikawa. She also started learning about statistical process control (SPC) in 1983. Before transferring to Normandale from Control Data in Burnsville, she followed traditional supervisory practice; but at Normandale she began experimenting with JIT applications. She and several others attended seminars given by R.J. Schonberger and continued the gradual evolutionary process toward JIT/VAM.

Because she had worked under a traditional supervisor and had been one herself, Hein was able to contrast the two systems. Before switching to JIT, she supervised about twelve people. She checked attendance, made sure everyone was on time, confirmed that employees complied with safety rules, and tried to keep her manager and workers happy. She had no role in planning, yet the bottom-line question was "How many did you ship today?" Now she supervises thirty-three people and is deeply involved with operators and staff in setting goals and planning personnel policy, work distribution, space layout, and capital equipment expenditures. She is a team leader rather than a boss and gives operators the freedom to be in charge of processes, maintenance, testing, and cross-training.

Production Operators

One of the assemblers on the removal-storage-drive (RSD) line was interviewed when he had been with Normandale-South for two years. He had been at Control Data for nine years before his transfer. In addition to performing assembly work he maintains SPC charts and graphs, audits processes four times per shift and makes adjustments as needed. Judy Hein, his unit manager, appointed him group leader—a responsibility he will hold until he transfers or is reassigned. As group leader, he also trains new people and coordinates cross-training in existing jobs. He likes Hein's style of managing and appreciates the fact that she lets him do his job. "In earlier years Judy was more of a watchdog," he says, "but now she has loosened up."

Joni Borning and Bev Geiken are operators working under unit manager Dianne Oney. Borning was with Control Data for nine years and is a group leader. Geiken has fifteen years combined tenure and sometimes serves as a trainer. Both transferred from Burnsville along with Oney about two years ago. They believe that

Oney was always inclined to be participative in her supervisory style but was not permitted to be under the old system. They are pleased with their freedom to try out new ideas and to help formulate their own rules. Borning explains:

> *In the old days our job was like a kindergarten class, and we checked our brains at the door. Now they respect our opinions and listen to us, and we are not frustrated by bureaucratic constraints. We can talk directly to engineers, production control, and schedulers; but out of courtesy we keep our managers informed of any changes we have worked out. We can leave our work area without permission simply by coordinating our absence with team members. We stand in or take over for absentees; the team will decide how to run shorthanded. Managers say 'handle it the best way you know how.' When a quota exists, our manager asks us what we need in terms of personnel and equipment to do the job. It gives us the feeling, 'We can perform miracles!' or 'We'll show you we can do it!' Because we are able to influence decisions that count, we have more ownership in the company.*

Geiken adds:

> *Everybody is everybody's customer—these are not just words. It really works. We have opportunity to have input with vendors and go to vendors' sites and talk to operators, and vice versa. We have the opportunity to participate in JIT training programs provided by Control Data Corporation and outside consultants and take part in brainstorming sessions on how to make training better. Managers sit down and have lunch with us, and we can join them on a first-name basis. Dale Hooper plays softball with the group. We occasionally participate in a managers round table with a group of about twelve operators and vice presidents and have lunch and talk about whatever we want on an informal and friendly basis.*

Interdisciplinary Teamwork

Although it is true that at Normandale-South "everybody is everybody's customer," it is also clear that production operators and their unit managers are the most important in-house customers of staff support people. Engineers and other staff personnel are available on the shop floor and may be seen huddling with the operators in planning and problem-solving sessions. And because everyone is wearing a blue jacket, outsiders cannot distinguish among operators, technicians, engineers, and managers. In other words, staff support people do not summon production people to office meetings; production workers attend meetings on their own turf.

Employees at Normandale-South use interdisciplinary teamwork to deal with any matters related to production. The following examples illustrate the nature of interdisciplinary teamwork at Normandale. In each of these instances supervisors and operators function as clients of staff support people and top management.

WCM Team Meeting

The world-class manufacturing (WCM) team at Normandale-South is composed of a production manager, a manufacturing engineer, assemblers, a test technician, a materials-quality engineer, an SPC resource representative, and a guest member. A weekly one-hour meeting is held at the RSD (removal storage drive) disk-drive production line to discuss problems concerning procedures, parts, tooling, equipment, facilities, and other matters affecting the production line. Participants begin the meeting by reviewing the previous week's action items. The driving force of the meeting is the list of nonconformities logged during the week by production operators at each work station. All defects are entered into a microcomputer for ready display, reconfiguration, and printout. The team focuses on the top ten defects, ranked in terms of frequency and importance. A standard form is used to list each nonconformity, the number of occurrences, the person responsible, and corrective action. Team members brainstorm an analysis, a solution, and a follow-up action for each problem identified. Some problems are solved during the course of the meeting; others may require extensive follow-up meetings with suppliers, customers, and in-house resources.

The Scheduling Team

Prior to the start of each month the scheduling team meets to determine what must be done to achieve "linearity" against the daily-rate-based schedule. Team members include the master scheduler, the unit manager, the lead assembler from each build area, and a lead test technician. Team meeting agendas include production rates, customer delivery dates, throughput times, specialized testing, and incoming-material delivery dates. Participants also discuss employee training, information derived from assembly/test team meetings, less-than-full-capacity scheduling, and kanban techniques. (A discussion of kanban is offered in this chapter under the subhead "Key Roles of Measurement and Visual Controls.")

Before JIT/VAM and the formation of the scheduling team, work schedules for all the units were organized by the staff in production control on a full-capacity basis with no time allotted for team meetings or assembly problems. Each work center received its own schedule, a plan that contributed to an individualized rather than a teamwork culture. Unique customer requirements and schedule changes created confusion. Frequently, the planners did not know whether there were enough parts available to support the schedule they had planned.

With the formation of the scheduling team, more complete information became available to people on the build site. Visible schedule boards replaced printed handouts. Units are now scheduled to less than full capacity to allow for planning and problem solving, and no units are started in assembly until all parts are available throughout the flow. Normandale's kanban system (called *full-pull*) brings parts from the stockroom to the line dependably. All participants are now on the same data base.

Calibration of Tools

The calibration of hand and torque tools was an ongoing problem that resulted in defects and delays. Operators were never sure whether their tools were calibrated and consequently hoarded backup tools. Sometimes workers inadvertently used uncalibrated instruments. Torque tools were graded in the calibration department by a simulation process that did not always replicate actual conditions. Bureaucratic procedures and paperwork caused delays of up to three days, and the calibration department would charge a cost to the work area whether or not the tool was used or calibrated.

Under JIT a calibration team was formed, made up of six production operators, two engineers, and two managers, including a member of the calibration department. The team brainstormed the problem with a fishbone chart (cause-and-effect-diagram), analyzing problems associated with manpower, materials, methods, machines, and environment. Technicians from the calibration department taught operators how to calibrate torque tools, and the unit purchased a torque analyzer. Production operators and engineers wrote a calibration procedure.

The new process reduced the number of tools in each area by 50 percent and eliminated most of the paperwork. Each tool is now tracked by the operators on X-bar and R charts so that no uncalibrated tools are used. Calibration is more accurate because it is now based on actual rather than simulated tasks, and operators now have ownership and control of their torque tools and of the calibration process. Except for the nominal initial investment in the torque analyzer, no calibration costs are charged to the work area.

Suggestion-Evaluation Team

Employee suggestion plans in most companies are plagued by delays, incomplete feedback, restricted participation, proprietary conflict, and overloading of the engineering department. Normandale-South overcame these shortcomings by forming suggestion-evaluation teams with rotating membership. The teams include the individuals who turn in suggestions plus people from the engineering group; an effort is made to have more direct-labor people than indirect-labor people on the team. A team usually has six to ten members: a unit manager who serves as team leader, a mechanical engineer, an electrical engineer, and an assembler and technician from each area within the department. Team membership rotates monthly. To provide continuity the new team leader attends the last meeting of the previous group, and a previous team leader attends the first meeting of a new group. Each team is obliged to complete the processing of suggestions within a one-month time frame.

During the past year 1,174 suggestions were made by 198 suggesters out of a population of 690. Most of the suggestions were made by team members. About 39 percent of the suggestions were adopted, with a payout of $18,035 for awards and a net savings to the company of $429,262.

The team approach overcomes many of the disadvantages of the traditional system. Anyone can make suggestions; and suggesters more readily accept evaluations of their ideas, because those appraisals are based on the judgments of a team rather than on individual opinions. Team members interview suggesters so that all ideas are fully understood, and engineers (who previously were ineligible to make suggestions) are not saddled with the sole burden of processing suggestions. Idea throughput is reduced to one month or less. Because technicians and assemblers have a better understanding of production processes and the suggestion program, higher-quality and more realistic suggestions are received.

Diversity of Operator Influence

The previous examples do not fully reflect how widely initiative and teamwork are expressed at Normandale-South. Further examples, summarized below, illustrate the variety of forces that help shape the culture of the company:

- Operators track variations in processes through SPC and adjust equipment as necessary to reduce the costs resulting from rejects, inspection, waiting, and wasted motion and inventory.

- Operators are responsible for their own plotting and inspection charting and for reporting of nonconformities. They no longer rely on inspectors.

- Buyers and planners now occupy the manufacturing building, thus improving communications with factory managers and work teams.

- Operators collect data on failed components and present the findings to design engineers, allowing new tooling, changed dimensions, and improved yields.

- Operators write their own manufacturing procedures or rewrite them in their own terms, using sketches, hints, and so forth. Manufacturing engineers do not have to provide procedures, and the instructions are more easily understood.

- Small hand-tool storage has been transferred from industrial engineering to operators in order to increase ownership and flexibility and to improve safety.

- Work-station layout is planned by operators rather than by industrial engineers, thus increasing ownership and flexibility and improving safety.

- Operators maintain a "conditions board" on which they list problems for the purpose of making them visible to people who can help solve them.

- Operators visit suppliers to help resolve nonconformity problems and thus improve material quality through better user-supplier understanding.

- Managers and operators jointly experiment with process changes in their work areas and revise policy and procedures as appropriate.

- Operators use computer terminals for JIT ordering from the warehouse, cutting delivery time from one week to two hours.

- Work teams schedule their own coffee breaks and lunch periods to accommodate optimum machine usage.

- Technicians and assemblers have devised visible tool boards for each work station to replace the previously jumbled toolbox system.

Conditions of Ownership

The foregoing examples illustrate one plant's approach to creating a JIT/VAM work culture geared to continual improvement and led by those closest to the action. In a JIT/VAM culture the employees assume process ownership so that they can act and respond with little or no delay. The conditions for process ownership are summarized into four categories: shared information, operator control, employee versatility, and an equitable reward system.

   1. *Shared Information.* Operators, managers, and staff people share a common data base regarding the mission of the organization. Managers are sensitive to the latent and underused talents of line people and acknowledge their concerns about job security, dignity, and career opportunities. Managers and operators share information about product quality and engineering; price competitiveness and margins; and how to speed up response through rapid changeovers, low inventory, and shorter lead times. Operators have networking relationships with people who precede and follow them in the work flow, including joint-stake suppliers and users; operators also interact with experts who can help solve problems. This kind of interac-

tion works best in an egalitarian culture (see Figure 2-3). The vision that people share must be broader than their individual job responsibilities. The larger picture should include the duties of each employee, but within the total system framework envisioned by the plant manager. Figure 3-2 is a diagram that enables all employees to see the organization through the eyes of the plant manager; the diagram allows workers to understand their individual and collective roles in supporting organizational and personal aims.

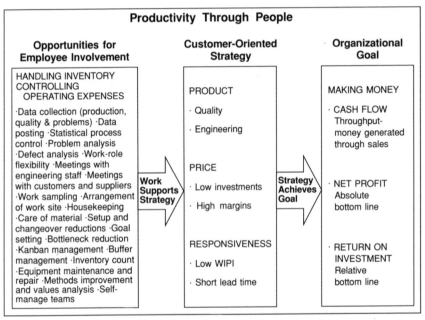

**Figure 3-2. How Individual Responsibilities
Support Organizational Goals**

For instance, an understanding of the organizational goal (to make money, measured in terms of cash flow, net profit, and return on investment) can help workers to link this goal to the joint-stake interests of employees, shareholders, customers, and suppliers. Employees can see that the company strategy (providing a well-engineered, high-quality product at a competitive price in quick response to customer demand) is a bridge between the work and responsibilities of the employees and the organizational goal. They also acquire a better understanding of the vital link between lead time and work-in-process inventory (WIPI).

2. Operator control. Operators and first-line supervisors hold first-mortgage ownership of the production processes. At Normandale-South, these two jobs constitute the only levels below plant manager. Operators and first-line supervisors not only run the system but also modify and maintain it, plan work goals, and measure, evaluate, and correct production processes. First-line people receive fast, direct feedback from the process itself rather than from staff-controlled reports and computer printouts.

3. Versatility. Ownership is broadened when employees can change roles often and move to wherever the work is. At Normandale-South all operators are listed under a single job classification to facilitate cross-training and employee versatility. Problem-solving efforts span craft lines; and the scope of interdisciplinary teamwork includes engineering, maintenance, materials handling, purchasing, suppliers, and customers. Because each operator has ownership of his or her responsibilities, operators are assigned analytical functions usually given to staff people, such as work simplification, statistical process control, work sampling, and cause-and-effect diagnosis.

4. Equitable rewards. Shared ownership justifies shared rewards: employees at Normandale-South receive pay for knowledge and pay for performance, including merit pay to individuals and gain sharing for collective achievements. Employees have ample opportunity to earn recognition and freedom commensurate with responsible and meritorious performance.

Key Roles of Measurement and Visual Controls

Normandale-South, like most other successful JIT/VAM plants, has recognized the importance of incorporating certain measurement duties into the jobs of production people. This step is pivotal in assuring the transfer of ownership to factory-floor people. The best measures of accomplishment call for continual improvement, not for the achievement of a static goal. These measures should be visual, preferably charts on the wall that are frequently updated; Normandale-South uses computer terminals and screens on the shop floor. Just-in-time purists will furrow their brows and say that computer terminals are an unnecessarily complex way to track process improvement, that they cost too much and are themselves another breakdown-prone process. However, a computer company such as Seagate can argue that operators who use computer products feel closer to the basic source of the firm's revenue and understand the company's reason for being in business. Employee involvement in defining and monitoring improvement is a powerful influence in giving management, staff experts, and operators a common data base and uniting them in a common cause. Although measures of improvement can number in the dozens, most can be grouped into five categories: quality, inventory, flexibility, lead time, and space management.

1. *Quality.* Upon receipt of the product or service and during its expected life, the customer is the ultimate judge of quality. The final customer, the buyer, exercises final judgment. The intermediate customer, the employee who must complete the next step in the production process, makes a more immediate judgment. (At a JIT organization this intermediate customer should receive the product in a timely fashion and, if necessary, should be physically close to his or her neighbors in the production process.) Measures of quality are varied and may include consideration of cutoff length or the inner diameter of a component part, elegance of design, the taste of a hamburger, the bouquet of a wine, the tone of a piano, the durability of a tire, or the courtesy of a bank teller or airline cabin attendant. The quality goals of any manufacturing firm—for example, zero defects and continual reduction of process variability—are influenced by all of the firm's organizational functions and are assessed in several ways: evaluators consider product design, process capability and reliability, percentage yield, defects, scrap or rework, and customer feedback. In service industries the quality of customer interaction is pivotal. Quality is widely acknowledged to be a key to competitive advantage, and quality improvement clears the way for JIT achievements in reducing delays and symptoms of waste, such as inventories.

2. *Inventory.* Although inventory represents potential sales, it often consists of items not currently selling well. Inventory also freezes large amounts of working capital, consumes valuable storage space, and requires a costly army of handlers and controllers. Furthermore, inventory is the most obvious source of delay in error detection and response to change. The work-in-process component of inventory (which—for durable goods manufacturers, at least—

has usually been the largest component) ties up plant capacity and kills flexibility. The JIT view is that, in general, inventory is more a liability than an asset. Inventory measures include purchase price, raw material, work-in-process, batch size, buffer stock, queue time, finished goods, and annual inventory turnover. "Zero inventory" or "stockless production" is the JIT ideal; when a company is operating with stockless production, all inventory on hand is undergoing error-free "value-added" processing synchronized with customer demand. Paperwork (invisible inventory) is a considerable source of delay and cost and also belongs in the waste-reduction equation of a JIT campaign.

3. *Flexibility.* Quick customer response requires factory flexibility, defined as the number of different models or products producible per unit of time. Quick response is a function of the changeover time between the end of the previous production and the completion of the first good piece in the new process. Rapid setup requires shop-floor teamwork; workers must ready tool changes while equipment is running a previous job. Readiness to handle new work on short notice is also facilitated by short production runs and by a product design approach that emphasizes producibility and rapid engineering changes. Flexibility is inhibited by adversarial attitudes and restrictive work rules and is supported by employee versatility.

4. *Lead Time.* Total lead time is measured from order entry to delivery. It encompasses engineering design, order preparation, receiving, production, queuing, transport, and delivery. When a plant's first success is in slashing production lead time (also known as throughput or flow time), its priorities shift to reducing time-consuming bureaucratic paperwork. Shorter quoted lead time is often a key to competitive advantage.

5. *Space.* Manufacturing space contains production equipment and people, tools and materials, and storage and handling facilities. The JIT mandate to stamp out delay, error, and variability requires a tidy workplace; orderly placement of materials, tools, and equipment; removal of unnecessary material; compact arrangement of people and machines to tighten human linkages and eliminate or minimize storage and handling; and visibility of work in process.

It is possible to expound in detail on the many types of measurement techniques that apply to each of these five groups of measures. However, because of their dominant roles in JIT/VAM, only two will be mentioned—SPC and kanban. Statistical process control is probably the most respected process-tracking tool. It directly monitors and corrects the processes that are causing errors. Companies using SPC do not have to wait for defects to be found when bad products are sorted out of large lots. Statistical process control avoids errors by measuring central tendency, deviation, distribution patterns, and predetermined limits.

Kanban is another important device, one that cuts inventories and lead times and reduces potential scrap and rework. Kanban is a "pull" signal authorizing production and delivery of one part (or just a few parts) of a particular item. The parts arrive exactly when they are needed, and the system will not authorize another part until the user has utilized one and sends out another kanban signal. The pull feature of kanban is quite different from an ordinary schedule, which acts to push parts upon a user with little regard for rate of use. Kanban gives the user control of work flow—one more element of process ownership.

At Normandale-South, kanban devices include abacuses with red and green beads and poker chips painted red on one side and green on the other. Each chip has a hole in it so that it can be hung on a hook on a visible board, which calls for production to stop or go.

In the pre-kanban era a final assembler had little contact with the next operator in final assembly, who had little contact with the packer at the next operation in the packing department. No contact, no teamwork. The tight time linkages arising from the pull system not only reduce waste associated with unsynchronized inventory flow but, more importantly, tie people together into a production team that works as a unit.

CHANGING A CULTURE

The act of changing a culture from push to pull, from individual to team, from slow response to JIT, from static to continually improving is accomplished through three interrelated efforts:

1. Assembling a vision of the new culture;

2. Obtaining commitment to that vision; and

3. Institutionalizing the vision.

This three-part process cannot be implemented as separate sequential steps. Initiation of the first step must simultaneously trigger the second and third. A top-down manager who tries to assemble a vision within the four walls of a conference room and who then tries to give it the hard sell to the troops usually fails to get beyond the first step.

Ray Flygare, Judy Hein, and Dale Hooper have not assembled a final vision of the culture that they and others hope to institutionalize at Normandale-South, because the vision is constantly evolving with the help of all members of the work force. They are all learning together, sometimes on a trial-and-error basis. But commitment to the emerging vision remains high because of widespread involvement in and ownership of the evolving processes. Employees became committed to the vision and began to institutionalize it while it was still being assembled, and all three steps are in a continual state of change and mutual reinforcement. Should the vision ever be cast in concrete, beyond further modification and refinement, all three steps would be adversely affected; and the desired culture change would be derailed.

The most serious barrier to creating a JIT culture is the enduring gulf between management and operators. Throughout industry the mentality of production people has shifted in recent years, but managerial styles have not always kept pace. The "working stiffs" of previous eras are being replaced by more knowledgeable people who respond positively to earned rewards (both monetary and nonmonetary) particularly and egalitarianism. Less tolerant of boss power, they want to make their influence felt; and they resent the symbolism of the two-class system that suppresses their talents. Their irreverence for traditional chain-of-command protocol is seen in their clothing and conduct. Although they have been conditioned to defend their circumscribed job descriptions at work, they find ways off the job—through civic involvement and a variety of avocational pursuits—to be creative and responsible. In other words, today's line employee is ready and able to help run the plant if allowed to; but that orientation, if blocked, results in disengagement and displaced talent. Although managers are products of the same societal culture, many seem to view production people through filters handed down from obsolete role models and may not discover the bottled-up talents that are a rich resource for putting JIT/VAM to work.

New Roles and Relationships

The new culture is achieved through changes in the mind-sets and roles of all members of the work force, but the launching signals and empowerment originate at the top. If the organization is unionized, employees must be empowered simultaneously by both company and union leaders. If a deeply entrenched adversarial relationship exists between company and union, the first step is a joint educational process to interrupt the win-lose cycle and to place the two parties on a common data base for joint pursuit of mutual gain. The first changes must take place in the roles and relationships of managers and union leaders; these former adversaries must become collaborators.

The more job-grade levels there are between plant manager and operators, the more difficult the empowerment process becomes. People in surplus organizational layers are often so busy protecting their empires that they are not inclined to be conduits of downward or lateral empowerment. Not only do such empire builders tend to practice top-down control within their own functions but they also tend to maintain separate and uncoordinated silos, as described in chapter 1. In a JIT organization middle managers move out of these protected kingdoms into a matrix relationship better suited to serving the chain of customers. In most organizations this move requires a radical reduction in the layers between the CEO and the operators. At Normandale-South the structure evolved until there was only a single layer between operators and the manufacturing manager.

Supervisors and staff support personnel at Normandale-South no longer operate from a power base of official authority but rather from a knowledge base shared with operators. Leaders who once performed in a Parent-Child role as watchdogs are learning the Adult-Adult skills of advisers, consultants, and facilitators. Where they once set goals, rated performance, controlled information, applied discipline, introduced methods changes, and directed career development, they now use positive reinforcement to induce operators to take charge of these matters. They involve people in problem solving and goal setting and encourage networking to promote open access to information. Just-in-time supervisors attack the problem rather than the person when infractions occur and often let the team deal with counterproductive behavior. They encourage methods improvement by people closest to the job, reward teamwork, and give employees the means and the freedom to take charge of their own careers. The contrasting roles of authority-oriented bosses and goal-oriented leaders are discussed in Chapter 9 and summarized in Figure 9-1.

Staff-support people at Normandale-South have moved their desks closer to the workplace and are on call to help solve the problems that, under JIT/VAM, require an immediate response. Support people also involve operators in the development of the systems and policies that affect them. Many of the processes that were used at Normandale-South before the advent of JIT still exist, but they are administered differently:

- The industrial engineer no longer carries a clipboard and stopwatch for motion-and-time studies but instead teaches principles and techniques of work sampling, flow-process charting, Pareto and fishbone analysis, work simplification, and value analysis to job incumbents and lets them take the lead in devising improvements.

- The quality engineer no longer heads a team of inspectors but turns the job over to the operators. The engineer teaches them the necessary skills of statistical process control, enabling them to track and correct operating processes.

- The maintenance manager reduces his own fiefdom by teaching preventive maintenance to the people who run the machines.

- Manufacturing engineers teach new skills to operators and participate with them in implementing group technology, rapid changeovers, materials handling, kanban, and other principles of the pull system and synchronized manufacturing.

- Accountants and other financial specialists no longer evaluate organizational performance in terms of the usual narrow measures, such as direct labor cost. Instead, members of the financial staff downplay or abandon irrelevant criteria and engage in management accounting by working with operating people in reducing causes of cost related to delays, variability, and other wastes.

- Human resource development (HRD) staff no longer generate voluminous procedure manuals or job descriptions or maintain large platoons of trainers. Instead they let job incumbents revise and update their own missions in cooperation with peers and team leaders. Normandale-South maintains a lean corps of trainer-trainers who transfer the training function to the shop floor. Just-in-time organizations require a much greater investment in training than do traditional companies, but the return on investment is far greater when it is institutionalized in the hands of the people who must apply the new skills. In Normandale-South, HRD people attend unit managers' staff meetings to improve staff support services to the line.

- Labor relations are improved when operators and managers are on the same data base. Under these conditions the company is not burdened with the usual backlogs of grievances nor does it have to engage in adversarial collective bargaining. Labor-relations specialists convert adversarial relationships to collaboration by teaching communication, goal setting, and conflict-resolution skills to former adversaries.

CONCLUSION

JIT/VAM requires levels of operator involvement that in the past were not even imagined by the most avid fans of employee participation and team building. Fortunately, the necessary tool is simply training, and training is cheap when compared with the cost of other spending decisions made by management. Still, the very idea of investing in training for direct labor is usually foreign to North American industry. In the words of a United Auto Workers (UAW) union representative at the new United Motors plant in Fremont, California, "Training in the old days consisted of grabbing someone off the street, giving him a wrench and a five-minute introduction about the job, throwing him on the assembly line, and telling him to work like hell."

Top Western companies have seen the light. For example, Motorola, 1989 winner of the Malcolm Baldridge Quality Award, spends about 2.4 percent of its payroll on employee training. In

Normandale-South, training is not broken out as a separate budget item but is lumped in with the cost of doing business. When considering the cost of the various kinds of waste and the impact on customer-credibility resulting from inadequate training, Ray Flygare estimates a seven-to-one return on investment from up-front and continuous training.

Actually, as comprehensive as JIT/VAM is, training costs can be comparatively modest because JIT/VAM is mostly applied common sense, which is not very complicated. The Seagate example demonstrates that a lot of the continuous training that accompanies JIT occurs in connection with problem solving and centers on techniques of measurement, data analysis, diagnosis, brainstorming, goal setting, and proposal presentation.

Just as improving management is a never-ending mission, learning must also be unending. Perhaps the most important kind of learning in an organization is the trainer-training that teaches operators to carry the learning process forward in the workplace. Internal facilitators teach work simplification, SPC, work sampling, cause-and-effect diagnosis, workplace layout, measurement techniques, kanban, and setup-time reduction. (Appendix B is a learning instrument for analyzing waste. Appendix C is a learning instrument for JIT/VAM.)

For all its simplicity, JIT/VAM requires wholesale changes in the physical operation of the workplace; but those alterations must be accompanied by role changes for the operators and the supporting experts and managers. Without changes in roles and mindsets, the best that can be expected is a limited one-shot JIT improvement. Here is a summary of the role changes required by JIT/VAM:

- Jobs are broader and include more planning and diagnosis and both operating and maintenance responsibilities.

- Work teams manage the more tightly linked work roles and synchronized stages of production.

- Operating decisions are pushed down to operator level to meet the need for immediate action on production problems.

- Supervisors and staff-support people are viewed as resources whose primary in-house customers are the operators.

- Management and unions develop innovative ways to recognize tenure and experience while matching jobs with aptitudes.

- Pay schemes are tied to teamwork and versatility to encourage mastery of a progressively broader range of tasks.

- Managers and operators show significantly greater concern for training and a greater willingness to invest in it.

The formula requires stem-to-stern overhaul of the work culture and the mind-sets that make that culture. Although the arguments for team building are not at all new, having a unifying purpose for team activities is still a recent innovation. In a JIT organization employees are united by common goals that motivate the JIT response to change and customer needs. Those common purposes offer an ideal rallying point for team building and employee involvement. In the same vein, team building and employee involvement appear to be the surest, most logical method for molding the organization into a quick-reacting, highly competitive change machine.

REFERENCES

Myers, M., & Schonberger, R.J. (1988, June). *Team-driven JIT*. Presentation to panel on "Supervisors as Team Players," sponsored by the Work in America Institute, Scarsdale, NY.

4

Compatible People

This chapter and the following two chapters discuss three components necessary for organizational effectiveness: people, goals, and systems. All organizations have goals, systems for achieving them, and people who work together to achieve those goals. These three dimensions will be discussed as *compatible people, meaningful goals,* and *helpful systems,* as shown in Figure 4-1. This chapter focuses on the *compatible people* block.

INTERPERSONAL RELATIONSHIPS

People usually get along with one another when they are pulling together toward common goals. Even people who normally do not socialize because of differences in ethnic background, age, gender, religion, or education become compatible if bound together by a common mission. Conversely, people who might otherwise be socially compatible can be fiercely adversarial if they are pursuing conflicting goals.

Organizational relationships are usually defined formally through organization charts and job descriptions. Although formal relationships are the basis for many informal ties, social and technical relationships often develop independently of the formal organization. Social or primary groups form because people do the same kind of work, are of similar ethnic or regional origin, have similar interests, are the same age or gender, or have similar seniority in the firm (Brown, 1965). However, more often people come together simply because they are near one another in the work area. The structure of a primary group is not stable; it changes as membership, job relationships, and work assignments change and as events alter the roles of individuals within the circle. Primary groups based on

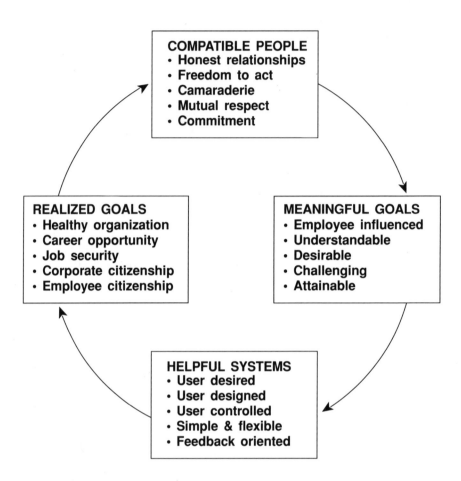

Figure 4-1. Conditions for Organizational Teamwork

work-station relationships may be pre-empted by other primary-group ties, such as those formed in ride pools, coffee bars, lunch rooms, and bowling teams. However, these other groups do not . detract from the work-group membership and may even enrich it.

Large organizations are composed of small, informal groups held together by the process of face-to-face communications. A primary group will sometimes develop its own jargon, which promotes group solidarity and identifies members of the group. These small primary groups vary in size but average six to ten people. Because problems of communication increase as the group grows larger, a group tends to break up or subdivide after it has reached a certain critical size.

New employees who hope to do well at their jobs often try to develop primary-group relationships. These relationships may actually help the newcomer to succeed: primary groups are most likely to function successfully and foster competence in skilled trades in which turnover is low, if the plant is situated in a relatively small and stable community, and if the work force is stable and not subject to fluctuations brought about by such factors as seasonal employment, temporary help, layoffs, and high turnover.

The primary group is the medium through which people acquire their attitudes, values, and goals. It is also a fundamental source of discipline and social control. In most organizations, members of primary or natural work groups expect each member of the circle to perform his or her fair share of the group's work and will rally against the member who benefits at the expense of another. Because the informal work group is the main source of social control, attempts to change human behavior should be made through the group rather than by addressing individuals. The supervisor should try to exercise legitimate influence through such groups and should avoid breaking them up.

People relate to one another in the workplace through the languages of words, behavior, and systems. The language of words consists of the spoken or written words that people hear or read. The language of behavior consists of nonverbal communications such as facial expressions, gestures, supervisory styles, social interactions, recreational groupings, task-force endeavors, and freedom of action. The language of systems includes procedural media such as kanbans, time clocks, attitude surveys, job posting, grievance procedures, public-address systems, performance reviews, work methods, and other processes that utilize standardized forms and equipment. The holistic JIT/VAM processes described in Chapter 3 represent a powerful combination of these three languages. Hence, JIT/VAM, appropriately administered, comprises a basis for productive work teams, which tend to override counterproductive forces stemming from other groupings mentioned above.

Behavior and systems may be thought of as the language of action and usually carry more weight than the language of words. When the language of action differs from the language of words, it is the only one "heard." For example, a management spokesperson may say, "People are our most important assets," but with the language of behavior may convey a contradictory message. In addition, the language of systems may reinforce this contradiction through inappropriate use of time clocks, signal bells, work standards, and status symbols.

Some standard practices in communication have become less appropriate as people have become more enlightened. Enlightened employees usually resent bosses who talk down to them as some parents talk down to children. Most people respond better when addressed as adults. However, unenlightened employees who are more accustomed to dependency relationships may expect to hear the voice of authority, accept it as normal, and even welcome it as an expression of protective parental concern. During the 1990 political revolution in Russia, enlightened Russians expressed their revulsion toward Joseph Stalin to a *60 Minutes* interviewer, but less enlightened citizens wanted him back.

The late Eric Berne (1961), borrowing from the Freudian concepts of superego, ego, and id, labeled personality components as *Parent*, *Adult*, and *Child*, respectively. According to Berne's principles, which he termed *transactional analysis (TA)*, each person has these three components in varying proportions, ready to respond to appropriate cues. The Parent is talking when a supervisor says, "I warn you not to be late again"; the Adult says, "We needed you at eight o'clock this morning"; and the Child says, "Please don't come in late; you'll get us both in trouble."

When the Parent part of the personality is being asserted, it may be expressed in one of two ways—as *critical* or as *protective*. The Critical Parent may be judgmental, fault-finding, self-righteous, hostile, tough, or dogmatic. The Protective Parent may be sympathetic, kind, helpful, nurturing, indulgent, and lenient.

The Adult component of the personality is rational, logical, factual, and unemotional. It is the data processor within us, and sometimes it is referred to as our computer. It is also the component of personality that enables us to understand the influence of the Parent and the Child. The Child component of the personality may be expressed in one of two ways—as a Natural Child or as an

Adapted Child. The Natural Child may be creative, intuitive, fun-loving, charming, and optimistic; or self-indulgent, selfish, stubborn, and manipulative. The Adapted Child tends to be compliant, courteous, whining, withdrawn, and dependent.

The concepts of Parent, Adult, and Child, as used here, are not related to chronological age or to roles in a family. People of all ages have these three components in their personalities. For example, all people have strong Parent tapes imprinted in their minds; that is, they may have powerful instructional memories imprinted by their parents or other authority figures. The memories, like cassette tapes, replay whenever an appropriate situation arises:

- Get plenty of sleep.

- Eat your vegetables.

- Big kids don't cry.

- Never leave a job unfinished.

By the same token, older people may have strong Child components, and hence we see sixty-five-year-olds enjoying a party, going to a picnic, eating ice cream, pouting about a disappointment, or withdrawing within themselves.

People of all ages, then, have active Parent, Child, and Adult personality components. The Adult component enables us to take an objective look at ourselves, to understand how our Parent and Child are influencing our behavior, and to help us decide whether or not to permit this to happen. For example, the obese person who spots coconut cream pie when he or she goes through the cafeteria line hears three voices:

Child: "Wow! Coconut cream pie! That's what I want!"

Parent: "You shouldn't eat it, fatty."

Adult: "I'd enjoy it for five minutes and carry it around for five weeks."

The Child may dominate and the Parent may arouse guilt feelings, but the Adult may analyze what is happening and, if the desire for pie is strong enough, work out a calorie budget to compensate during the next meal.

In the work place, a person's perceptions and expectations are influenced by the component that may be dominant. Consider, for example, the immediate reaction of the individual who is told, "Hey, Joe, the boss wants to see you in his office—right now." Depending on which component of his personality is activated at that time, Joe may experience any of the following feelings:

Critical Parent:	"Why can't he leave me alone when I'm busy?"
Protective Parent:	"Don't worry, Joe; everything will be OK."
Adult:	"I wonder what he wants to see me about."
Natural Child:	"Wow, maybe I'm getting a promotion!"
Adapted Child:	"Oh, no—I hope I didn't do anything wrong."

In his supervisor's office, Joe may receive either positive or negative strokes. Speaking from his Adult, the supervisor may give a positive stroke: "Thanks for coming in, Joe. I would like your advice. The superintendent wants to know when we could get the new compressor installed. What should I tell him?" Speaking from his Parent, the supervisor could give Joe negative strokes on the same subject: "Where the devil were you, Joe? I promised the super we'd have the new compressor installed by tomorrow noon. Drop whatever you're doing and get on it, or it's your neck and mine. Now don't tell me your problems; I don't want to hear from you till the job is done."

The use of positive strokes is more likely to evoke an Adult-Adult discussion between Joe and his supervisor, resulting in mutual respect and self-confidence. Negative strokes clearly represent a Parent-Child encounter, which evokes a "Yes, sir" from Joe's Adapted Child, resulting in lingering resentment and conformity. Or it could evoke an "I don't need this job" from Joe's rebellious Natural Child.

A positive stroke in its simplest form may be a smile or a friendly gesture—a warm sign of acceptance. A negative stroke may be a frown, a sneer, or a criticism—a put-down. In the work environment, asking for suggestions and listening to them are positive strokes. Giving "idiot-proof" job instructions or not listening to ideas are negative strokes. Not all positive strokes have to convey good news. In a performance review discussion, for example, adverse information handled as feedback rather than as criticism represents a display of confidence and respect that makes it a positive stroke.

Depending on whether they have received mostly positive or mostly negative strokes, people tend to develop a rather permanent set of attitudes toward themselves, others, and life in general. This attitudinal life position is sometimes referred to as degree of "OK-ness" (Harris, 1976). A person who is consistently treated as an adult and given many positive strokes tends to develop feelings of OKness about self and others. This person's basic position is "I'm O.K., you're O.K.; the world is a pretty good place, and it's fun to be alive." But the person who is given many positive strokes from permissively protective authority figures may develop a spoiled-brat syndrome: "I'm O.K., you're not O.K." Individuals who have received a lifetime of negative strokes may develop the position "I'm not O.K., you're O.K." or "I'm not O.K., you're not O.K." This is particularly true of people whose initiative has been continually quashed or who have been unfairly and inescapably disadvantaged in competitive pursuits.

Some individuals appear to carry through life a characteristic position of OKness that manifests itself predictably in almost all circumstances. For most people, however, feelings of OKness are situational. For example, an employee may feel in the workplace, "I'm O.K., you're not O.K."; in church, "I'm not O.K., you're O.K."; and at home, "I'm O.K., you're O.K."

People are sometimes polarized into positions through their group identity. In a company with adversarial labor relations, management people sometimes assume a uniform position toward workers of "We're O.K., they're not O.K." Workers, in turn, assume the same position: "We're O.K., but management is not O.K." As long as these basic group postures exist, it is not realistic to expect collaboration between the two parties.

Strokes and life positions are interdependent. When our Critical Parent or defiant Natural Child causes us to dispense negative strokes, we may evoke an "I'm not O.K." or "You're not O.K." attitude from the recipients. When our Adult or Natural Child applies positive strokes, we usually evoke "You're O.K." responses. However, people in the "We're O.K., you're not O.K." position find it unnatural and difficult to dispense positive strokes to an adversary, so the mutually self-defeating, win-lose cycle is perpetuated. This win-lose cycle can be interrupted by applying the JIT/VAM process described in Chapter 3 in combination with the appropriate reward systems described in Chapter 2.

THE ROLE OF ASSUMPTIONS

Douglas McGregor's classic book, *The Human Side of Enterprise* (1960), illustrates the concept that each person's behavior reflects his or her values or attitudes. One type of attitude, which McGregor called "Theory X," embodies assumptions that tend to bring out undesirable behavior in people. A contrasting set of assumptions, which he labeled "Theory Y," is likely to bring out the best in people. Although the terminology of transactional analysis was not widely known when McGregor wrote his book, Theory X values are usually expressed as Critical or Protective Parent in Parent-Child relationships from the position "I'm O.K., you're not O.K." Theory Y generally finds expression in Adult-Adult relationships, though at times it is also expressed as Parent-Child, Adult-Child, and Child-Child transactions. Theory Y is usually a manifestation of the position "I'm O.K., you're O.K."

Goal-oriented, developmental (Theory Y) supervisors embrace values that reflect confidence in other people. Although this kind of supervisor recognizes that some employees may not yet have earned that respect and confidence, he or she assumes that they are capable of doing so. Theory Y supervisors in effect activate a self-fulfilling prophecy by treating people as though they merit respect and confidence.

Theory Y supervisors recognize that some people are counterproductive but tend to interpret this as the fault of job design or supervisory style rather than as a reflection on the inherent characteristics of jobholders. Such leaders believe that freedom and responsibility go hand in hand and that if managers share information with employees, the employees will tend to think and behave responsibly. These leaders have consistently high expectations of others and assume that given access to information and freedom to act, employees will set and achieve high goals on their own. [1] Theory Y leaders

---

[1] For further information on the role of a manager's expectations, see "Pygmalion in Management," by J.S. Livingston in the *Harvard Business Review*, July-Aug. 1969, pp. 81-89.

are not mollycoddlers and believe in giving people both good and bad news; they believe that most people want and are capable of accepting the whole story, regardless of how painful it is. Theory Y facilitators assume that mistakes are inevitable and should provide a basis for learning and that punishment tends primarily to evoke defensiveness. Although they recognize the importance of money, they believe in the broader concept of reward systems described in Chapter 2.

Authority-oriented, reductive (Theory X) supervisors, in contrast, tend to quash initiative or to evoke defensiveness through behavior that reflects lack of confidence in others and, through such signals, also activate a self-fulfilling prophecy. Hence, Theory X bosses find that people tend to do as little work as possible and that they require close supervision and a little fear to prevent them from lowering their standards. In their eyes few people have imagination or ingenuity; these managers tend to discount employee suggestions because they believe that most workers have too limited a perspective. Moreover, Theory X supervisors assume that their positions in the hierarchy entitle them to respect and believe that their prestige would be weakened if they asked for advice or admitted the superiority of a subordinate's ideas. They filter and screen information that they spoon-feed to subordinates on the assumption that they will abuse information and are incapable of accepting bad news. Although reductive bosses readily admit that people like responsibility and recognition, these managers think that such concerns are "mollycoddling"; that employees are bound to gripe about something; and that the only real way to motivate workers and keep them happy is to give them enough money. Theory X supervisors are usually unable to differentiate between happiness and motivation.

The trend in organizations is to favor goal orientations over authoritarian orientations as a foundation for human effectiveness. Few thoughtful managers today would deliberately defend the traditional application of authority. Often managers have helped to prepare formal statements of philosophy that idealize their organizations as democratically goal oriented; they might have conscientiously committed themselves to goal-oriented principles through both written and spoken words. However, in many ways, both subtle and obvious, as a result of habit, tradition, policy, systems, insensitivity, and introspective myopia, some of these same managers continue to use delegated authority as their primary source of power.

The Reductive Use of Authority

The most overtly authoritarian managers form *superior-subordinate* or *reductive* relationships that imply ownership of subordinates by the supervisor. These managers demand, rather than request, actions from their employees. They will summon employees without apparent regard for their convenience or will otherwise interrupt employees' activities. They phone orders to underlings without inquiring about their schedules or simply bark to the subordinate's secretary, "Tell Bill to come to my office!" Although this kind of manager may drive points home in meetings by shouting and pounding the conference table, it is generally understood that subordinates will not respond with similar shouting and table pounding. This manager is likely to pre-empt conference rooms reserved by subordinates, call subordinates out of training programs, by-pass their secretaries, interrupt their staff meetings, make disparaging remarks about modes of dress and hairstyles, and disregard social relationships and commitments.

Managers have been endowed with privileges for so long that these signs of rank find unquestioned acceptance; often people are no longer consciously aware of the original and lingering significance of these entitlements. Class distinctions are created or reinforced through authority-based privileges and through symbols such as exclusive dining and parking facilities; larger, better-furnished offices; distinctive identification badges; and more formal modes of attire. Special coffee service, exemption from parking rules, disregard of time signal bells, nonobservance of lunch and coffee schedules, and circumvention of job-posting procedures are among the common privileges of rank, unthinkingly and flagrantly perpetuated by managers long after the company has declared itself officially against an authoritarian orientation. Symbols associated with these privileges tend to increase social distance and inhibit communication, thus creating and exaggerating cleavages between groups at various levels of the organization.

An authority-oriented supervisor rarely forms convictions on the basis of professional competence but instead aligns himself or herself with the power structure of the organization. If a project managed by a subordinate is viewed favorably by upper management, this supervisor becomes identified with it and gradually and subtly reverses the delegation process until he or she is pulled into the limelight and becomes the official spokesperson for the project. The subordinate, expecting to present a proposal personally, completes the necessary research-and-development work, only to have the supervisor whisk it away to an unknown fate. If the project loses favor in the eyes of upper management, the supervisor quickly denies responsibility by redelegating it.

The chain of command is the authoritarian's primary basis for both official and unofficial relationships. He or she expects all information to flow upward or downward through "official channels." A subordinate who wishes to contact another employee at the supervisor's level or above—hoping, for example, to secure a guest speaker for a graduation banquet—soon learns that the message must be channeled through the boss. However, subordinates are free to contact those at their own levels or below. Authority-oriented people tend to choose employees at their own levels or above for luncheon dates or social activities, though they would find it acceptable to accompany a group of their own subordinates to lunch. For this manager, social stratification within, and even outside, the organization is determined largely by position in the official hierarchy.

If one of the subordinates of an authoritarian manager loses favor with a higher-up, for whatever reason, the manager's own perception of the subordinate is altered; and he or she readily turns and "takes the second bite" at the heels of the unfortunate employee. The supervisor may salve his or her conscience by uttering feeble demurrals and by damning the subordinate with faint praise but will ultimately acquiesce and obediently perform the painful ceremony of admonishment, transfer, demotion, or termination with the courage displayed by all official axmen.

Occasionally, goal-oriented work groups, made up of individuals whose professional competence immunizes them against the arbitrary use of power, form within the authoritarian's organization. The supervisor holds them in awe because he or she respects power of any kind; and as long as they incur top management favor and support, the supervisor does not stand in their way. However, his or her relationship to these individuals is not usually one of goal-oriented reciprocity. For authoritarians, solidarity or equality is an uncomfortable experience. Hence, the authoritarian supervisor tends to abandon these employees or disengage from involvement in their efforts. If the group finally disbands and leaves the organization in reaction to the authoritarian's style of leadership and he or she must restaff the vacated positions, this type of manager will vow never again to let another "power-base" develop.

Slightly more subtle are the cat-and-mouse tactics employed by a manager to remind underlings that their security and freedom exist only through official magnanimity. Such ploys include the arbitrary withholding and dispensing of information according to whim, the last-moment scheduling or canceling of meetings, the delaying and extending of staff gatherings, the extraction of reasons for personal leave, the selective distribution of homemade Christmas cakes to favorites, and the authorization to use company-financed club facilities.

When the authoritarian supervisor chairs a staff meeting, subordinates follow an infallible method for taking the "right" position on any issue: they learn to read the supervisor's facial expressions. They sit in watchful silence until the chief speaks and then converge on an elaboration of his or her viewpoint. So firmly established become the cue-reading patterns, that subordinates—as well as the supervisor— are often deceived into interpreting conformity as consensus.

The manager's authority is often adopted by his or her secretary through a process of power by association. The secretary's requests for information frequently come through as orders to subordinates and their secretaries. Exempted from timekeeping regulations, rotational relief assignments, and many standard ground rules, the secretary gradually becomes more imperious while subordinates become acquiescent and alienated. Attempts to give feedback to the manager about the secretary's "little-dictator" syndrome characteristically evoke a defensive response, shutting off future feedback attempts.

Perhaps the most discouraging aspect of this misuse of authority is the supervisor's insensitivity to the problem. Authority orientation is not usually an expression of intentional or deliberate malice. It is more often a form of conditioning, perhaps resulting from years of adapting to authoritarianism at home, in school, in the armed forces, and in previous jobs. The intelligent authoritarian typically experiences flashes of insight. When alienation among subordinates becomes obvious, this type of manager may attempt to win goodwill through the paternalistic generosity of an office party, a home barbecue, a Christmas turkey, or other forms of bribery. Paternalism, of course, only increases social distance. These attempts to change are sincere but are merely superficial veneers that fail to conceal the real attitudes exposed through the day-to-day language of action. What the boss is speaks so loudly that his subordinates can scarcely hear what he says.

Finally, authority-oriented supervisors should not bear the full brunt of their ineptness. The bosses above them who appointed them and reinforced their behavior through rewards, authoritarian systems, and their own leadership styles, are the primary problem. If these supervisors can change, they certainly will not do it until they get different cues from above. Their behavior usually reflects their subconscious attempts to build themselves in the images of their superiors.

Figure 4-2 shows how 1,344 managers were described by highly motivated and poorly motivated subordinates. Highly motivated employees use descriptors characterizing goal-oriented supervisors. Poorly motivated employees were almost evenly balanced in describing their managers as authority-oriented or goal-oriented, with more emphasis on reductive descriptors. These results suggest that a manager's competence in interpersonal relationships is a necessary—but not the sole—factor in highly motivating employees. Meaningful goals and helpful systems are also necessary.

Effective Teams

In research conducted at the MIT Sloan School of Management during the 1950s, Douglas McGregor found that successful teamwork was based on Theory Y assumptions. For instance, when observing task-oriented groups or teams engaged in problem-solving and goal-setting missions, he found that successful groups with a genuine unity of purpose tended to operate under the following conditions:

1. Climate. The atmosphere, which can be sensed in a few minutes of observation, tends to be informal, comfortable, and relaxed. There are no obvious tensions. It is a working environment: people are involved and interested, and there are no signs of boredom.

2. Discussion. There is a lot of discussion in which virtually everyone participates, but it remains pertinent to the task of the

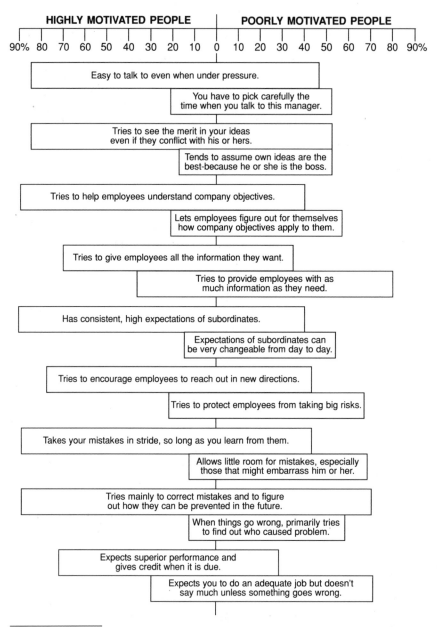

HIGHLY MOTIVATED PEOPLE | **POORLY MOTIVATED PEOPLE**

90% 80 70 60 50 40 30 20 10 0 10 20 30 40 50 60 70 80 90%

Easy to talk to even when under pressure.

You have to pick carefully the time when you talk to this manager.

Tries to see the merit in your ideas even if they conflict with his or hers.

Tends to assume own ideas are the best-because he or she is the boss.

Tries to help employees understand company objectives.

Lets employees figure out for themselves how company objectives apply to them.

Tries to give employees all the information they want.

Tries to provide employees with as much information as they need.

Has consistent, high expectations of subordinates.

Expectations of subordinates can be very changeable from day to day.

Tries to encourage employees to reach out in new directions.

Tries to protect employees from taking big risks.

Takes your mistakes in stride, so long as you learn from them.

Allows little room for mistakes, especially those that might embarrass him or her.

Tries mainly to correct mistakes and to figure out how they can be prevented in the future.

When things go wrong, primarily tries to find out who caused problem.

Expects superior performance and gives credit when it is due.

Expects you to do an adequate job but doesn't say much unless something goes wrong.

From M.S. Myers, "Conditions for Manager Motivation," *Harvard Business Review,* January-February, 1966, p. 63. Adapted by permission of *Harvard Business Review.*

Figure 4-2. How Employees Describe Their Supervisors

group. If the discussion gets off the subject, someone redirects it in short order.

3. Goals. The task or the objective of the group is well understood and accepted by the members. There is free discussion of the objective until it can be formulated in a way that allows the members of the group to commit themselves to it.

4. Listening. The members listen to one another. The discussion does not jump from a given issue to an unrelated concept. Every idea is given a hearing. People do not seem to be afraid of appearing foolish by putting forth a creative thought, even if it seems fairly extreme.

5. Disagreement. There is disagreement. The group is comfortable with this state of affairs and shows no signs of trying to avoid conflict or of struggling to maintain a false impression of sweetness and light. Disagreements are not suppressed or overridden by premature group action. The reasons for dispute are carefully examined, and the group seeks to resolve them rather than to dominate the dissenter. On the other hand, there is no domination by a vocal minority. Individuals who disagree do not appear to be trying to control the group or to be voicing hostility. Their disagreement is an expression of a genuine difference of opinion, and they expect a hearing so that a solution can be found. If there are basic disagreements that cannot be resolved, the group finds it possible to live with these differences, accepting them but not permitting them to block its efforts. Under some conditions, action will be deferred to permit further study of an issue by the members of the group. On other occasions, where the disagreement cannot be resolved and action is necessary, it will be taken, but with open caution and with recognition that the action may be subject to later reconsideration.

6. Consensus. Most decisions are reached by a kind of consensus in which it is clear that everybody is in general agreement and willing to go along. However, individuals who oppose the action rarely keep their opposition private or let an apparent consensus mask real disagreement. Formal voting is at a minimum; the group does not accept a simple majority as a proper basis for action.

7. Criticism. Criticism is frequent, frank, and relatively comfortable. The focus is on issues and problems rather than on personal attack, either open or masked. The criticism has a constructive flavor in that it is oriented toward removing obstacles that face the group and that prevent it from getting the job done.

8. Candor. People are free in expressing their ideas and their feelings. Group members reveal both their reactions to the problem at hand and their views of the group's operation. There is little pussyfooting; there are few hidden agendas. Everybody appears to understand how everybody else feels about any matter under discussion.

9. Action Plan. When action is taken, clear assignments are made and accepted.

10. Chairing. The person chairing the group does not dominate it, and the group does not defer unduly to the leader. In fact, leadership appears to shift from time to time, depending on the circumstances. Specific members of the group, because of their knowledge or experience, at various times act as resources for the other participants. The members of the group utilize one another in this fashion, and the resource people occupy leadership roles while they are serving in this capacity. There is little evidence of a struggle for power while the group operates. The issue is not who controls, but how to get the job done.

11. Feedback. The group is self-aware in relation to its own operations. Frequently, it will pause during the meeting to examine how well it is functioning and to decide what factors may be impeding its progress. The problem may be a matter of procedure, or it may be an individual whose behavior is interfering with the accomplishment of the group's objectives. All issues are discussed openly until a solution is found.

Ineffective Groups

In studying groups that are relatively ineffective in accomplishing their purposes, McGregor reported the following characteristics:

1. Climate. The atmosphere is likely to reflect either indifference and boredom (people whisper to each other or carry on side conversations, and some individuals are obviously not involved) or tension (there are undercurrents of hostility and antagonism, stiffness and undue formality). The group is clearly not challenged by its task and is not genuinely involved in it.

2. *Discussion.* A few people tend to dominate the discussion. Often their contributions are off the point, but little is done by anyone to keep the group clearly on track.

3. *Goals.* From the conversation, it is difficult to identify what the group's objectives are. These aims might have been stated by the chairman initially, but there is no evidence that the group either understands or accepts a common goal. On the contrary, it is usually evident that members of the group have differing, private, and personal objectives that they are attempting to achieve through the group. These objectives are often in conflict with one another and with the group's task.

4. *Listening.* People do not really listen. Ideas are ignored and overridden, and the discussion jumps around with little coherence and no sense of directed movement. Members of the group appear to be talking for effect: people make speeches that are obviously intended to impress rather than to address the task at hand. Some members believe that the leader or other members are constantly judging everyone's contributions, so the suspicious participants are extremely careful about what they say. Conversations with members after the meeting reveal that fear of being criticized or regarded as silly kept them from expressing their ideas or feelings.

5. *Disagreement.* Disagreements are generally not dealt with effectively by the group. Dissent may be completely suppressed by a leader who fears conflict; or it may result in open warfare, the consequence of which is domination by one subgroup over another. Disagreements may be "resolved" by a vote in which a very small majority wins the day and a large minority remains completely unconvinced. There may be a tyranny of the minority in which an individual or a small subgroup is so aggressive that the majority accedes in order to preserve the peace or to continue with the task. In general, only the ideas of the more aggressive members are considered, because the less aggressive people tend either to keep quiet altogether or to give up after short, ineffectual attempts to be heard.

6. *Consensus.* Actions are often taken prematurely before the real issues have been examined or resolved. There is a lot of complaining

after the meeting by people who disliked the decision but failed to speak up during the meeting itself. A simple majority is considered sufficient for action, and the minority is expected to go along. Most of the time, however, the minority remains resentful and uncommitted to the decision.

7. Criticism. Criticism occurs, usually in the form of attacks that produce tensions and embarrassment. Criticism of ideas tends to be destructive, putting certain members on the defensive. Sometimes every proposal is clobbered by one participant or another. After a while, no one is willing to take the risk of offering another idea.

8. Candor. Personal feelings are hidden rather than brought out in the open. The general attitude of the group is that feelings are inappropriate for discussion and would be too explosive if revealed.

9. Action plan. Action decisions tend to be unclear; no one really knows who is going to do what. Even when assignments of responsibility are made, there is often considerable doubt as to whether the duties will be carried out.

10. Chairing. The leadership remains clearly with the committee chairperson. This person may be weak or strong, but he or she always sits at the head of the table.

11. Feedback. The group tends to avoid any objective discussion of how it is functioning as a unit. After the meeting there is often some talk about what went wrong and why, but these matters are seldom brought up during the meeting itself when they might be resolved.

How a Group Can Measure Its Effectiveness

The principles elaborated above can serve as guidelines for conducting successful meetings and for helping a group to critique itself. Figure 4-3 summarizes these evaluation criteria in a group-feedback form. The recommended use of this form is to have a supply on hand and when a meeting is not functioning as desired, to stop and have each member complete a form. A highly successful meeting might be followed by the same sort of self-assessment. The group average or median for each item is the score for that item. The potentially perfect score for the whole form is 99, and the absolute low is 0. In practice, groups do not hit these extremes; but a well-functioning group scores above 75 and a poorly functioning group below 50.

1. Climate   0   1   2   3   4   5   6   7   8   9
indifference, boredom   involvement, interest

2. Discussion   0   1   2   3   4   5   6   7   8   9
unbalanced, irrelevant   widespread, relevant

3. Goals   0   1   2   3   4   5   6   7   8   9
unclear, conflicting   understood, accepted

4. Listening   0   1   2   3   4   5   6   7   8   9
ideas ignored, overridden   attentive, respectful

5. Disagreement   0   1   2   3   4   5   6   7   8   9
conflicts suppressed, open   thoughtful acceptance of
warfare, or tyranny of   conflict, rational expression
the minority   of differences

6. Consensus   0   1   2   3   4   5   6   7   8   9
premature action, resentful   working through
minority(ies)   to agreement

7. Criticism   0   1   2   3   4   5   6   7   8   9
tension-producing, personal   obstacle-directed
attacks   discussion

8. Candor   0   1   2   3   4   5   6   7   8   9
hidden feelings   free expression of feelings

9. Action Plan   0   1   2   3   4   5   6   7   8   9
unclear assignments,   clear, accepted assignments
uncommitted acceptance

10. Chairing   0   1   2   3   4   5   6   7   8   9
domineering, arbitrary,   democratic, thoughtful,
Parent-Child   Adult-Adult

11. Feedback   0   1   2   3   4   5   6   7   8   9
faultfinding   self-examination
after meeting   during meeting

Figure 4-3. Group-Feedback Form

REFERENCES

Berne, E. (1961). *Transactional analysis in psychotherapy*. New York: Grove.

Brown, J.A.C. (1965). *The social psychology of industry*. Baltimore, OH: Penguin.

Harris, T.A. (1976). *I'm O.K., you're O.K.* New York: Avon.

McGregor, D. (1960). *The human side of enterprise*. New York: McGraw-Hill.

5

Meaningful Goals

Everyone has goals. Some goals are set by the individuals pursuing them, some are set with the participation of others, and some are set exclusively by others. Generally speaking, individuals most actively pursue the goals they set themselves. When too many of a person's goals are set by others, he or she reacts individually or collectively to circumvent, violate, or change these goals. These goals of avoidance and rebellion then become personal goals. Therein lies the crux of the problem of goal setting in industry.

The higher a person's position in the organization, the more freedom he or she has to set goals. If the person at the top defines his or her goals with the genuine involvement of the people at lower levels, his or her goals become their goals.

However, if goal setting is a top-management function to be sold downward through the use of persuasion, authority, bribery, and manipulation, people respond with words and actions that say, "Those are not my goals, they are management's goals." If management is seen as an enemy, the individual fights back in subtle or overt ways, often ingeniously, sometimes subconsciously, to thwart management goals. If management is perceived as benevolent and friendly, the individual may curb inner frustrations, turn out a fair day's work, and appreciate any well-intended praise and rewards. In any case, when they are not part of the decision-making process, workers think and talk most of the time about their own goals—which they find off the job.

DYNAMICS OF GOAL SETTING

The relationship of goals to satisfaction may be expressed in the following equation:

$$\text{Satisfaction} = \frac{\text{achievements}}{\text{goals}}$$

Goals nearly always exceed achievements, hence satisfaction increases as achievements approach goals. In reality, even this satisfaction is illusory and fleeting, because people begin raising their expectations or directing their attention elsewhere as soon as they realize they are approaching their goals. For example, a person who decides to jog a mile per day may adjust that goal to three miles per day when the earlier objective becomes easy. When a man is hungry, his immediate goal is to eat. Having satisfied that need, he redirects his concern and plans to read a chapter of a book or to complete some office homework.

The equation also has long-range application. For example, a high school graduate's goal may be a Bachelor's degree in electrical engineering. As the student nears the attainment of this goal, he or she sets a new goal—perhaps to get a job as an engineer in a certain company or to pursue an advanced degree. While working toward these long-range goals, he or she has set and achieved (or set, failed to achieve, and readjusted) many short-range goals, such as pledging a fraternity or sorority, earning an A in calculus, getting a passing D in history, going with a particular person to the spring dance, winning a tennis match, and learning to ski.

Victor Vroom (1964) defined the attractiveness of a particular goal as a function of the net desirability of any number of consequences of its attainment. The level of motivation with which an individual pursues a goal is determined by how much he or she values the consequences that will result when the goal has been achieved. For example, a high school graduate may volunteer for an uninteresting military job to earn educational assistance for a college education. While performing uninspiring military duties, the student may unexpectedly discover an opportunity to apply for a military-sponsored educational assignment that is relevant to his or her professional interests and that may also offer college credits. The enlistee pursues the assignment with newly kindled enthusiasm because now the perceived negative value of the military job itself has the potential of leading to a positive outcome to be coupled with the positive value of the long-range college plan.

Goal-setting problems often arise when managers assume that people have little interest in organizational objectives. Many supervisors, not understanding the characteristics of meaningful goals, assign only tasks or duties. Tasks and duties are performed to achieve the supervisor's goals, but employees rarely perform such tasks with the enthusiasm felt by the boss. Tasks and duties take on meaning when those who perform them can see the relationship between their efforts and the attainment of their own as well as the company's goals.

Finding A Goal-Setting Arena

Through trial and error most people ultimately find the arena in which they can achieve their goals. The new college graduate entering industry often finds ever-blossoming opportunities for setting and achieving increasingly higher goals. Because a college degree opens many doors, success in the company is largely a function of ambition and talent. The graduate's economic needs are routinely met through an expanding compensation package and are not a primary concern as long as a broadening professional role in the organization provides noneconomic rewards in the form of growth, responsibility, and recognition for the achievement of challenging goals. New employees may become so engrossed in these rewarding experiences on the job that gradually, voluntarily, and sometimes unconsciously, they disengage from outside interests and devote ever-increasing amounts of time and energy to the job, which becomes a primary arena for goal setting and achievement.

However, the employee's former high school classmates who entered industry without college degrees usually find the industrial workplace only temporarily rewarding. Having escaped parental control and having satisfied immediate maintenance needs, they cast about impatiently for new opportunities, only to find those opportunities reserved for the newcomer with a degree, who is often a younger and less experienced employee. Their alternatives are few, difficult, and often not satisfying. They can do double duty and acquire the necessary academic credentials by attending classes after working hours; they can earn advancement through sheer talent, initiative, and perseverance; or they can abandon the organization—physically or mentally.

Most who enter industry without benefit of a college degree stay in the work force physically, job-hopping occasionally, preoccupied during duty hours with wages and working conditions, finding and gradually accepting their identity through their work roles and memberships in peer groups. However, the compliant performance of simple tasks does not demand much of their talents; and their interests and energies are channeled outward to their own arenas for self-actualization—off the job.

When on their own time, these people can satisfy growth needs through travel, reading, music, group memberships, and any number of challenging pursuits. They look for achievement opportunities in bowling, fishing, painting, stock speculation, and mountain climbing; they seek responsibility as scoutmasters or Sunday school teachers and through school-board membership, public office, and participation in social-action groups. Recognition needs may be satisfied through many of the foregoing activities, plus undertakings such as little theater, ballroom dancing, public speaking, competitive sports, and social-group memberships.

People with degrees gradually channel more of their energy into the pursuit of organizational goals, while their contemporaries without degrees are gradually disengaging themselves from organizational commitment and finding expression for their talents in the pursuit of meaningful goals off the job.

Hence, the manager and the worker go separate ways in pursuit of goals. The problem is circular and self-perpetuating. The manager finds that he or she must do extra duty to make up for the lack of commitment at the lower levels. But people at the lower level pursue goals outside the organization because managers have reserved the more interesting work for themselves.

Consequences of Overcommitment

It is not uncommon to encounter overcommitment to the job at the higher management levels—overcommitment in the sense that the individual is deprived of a well-rounded life of responsible citizenship. Avid corporate goal setters rarely have enough energy and time left over from company duties to attend to personal and professional growth, physical well-being, or family and community responsibilities. The more engaged they become in the pursuit of meaningful goals on the job, the more tunnel-visioned they become and the more disengaged they become from involvement with the members of their families, and hence, the less opportunity they have to experience goal setting within family and community units. Moreover, spouses and children have only fragmentary familiarity with the vocational roles of these managers and cannot experience their achievements vicariously.

Members of the corporate goal setter's family often have life roles similar in many respects to the work roles of lower-level employees. Like traditional hourly paid workers, they do not share the manager's corporate goals as a foundation for their own goal setting. Yet each family, like each organization, has unique aims that need the involvement, support, and commitment of all members of the family unit, including the people whose incomes pay the bills. Checkbook benevolence is not an adequate substitute for personal participation. Many business organizations, however, seem to thrive, at least temporarily, at the expense of a society that suffers because of absentee spouses and parents who are overcommitted to corporate goals.

Consequences of Undercommitment

Hourly, nonexempt workers sometimes have just as much imbalance in their lives. Their goal-setting efforts within the organization are often unofficial and counterproductive, aimed at overcoming the limitations imposed by corporate goal setters. Because their jobs are not challenging and because they cannot influence company goals, these employees use their talents to pursue aims associated with issues that are unrelated to the work itself, such as wages, paid leave, broadened insurance, liberal retirement benefits, and shorter hours. These are only intermediate goals, of course, providing people with the means to achieve the ends that they are pursuing off the job. In addition, the fun of engaging management in adversary bargaining breaks the monotony of an otherwise humdrum existence.

Disengaged workers seem to have capricious and vacillating interests in issues peripheral to the jobs, such as improving the grievance procedure, revising work rules, changing the content of the company newspaper, upgrading job titles, varying the cafeteria menu, and improving the parking facilities. Their goals often relate to social needs, such as gaining acceptance and status within work groups, organizing office parties, finding congenial ride pools, and planning recreational outings.

Most nonproductive or unofficial workplace preoccupations serve primarily to make time at work more bearable or to reinforce off-the-job pursuits. Efforts directed toward these activities may seem wasteful to corporate goal setters, but at least off-the-job activities involve family members in ways that company activities do not and therefore contribute to family cohesiveness and community stability. Wage earners, because they tend to direct their talents and energy to issues outside the workplace, have a disproportionately greater influence on the values and behavior patterns of a culture. Their impact on society is also great because they vastly outnumber their managers.

Unfortunately, people who have the most highly developed administrative skills may not have the time to be responsible citizens. The corporate goal setter, whose leadership talents are often being challenged and developed through involvement in responsible roles on the job, has little time to utilize this competence in the community. On the other hand, wage earners who have not been able to grow or to influence decision making on the job may become culturally conditioned into habits and attitudes that handicap them when they try to exercise effective leadership in their communities. Ideally, a balance should be sought in which the corporate goal setter can devote more attention to family and community and the wage earner can develop leadership talents through responsible goal-oriented job activities. The JIT/VAM process described in Chapter 3 represents a significant shift toward this better balance.

REQUIREMENTS FOR MEANINGFUL GOALS

Attractive goals can give meaning to almost any type of activity, on or off the job. The hope, of course, is that work itself is intrinsically interesting. However, even distasteful, enervating, and humdrum activities are usually tolerated as long as they lead to meaningful goals. Otherwise, diapers would not be changed, dishes would not be washed, and lawns would not be mowed.

Company goals are meaningful if they are understandable, challenging, and attainable and if they are desired by the goal setters. In addition, these aims must satisfy employees' maintenance requirements and their need for growth, achievement, responsibility, and recognition.

Organizational success can be an adequate motivational goal when it fulfills these conditions, but only when the goal meets criteria meaningful to each job holder. To the CEO organizational success might mean good return on investment, enlarged share of the available market, or increased profitability. An engineer's goal might be a technological breakthrough that solves a product performance problem. Members of an assembly line feel that they are contributing to company success when they see their creative and productive effort in the perspective provided in figure 3-2.

Company goals are much more likely to be achieved when they are formed through the participatory task-force approach of JIT/VAM described in Chapter 3 than when developed through the traditional supervisory mode. When the participatory process is used, operators, a supervisor, and an engineer might convene as a task force to decide how to reduce costs to meet a company commitment. Suggestions obtained through this collaborative brainstorming approach can lead to process improvements, shortened cycle time, greater cooperation and commitment, and the attainment of goals that surpass the benchmark standards for the industry.

When participatory and supervisory goal-setting procedures are analyzed in terms of eleven characteristics common to all meaningful goals, the group approach is found to be preferable to the boss approach on every point (see Figure 5-1). The relative importance of any one of the eleven factors varies among individuals and may fluctuate for any given individual. Moreover, even meaningless work satisfies the need for money and a number of other needs detailed in Chapter 7. As noted earlier, some goals are desirable simply because they represent stepping-stones to other goals.

Value of Goal Setting

Two kinds of goal-setting opportunities exist within an organization. Employees can set goals within the context of the work for which they were hired; and they can set goals that relate to managing systems peripheral to their own work, even though those systems are normally administered by staff people. Both of these goal-setting

Characteristics of Meaningful Goals	Participative Goal Setting	Supervisory Goal Setting
1. Influenced by goal setter	Operators participate with supervisor and others to help set goals based on analysis of problems.	Operators receive goals from supervisor, usually in terms of engineered standards.
2. Visible	Operators see goals in quantative terms and receive visible feedback on quality, costs, delivery dates, and other customer requirements.	Operators are in the dark regarding goals and feedback.
3. Desirable	Achievement of goals desirable to meet personal commitments and earn better rewards.	Achievement of goals to earn money and to avoid punishment.
4. Challenging	Both mental and physical challenges to achieve self-established goals.	Physical challenge to meet quantity and quality goals, and sometimes mental challenge to beat the system.
5. Attainable	Attainability determined by group problem solving, consensus, and cooperation.	Goals are usually established at levels where a majority can meet standards.
6. Growth oriented	Operators broaden perspective, develop problem-solving skills and mature attitudes.	On-the-job learning opportunities usually restricted by job descriptions and work rules.
7. Achievement oriented	Achievement motive recurrently stimulated and satisfied by goal setting.	Achievement motive is satisfied by attaining and exceeding standards or by thwarting system.
8. Responsibility oriented	Responsibility for the project results naturally from process ownership.	Responsible for following instructions and being loyal to the supervisor and the company.
9. Recognition oriented	Recognition granted from within and outside the group for attainment of goals and from prestige of group membership.	Praise comes from supervision for high performance; acceptance from peers for supporting unofficial goals.
10. Affiliation oriented	Joint-stake effort increases interpersonal and group cohesiveness.	Social needs are satisfied through informal cliques.
11. Security oriented	Feelings of self-confidence fostered by knowledge, competence, and empowerment.	Feelings of insecurity are fostered by unpredictability of the job situation and dependency relationship.

Figure 5-1. A Comparison of Goal-Setting Techniques in the Workplace

arenas, which are discussed later in this book, allow employees an entrepreneurial stake in the success of their efforts.

When managers involve individuals and groups at all work levels in goal-setting processes, organizations make better use of available talent, develop better systems, and foster understanding and acceptance among the people who are affected by organizational decisions. Although the involvement of employees in planning and control functions is sometimes perceived by traditionalists as nonproductive use of time, in practice, systems introduced top-down by upper-level management often create more misunderstanding and resentment and therefore more nonproductive efforts than systems designed with the involvement of the users.

Entrepreneurial behavior by managers is sometimes discouraged on the assumption that it stifles the spirit of people at the lower levels of the organization. The indictment should not be made against entrepreneurial behavior, per se, but against the practice of restricting it to top management. Ideally every employee should be able to think of himself or herself as an entrepreneur (Pinchot, 1985), not working for a company, but working for himself or herself within a company, providing services and talents in exchange for compensation and other benefits, much in the same way that a service-station owner provides products and services in exchange for compensation. The difference in commitment between a service-station owner-operator and a hired service-station operator need not be so extreme as is usually the case. Given opportunities to utilize their talents, a stake in the success of their enterprises, and accountability for their behavior, hired operators can think and act like entrepreneurs.

REFERENCES

Pinchot, G., III. (1985). *Intrapreneuring: Why you don't have to leave the corporation to become an entrepreneur*. New York: Harper & Row.
Vroom, V.H. (1964). *Work and motivation*. New York: John Wiley.

6

Helpful Systems

When Jonathan Swift's tiny Lilliputians discover Gulliver asleep on their shores, they stake him to the ground so that when he awakens he cannot move (Figure 6-1). They are acting on the assumption that anyone as large and powerful as Gulliver must be dangerous. Gulliver's roar of protest evokes a panicky retreat and a retaliation with tiny arrows and spears. His initial entreaties for release and his offers of friendly assistance are rebuffed; but as the Lilliputians gradually become accustomed to his presence, and as he learns their language and wins their trust through helpful acts, they cautiously begin freeing him. He earns their respect and goodwill by adhering to their laws, by assisting them in their agricultural and construction activities, and by defending their shores against invaders. He is granted freedom within their specified guidelines, fed at a cost two thousand times greater than the amount required to feed a Lilliputian, and allowed to talk to the emperor.

Today Gulliver is reappearing in the form of advanced manufacturing technology. He still talks to and takes orders from the emperor, now known as the operations manager. He still has a voracious appetite, requiring a staggering budget; and until they learn that he will take orders from them, many Lilliputian employees feel dwarfed and frightened by him. He is often seen as a threat to job security, and many would like to see him deported. Even though they are assured by the emperor that he is friendly and helpful, they remain uneasy until they get to know him personally.

Business systems are growing in complexity. Computer technology, expanding exponentially, provides the ability to store, retrieve, manipulate, transmit, and display data at increasingly greater rates and lower costs. This capability, which serves the mainstream and support functions of an organization, accelerates the organization's growth and complexity, at the same time increasing its dependence

Figure 6-1. The Lilliputians Meet Gulliver

on massive and complicated networks of systems and their meticulously detailed and coordinated subsystems. These proliferating systems impose conformity. Increasing size depersonalizes the work environment, fostering alienation and apathy or hostility. Therefore, the systems themselves, depending on how they are developed, have a primary role in generating the attitudes and perceptions that cause them to succeed or fail.

Many systems encountered by people at work do little to bring out the best in people; instead, the systems evoke anxiety, resentment, and resistant behavior. Jobs are generally designed to fit the lowest level of talent. The design of a data-entry clerk's job, for example, is commonly guided by the directive "Assume that they cannot think." Creativity among data-entry clerks is seldom expected or rewarded and may actually provoke admonishments. When systems are more restrictive than helpful, workers may display remarkable ingenuity, or even dishonesty, in their efforts to circumvent them. Pressure from supervisors usually encourages employees to conform overtly, but that pressure also evokes covert counterproductive creativity.

System-controlled processes, such as the paced assembly line, though intended to increase efficiency, may do just the opposite. Men and women as appendages to a machine must share and sometimes exploit its inefficiencies. For example, operators in an ore refinery, geared to process one thousand tons per day, manage to look busy even when the intake of raw material drops to five hundred tons.

Some organizational systems compete to their mutual detriment. In a chemical company, for example, the engineering and operations divisions were inadvertently placed in conflict when managers applied inappropriate performance criteria. Engineering was rewarded for constructing processing plants at a lower cost per square foot, even though an increased expenditure would have resulted in greater efficiency by operations and, therefore, a greater return on investment to the company—another case of conflicting silos.

Inefficient systems are sometimes retained simply because they are required by tradition, protocol, or authority. Rules sometimes remain in the rule books long after people have devised informal and efficient shortcuts that disregard the official rules. Such a situation has a double-edged potential for punishment because people may be admonished either for violating rules or for slavish conformity. Finally, the most harmful of traditional systems are those that perpetuate social stratification by devising rules that vary according to employee status, such as time-keeping procedures, parking privileges, dining facilities, dress codes, paid leave, and benefits.

WHY PLAY IS FUN

Off-the-job recreational activities serve as models by which on-the-job systems can be improved. For example, a bowler might be attracted to the sport for a variety of reasons:

1. There is a visible goal.

2. The goals are challenging, but attainable.

3. The ground rules are clear.

4. The bowler is competing with self and with others.

5. Skills can be sharpened.

6. The activity was chosen by the bowler.

7. There is immediate feedback.

8. There is an opportunity for social interaction.

9. The exercise can dissipate hostility.

10. Bowling provides healthful physical exercise.

11. The bowler receives recognition.

However, the meaning and value of the bowler's activity could be taken away if someone did to bowling what seems to have been done to many jobs in industry. Consider, for example, the consequences of the following modifications of the game:

1. Eliminating the bowling pins, so the bowler is merely rolling a ball down an empty alley.

2. Hiding the pins from the bowler by hanging a drape halfway down the alley to prevent feedback.

3. Telling a bowler who cannot see the pins how poorly the game is going and then offering some "constructive criticism."

4. Changing the rules of the game and the standards of performance without involving the bowler in the change process or even explaining why the changes were made.

5. Making attendance at the bowling alley mandatory under threat of penalty.

6. Preventing social interaction among bowlers or discouraging team effort.

7. Giving most of the credit and recognition for the performance of the bowlers to the supervisor who oversees them.

8. Mechanizing the bowling process so the bowler need merely press a button to activate the bowling ball.

9. Keeping bowlers on the team by threatening them or by paying them enough money to make the time spent in the bowling alley worthwhile.

Bowling, under these conditions, would lose its meaning; and bowlers would look for activities away from the bowling alley to meet needs once satisfied by bowling.

WHEN WORK IS FUN

Effective management systems satisfy both motivation and maintenance needs. For instance, job posting, performance review, attitude surveys, work simplification, and problem solving require the creativity and commitment of the system users and also satisfy the maintenance needs of the employees.

A problem-solving/goal-setting system has many of the characteristics of the recreational bowling game. Both systems offer visible, challenging, and attainable goals; feedback; competition; social interaction; team involvement; and earned recognition. A problem-solving/goal-setting system can solve a workers's urgent organizational problems and become the most enjoyable aspect of the employee's job. People like to be creative, particularly when the new work affords an opportunity to break away from a monotonous assembly line. The following example illustrates what happened in one organization: The company was losing money on the production of radar units, and the workers were given the opportunity to apply their talents in remedying the situation. Their supervisor shared information with them regarding the duration of the contract time, the dollar magnitude of the project, delivery schedules, and the manufacturing costs stemming from overhead, materials, and labor. He asked them to suggest ways to reduce costs, particularly ways to lower the necessary labor hours below the one-hundred-hour break-even point. After a two-hour meeting to compile, discuss, discard, and select ideas, the group set a goal of eighty-six hours. As shown in Figure 6-2, they surpassed their goal and achieved a seventy-five-labor-hour level. During subsequent meetings in which the group was expanded to include engineers, inspectors, and assemblers from other lines (a chain of customers), the workers continued the goal-setting sessions. By the end of the year they reached a forty-one-hour level.

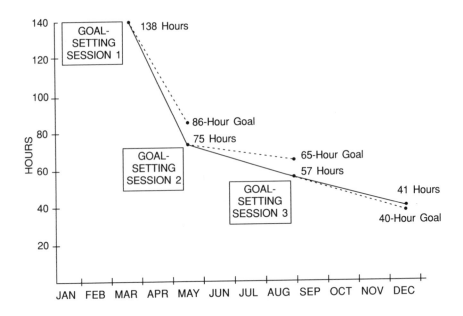

Figure 6-2. Goal Setting in Radar Assembly

In another application, when janitors and their supervisors became involved in a problem-solving/goal-setting process in an attempt to work more efficiently, they first established the criteria for
building maintenance and then the janitors took part in planning
their own work. The results reflected in Figure 6-3 show improvements in terms of labor costs, quality of performance, and turnover.
The work force was reduced from 121 to seventy, the reductions
being accommodated through job transfers and normal turnover.
Quality of performance increased from a cleanliness level of 65
percent to 83 percent, and turnover dropped from 100 percent to 20
percent per quarter. The reduction in turnover illustrates the potential, even in low-level jobs, for developing group cohesiveness and
pride through worthwhile goals and recognized achievements.

DESIGN OF EFFECTIVE SYSTEMS

A management system may be defined as a process by which people
interact to apply resources to achieve goals. Although we usually

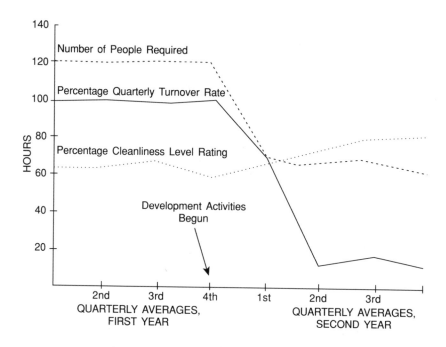

Figure 6-3. Team Improvement in Building Cleaning

think of systems in terms of hardware and software (technology), system effectiveness is primarily dependent on the human factor. Computers, machines, buildings, materials, and money lie idle and lifeless in the absence of human effort; therefore, all management is the management of that effort. The materiel with which people interact may be organized in a way that will either impede or enhance their performance. [1]

When people encounter administrative problems, they often blame the relevant system. For example, problems encountered in terminating a book-club membership, in changing a mailing address, in getting a charge-account error corrected, or in clearing an expense account are usually attributed to a faulty system. Systems

---

[1] Much of this section is abstracted from documents co-authored in 1968 with Charles L. Kettler, coordinator of Texas Instruments' management-systems development committee, and A. Graham Sterling, manager of control and administration in Texas Instruments' materials group.

are convenient scapegoats: a tardy report can usually be attributed to data lost in the computer.

Role of the System Designer

Attempts to remedy a system usually lead back to the system designer. System designers often defend their plans for software and hardware, asserting that a system failed only because people misused it. System designers often think of people as an extension of systems, rather than of systems as an extension of human beings. Within that point of view lies the crux of most management-system problems.

Systems designers are correct in diagnosing systems failures as human failures. However, systems designers often fail to recognize that any system design must include a plan for preparing or training the people who will be using it. This problem can be averted if the designer requires the users to take part in the design of the system. Because of job pressure, users are often prone to welcome the staff person's takeover and may thus avoid participating in the design process.

Sometimes failure occurs even when the users try to assist in designing their system. Although the system designer may urge the users to participate, and though the users themselves may be willing to do so, they are frequently stymied by the semantics of systems specialists. For example, terms such as *database normalization, timesharing, network gateways,* and *real time* are confusing to people not familiar with computer technology. System designers must adapt their terminology to the language of the users.

Informal Systems

Company systems may be official or unofficial, formal or informal, simple or complex; however, all come into existence because of the needs of individuals or groups at some level in the organization. For example, the office check pool (based on the highest poker hand in paycheck serial numbers) is an informal and unofficial system that forms almost spontaneously. It is perpetuated by a combination of the social, financial, and entertainment needs of the organization members and by their desire for excitement and risk taking. Failing to understand the check pool as a symptom of boredom, management may attack the activity as a violation of company rules on gambling and may try to develop a system for stopping it. Attempts to quash the check pool may be implemented through a system of posted notices, newspaper inserts, public pronouncements, and supervisory instruction, all reinforced by explicit or implicit threats of punishment. However, if the need to perpetuate the check pool is strong enough or if the joy of circumventing authority is great enough, the pool system will go underground, thereby satisfying a need for rebellion provoked by the management edict and perhaps increasing the system's value as a source of group cohesiveness, diversion, and excitement.

The check pool illustrates the circular nature of systems. Check-pool members contribute their dollars and obtain feedback by observing the payoff to winners. Attempts by management to intervene merely activate a countersystem for evading detection. This countersystem provides feedback on how to avoid detection and on the dangers of getting caught. Similarly, management's control system for preventing participation in the check pool gives feedback to managers in the form of official reports on conformity or violations. Feedback may or may not be valid.

Development of Formal Systems

Formal management systems are developed and refined through a continuous circular process that may be defined in terms of seven phases. Although any phase, and particularly Phase 5 (trial application), may lead directly back to any preceding phase, the development of a system generally follows a circular evolutionary process, diagramed in Figure 6-4.

Phase 1: Goal Setting. Goal setting is initiated to create a new system or to modify an old one. Intended users are involved in this and all subsequent steps. Goals are expressed quantitatively and qualitatively in terms of the results desired and the resources available.

Phase 2: Concept Study. The concept study is a systematic evaluation that determines how to achieve the stated goals. The study also evaluates the short- and long-range impact of the system on the user,

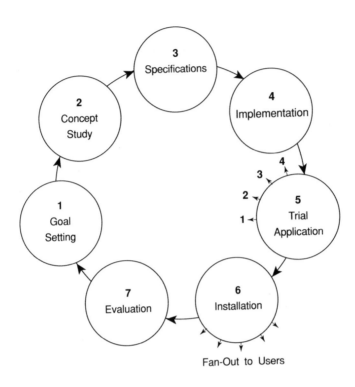

Figure 6-4. Seven Phases of System Development

on other systems, on uninvolved bystanders, and on the community, in light of social, economic, and legal considerations. The concept study ends with the selection of one of several alternative approaches for achieving the established goals.

Phase 3: Specifications. Specifications define precisely how the system will implement the concepts in order to achieve the goals. The specifications are established in terms of costs, time limits, personnel, machines, equipment, materials, facilities, responsibility, and evaluation criteria.

Phase 4: Implementation. The system is implemented by committing hardware, software, working hours, services, space, and budgets; by designing trial applications; and by defining error signals.

Phase 5: Trial Application. Trial applications are made with real or simulated data in representative situations. Errors are corrected, the system is refined, and management and user commitment is confirmed. Phase 5 may lead directly back to any previous phase.

Phase 6: Installation. Those who install the system must instruct users, transfer system management to users, inform affected segments of the public, establish review schedules, and monitor initial applications. Systems with potential for broad organizational application should immediately be fanned out (extended) to other operations to maximize system payout.

Phase 7: Evaluation. The system is evaluated by measuring performance against goals, by noting the impact on other systems and the deviations from design, and by identifying the necessary goal adjustments.

A Specimen System for Manufacturing

Advanced manufacturing technology (AMT)[2] refers to process technologies such as computer-aided manufacturing, computer-aided design and computer-aided engineering, manufacturing resource planning, computer-aided process planning, and the integration of these technologies in computer-integrated manufacturing. The relationships among the various technologies are illustrated in Figure 6-5.

Advanced manufacturing technology has the potential for reducing product cost, improving quality, and increasing flexibility. A growing number of companies are making major investments in AMT; their experience shows that organizations win greater benefits from these investments if, during the change process, managers give primary consideration to the role of people. The JIT/VAM principles described in Chapter 3 illustrate the philosophy and processes that govern the effective application of AMT.

Although the technology itself readily crosses the boundaries surrounding industries and countries, the human resource practices

---

[2] The AMT principles and conclusions summarized in this chapter are adapted from a report published in 1986 by the Manufacturing Studies Board, 2101 Constitution Avenue, Washington, D.C. 20418. The report was prepared by a committee of nine people composed of managers, union officials, and academics, who based their conclusions on their visits to sixteen sites where AMT was being implemented.

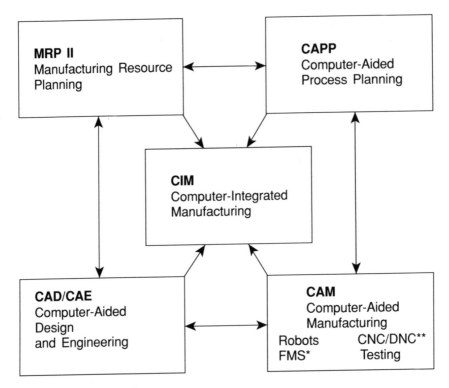

*Flexible Manufacturing System
**Computer Numerically Controlled/Direct Numerically Controlled

Figure 6-5. Advanced Manufacturing Technology

appropriate for its implementation are not so easily transferred. Some managers may be unable to change their human resource practices at the rate required to be competitive. In those automotive manufacturing plants where the focus was on technology rather than on human resource development, manufacturing has failed to become competitive. It is clear that manufacturers must spend more time and effort developing the organizational and human relations capabilities required for implementing and operating the new technology.

Advanced manufacturing technology requires a higher capital investment per employee and numerous changes within the organization. It requires a highly skilled, versatile, interactive, and committed work force capable of participating in its own problem solving.

Greater interdependence among work activities is necessary, and each unit has fewer employees responsible for each product, part, or process. In short, AMT requires a tightly united chain of customers, each of whom is in charge of process control.

Companies using AMT must have a flexible, humane, and innovative management organization with fewer levels, job classifications, and rank-oriented status symbols. Retention of well-trained workers is both more important and more feasible under these conditions. Productivity is strongly dependent on human skills, knowledge, and attitudes and on mental rather than physical effort. A malfunction in part of the production system has more immediate, pervasive, and costly consequences than those in companies without AMT.

Advanced manufacturing technology, administered according to the foregoing principles, develops a strong partnership between managers and workers. When the work force is represented by labor unions, a joint-stake relationship must prevail.

These principles are not unique to AMT companies, but are especially applicable to them. The dominant theme is that the axioms are designed to accommodate all parties with a stake in the organization and are intended to enlist their support. The company and its customers and shareholders profit through decreased costs, increased quality, greater flexibility, decreased cycle time, improved equipment up-time, and the company's increased ability to bring technology on line. Employees gain through learning and retraining opportunities, an increase in marketable skills, a chance for advancement, increased influence, and a more secure employment environment. Where employees are unionized, the union also gains through participation in a broader agenda of issues affecting its membership.

A Specimen System for Career Development

The job-posting plan described in the following pages is an example of an internal staffing system. The history of the plan illustrates the cyclical and evolutionary process that takes place when a management system is being developed (Shepherd, 1969). Job posting existed as a simple and informal process at Texas Instruments for several years. In its earliest form it consisted of duplicated lists of job openings that rarely crossed organizational and geographical boundaries. Feedback reached management through company gossip and the annual attitude survey; both reflected inadequacies in the job-posting system. Employees felt that supervisory practice was arbitrary and that ground rules were ambiguous.

The following complaints were among the list of system shortcomings: favoritism was a basis for many promotions, seniority was disregarded, education was emphasized to the exclusion of experience, qualifications for job openings were not specified, and advancement opportunities were restricted to the departments in which the opportunities occurred.

Complaints about supervisory practice included allegations that supervisors withheld information about job opportunities, sometimes resented transfer requests, refused or delayed transfers, and too often gave priority to outside applicants.

Viewed in terms of the system-development cycle illustrated in Figure 6-4, these reactions to the job-posting system represented an informal Phase 7 evaluation of an ongoing system. This feedback precipitated the formation of an official task force to improve the job-posting procedure.

Preliminary work by the Phase 1 (goal-setting) task force confirmed the Phase 7 evaluation described above and also noted the following shortcomings in the existing system:

- Job openings were published too infrequently.

- Many job openings were not posted.

- Posted openings were primarily for lower job grades.

- Dates for posting and closing job openings were not specified.

- Job postings were not easily accessible to all employees.

- Job specifications were too sketchy.

This systematic evaluation of the existing system helped the task force to define improvements. However, since most of the feedback came from the employees who were primary users of the system, it was necessary to broaden the scope of the goal-setting process; the evaluation included a balanced consideration of the goals of the organization and the impact of job posting on other systems. The system-development task force comprised a heterogeneous membership of line and staff people chaired by a seasoned industrial-relations generalist.[3] Although the permanent membership of the central task force numbered about eight, ad hoc involvement of people from all major functions and levels of the company through five satellite task forces totaled approximately nine hundred.

The task-force strategy led routinely and naturally into the Phase 2 concept study. Although managers believed that job posting could cause problems by increasing internal mobility, the task force concluded that the advantages of a job-posting system greatly outweighed its disadvantages:

- It would facilitate promotions, transfers, and reassignments— and thereby support the company's promotion-from-within policy, lead to better utilization of human resources, and encourage the retention of talent within the organization.

- It would reduce the loss of people from the work force due to faulty placement or work-force reduction and, therefore, would lead to increased organizational and community stability.

- It would facilitate the placement of people returning from leaves of absence and would upgrade workers who improved their qualifications through skills training and educational programs.

- It would lower interdepartmental mobility barriers and lead to broader unification of the total work force and implementation of an equal-opportunity policy.

- It would provide information, an incentive, and a viable procedure by which individuals could take charge of their own career development and would correspondingly reduce dependence on supervision.

After the concept study was complete, the task force developed Phase 3 specifications for the cost of overhead, hardware, software, and labor hours. Evaluation criteria were established to include employee (user) reactions as measured through attitude surveys,

---

[3] A.E. Prescott, manager of internal staffing for Texas Instruments, chaired the job-posting-system task force whose achievements are outlined in this section.

frequency of usage, and grapevine testimonials. The task force evaluated the effect on the organization in terms of reduced turnover and staffing costs, impact on work standards and schedules, and general acceptance by supervisors.

Phases 4 and 5 of development (implementation and trial application) were brought about through the joint efforts of a skeletal staff of corporate and division personnel who applied the job-posting system throughout Texas Instruments operations. Space, employees, and budget had been allocated by corporate personnel, with concomitant pledges of support from the relevant divisions. An immediate and favorable reaction to these initial applications resulted in an early commitment of support from top management. The corporation decided to expand the program to all domestic operations and to international operations that might be staffed from domestic divisions. Much of Phase 5 had been accomplished earlier during the application of the informal and local job-posting systems that had preceded the more formalized and comprehensive plan. To the users, the most apparent changes were that the job-opportunity bulletin, illustrated in Figure 6-6, offered increased coverage and that the procedure by which workers could apply for posted jobs had been simplified.

Phase 6 (installation) was formally and officially completed when capital, overhead, and expense budgets were approved; administrative staff and support personnel were selected and trained; and the system was described in the company newspaper. Approximately 10 percent of the domestic work force utilized the system for promotion and transfers during the first year. More than 20 percent of the positions filled were for exempt, rather than nonexempt, salary classifications. Administration of the program followed the procedure illustrated in Figure 6-7.

General reaction to the system, particularly from the user's viewpoint, was favorable. However, a gradual ground swell of dissatisfaction, largely from operating managers, reactivated Phases 7 and 1 (evaluation and goal setting). The central task force was reassembled with nineteen members to determine whether or not to continue the system and, if it were to be continued, to identify and correct the problems that had caused dissatisfaction. Nine geographically deployed division task forces, involving 125 system users from all levels and functions, compiled a list of problems and possible solutions and forwarded them to the central task force. The central task

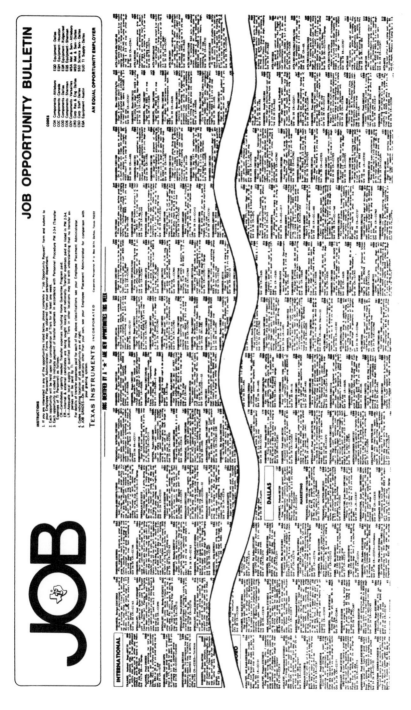

Figure 6-6. Job Opportunity Bulletin

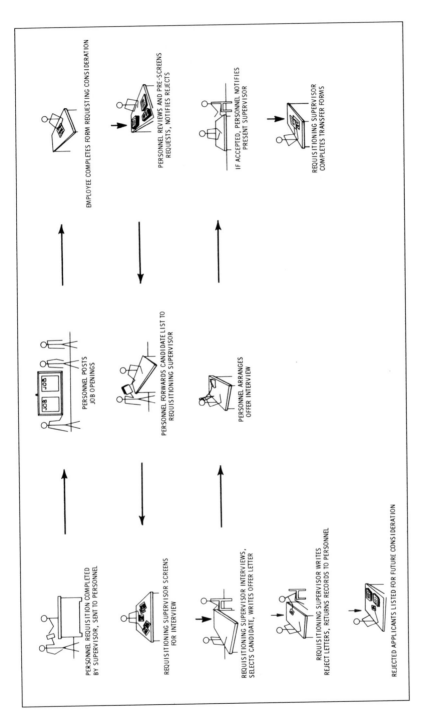

Figure 6-7. Job Posting

force consolidated the division recommendations and returned them to the divisions for review, revision, and ratification. Finally, the central task force consolidated the revisions for corporate review.

The company president and operating vice presidents held a day-long meeting to review the system, its problems, and possible solutions and to decide whether or not to continue it. The Phase 7 review, aided by testimonials from line and staff managers, revealed six problems associated with the job-opportunity system. A new Phase 1 goal-setting session resulted in appropriate modifications. The revisions are summarized in Figure 6-8.

These changes in the job-opportunity system were communicated to the work force via informal one-to-one and group discussions, the employee newspaper, and revisions in the procedure handbooks. During the decade following the Phase 7 evaluation described above, three similar evaluations were made, with necessary adjustments introduced into the system. This illustrates the important principle that systems are never cast in concrete but undergo continual improvement.

Why Systems Succeed or Fail

This evolutionary process, perpetuated by feedback from the users, represents an ideal model of an effective self-correcting management system. Tracing the evolution of the job-posting system through its seven developmental phases reveals characteristics common to most effective systems. Because of their involvement in the evolutionary process, users understand and agree with its purpose. It is a system they can activate simply by submitting a completed job bid to the personnel department, without fear of supervisory reprisal. Many people activate the system with covert inquiries. Their own initiative enables them to discover opportunities; and because the system minimizes dependency on supervisors, or their unsolicited intervention, the users are in control all the way. Finally, the system gives the users direct feedback regarding disqualification or acceptance. Figure 6-9 presents criteria by which the effectiveness of any management system can be judged.

Problems	Modifications
1. Large numbers of bids by a few individuals delayed the candidate-evaluation process and interfered with feedback to bidders.	1. Limit concurrent job bids to two per person, except for individuals made available for reassignment.
2. Employees who were not aware of the updated interim weekly bulletins posted on the bulletin boards bid on jobs listed in outdated monthly bulletins.	2. Simplify coding of new job postings.
3. Lateral transfers filled many positions that would have offered promotional opportunities to people from lower job grades.	3. Permit lateral transfers only when progress on the present job is blocked, the job category or salary schedule is being changed, the change is part of a planned career-development program, or the change is necessary to assign displaced personnel.
4. Operating efficiency in some departments was reduced by work interruptions caused by frequent transfers.	4. Effect a temporary "transfer-out moratorium" if necessary to protect vital understaffed work groups.
5. People transferred before achieving their competence levels, thereby depriving managers of a fair return on training or on time spent acquiring security clearances.	5. Require six months on the job for nonexempt personnel and twelve months for exempt personnel before bidding on a new job.
6. Some supervisors circumvented the system by delaying transfers or negotiating under-the-table arrangements under the pretense of following official job-posting procedures.	6. Provide continuing education and information to users regarding the system and its revisions.

Figure 6-8. Revision of a Job-Posting System

Effective Management System	Ineffective Management System
1. Users understand its purpose.	1. Users do not understand its purpose.
2. Users agree with its purpose.	2. Users disagree with its purpose.
3. Users know how to use it.	3. Users do not know how to use it.
4. Users are in control of it.	
5. Users can influence its revision.	4. Users feel they are unnecessarily restricted by it.
6. Users receive timely feedback from it.	5. Users believe it is hopeless to try to change it.
	6. Users receive inadequate feedback from it.

Figure 6-9. Criteria for Judging Effectiveness of Management Systems

Key Role of the User

Criteria in Figure 6-9 for effective and ineffective systems are almost exclusively functions of the attitudes and perceptions of systems users. When people believe that they belong to an organization, they tend to support its systems. This feeling of belonging grows when employees are allowed to participate in the development of company systems.

For example, compare the behavior of two groups of machine operators toward their respective assembly lines. One group, in a paper-carton factory, was idled for a few hours (with pay) while industrial engineers introduced process improvements into the assembly line. The operators clustered near the soft-drink machine—laughing, drinking Coca Cola, and smoking. When the engineers completed the installation, they briefed the operators on the changes and asked for questions. Receiving no comments, they assumed the installation would be an improvement. However, the system actually reduced the line yield; the line was less effective than before. The engineered changes had altered role relationships on the line; and even before giving it a fair trial, the operators had conspired, perhaps unconsciously, to make the system fail.

In contrast, a superintendent and a supervisor in an electronics assembly department involved the operators in planning and balancing their own assembly line and setting their first week's production goals. They achieved their Friday evening goal on Wednesday and went on to almost double their first week's goal. From an engineering point of view, the electronics assembly line was not so well designed as the paper-carton line; however, it worked because the operators made it work.

In general, the attitudes and perceptions of employees are crucial to the success or failure of a system. Such mind-sets can enable poorly designed systems to succeed and can cause well-designed systems to fail.

Qualifications of Systems Designers

As noted earlier, system designers now recognize that the attitudes of their users are critical. Designers try to familiarize themselves with their users' operations and to involve users in the development of the systems. It was also noted that these cooperative efforts are often made difficult because the users are pressed for time or the designers tend to speak in jargon. The discussion of the job-posting system at Texas Instruments demonstrates that sensitivity to the human factor—to the causes of commitment and alienation—is an essential ingredient for developing and managing effective systems.

System designers must apply three types of competence when developing workable systems: (1) knowledge of data-processing and production technology; (2) knowledge of the functions or operations to be served by the system and the proposed system's relation to, and potential impact on, other systems; and (3) sensitivity to the reasons for which people support or reject new and revised systems.

Management's Role

The hardware and software available for facilitating modern management systems have almost unlimited potential to be amplified or restricted by the people who interact with them. People also have untapped potential, to be utilized or limited by the systems with which they interact. If synergistic relationships are to exist between employees and their systems, human development and system development must be guided by designers who understand both people and systems.

Simply stated, leaders are responsible for managing the work force, materiel, and technology necessary to achieve organizational goals. Effective management systems cannot be established if system development is restricted to staff functions. A leader's responsibility when orchestrating management systems is to guarantee that system development is not an isolated, uncoordinated, or unilateral process, but a joint or task-force effort, appropriately balanced with systems technology, mainstream user participation, and human-effectiveness expertise.

REFERENCES

Shepherd, M. (1969, April). Process described by Shepherd, chairman of the board of Texas Instruments, in his EIA presidential address at the Industrial Relations Conference in San Diego, CA.

7

Work Itself

The emphasis on job enrichment and job enlargement in the 1960s and '70s has gradually been supplanted by a broader perspective reflected in the JIT/VAM principles described in Chapter 3. Job enrichment is still important. However, it is no longer seen as a target, but rather as a consequence of effective leadership, which empowers people to enjoy productive roles in their employing organizations.

Job enrichment for hourly paid operators is not always supported by supervisors and union leaders, particularly when those leaders are themselves being bypassed in the job-enrichment process. Some supervisors see the participative approach as erosion of their already diminished and ambiguous responsibilities. Certainly, autocratic supervisors who call all the shots feel threatened by an edict that, in their view, requires them to be soft with employees. The credibility of the participative approach is undermined further when the system is mandated by bosses who do not practice it themselves. Union shop stewards feel threatened when required to implement a process that violates a time-honored tradition of adversarial relationships. Employees who try to do the right thing do not know which way to turn when they sense foot-dragging on the part of their union leaders and supervisors.

Job enrichment, to be successful, must serve the needs of both the organization and its members. An effort to improve the quality of workers' lives at the expense of the organization will not be supported by executives who are themselves assessed in terms of bottom-line financial criteria. Conversely, a job-enrichment program that is undertaken to increase productivity, but that fails to consider employee concerns, is doomed to failure even though pay and job security are enhanced. In short, the long-term success of an organi-

123

zation depends on the pursuit of organizational goals that are synergistically related to the needs of its members. For purposes of this discussion, use of the term *quality of work life* assumes a balanced concern for organizational and individual goals.

The quality of work life in an organization is a function of the three basic ingredients described in Chapters 4 through 6: compatible people, meaningful goals, and helpful systems. These are not independent variables, because each influences the other two.

The systems of an organization are the vehicles through which employee needs are satisfied or thwarted. In this chapter quality of work life will be discussed as it relates to two kinds of systems: those associated directly with work itself (the classical concept of job enrichment), and those peripheral to the job or occupation for which the job incumbent was hired. Peripheral systems refer to nontask factors such as landscaping, eating arrangements, parking facilities, and dress codes.

HISTORICAL PERSPECTIVE[1]

Work was originally performed only as a means of survival; however, the attitude of mankind toward work has undergone significant changes over time. According to Maslow's hierarchy-of-needs concept (1968), when living is precarious, mankind devotes most of its attention to survival. Such was the case with cave dwellers, who were forced to spend most of their time seeking food and shelter. For prehistoric people, work and living were one and the same; work was meaningful because it was essential to survival. Their inability to predict or control their environment required them to react instead of to think. Efforts to control or cope with their surroundings through the use of crude weapons and fire resulted more from serendipity than from knowledge and logic. The more innovative individuals, who used and refined chance discoveries, were simply more likely to survive. Even social and status-oriented relationships developed because people had to band together for protection.

---

[1] The information in this section is adapted from Historical Perspective of Work, an unpublished paper by S. S. Myers. (1969, July). Southern Methodist University, Dallas, TX.

Through an evolutionary process, people in the medieval period found themselves more formally bound by social and status constraints. Tradition and environment had by then chained individuals to the economic and social orders to which they were born. Limited by inherited roles and positions, men born to families of artisans became artisans, and men born to royal families became kings, with virtually no mobility in between. However, within the limits of their inherited spheres, individuals had freedom to express themselves in their work and their social lives. In this respect, people during the Middle Ages were able to create, make, and market their own products, as long as they stayed within a particular product line and marketplace. At the same time, they enjoyed a certain amount of security and cohesiveness as a result of their membership in guilds, their attachment to an undivided and all-encompassing church, and their place in a highly structured and stable social order. Within their own spheres of influence, and in spite of being captives in the feudal system, individuals were free to set their own standards and goals and to experience the rewards of achievement.

Emerging Capitalism

Events during the Middle Ages charted another course for people, on which they could, for the first time in history, alter their own destinies. Skilled and motivated artisans reaped the benefits of quality work, and competition developed among them in a pattern that resembled what would later be called social Darwinism or survival of the fittest. The more successful artisans were able to hire less successful artisans to work for them, thus elevating their own social positions through increased wealth and status.

Along with the possibility of social mobility came an opportunity for geographical mobility as trade routes were opened throughout what is now Europe and between Europe and the Orient. The merchant classes of the Renaissance were comfortable, but the future of the exploited working masses was grim. As they lost their ability to maintain their traditional memberships and relationships in guilds, they lost proprietary interest in their work; and their social, economic, and political status deteriorated.

The combination of competition, capital, and economic opportunity enabled the most skilled and assertive of the artisans to survive and prosper, but at the expense of the weaker ones. The fittest became masters with entrepreneurial freedom and the power to act and realize their personal ambitions. Members of the working class were lucky if they were allowed to choose their crafts; their future was largely determined for them by their employers. Work was then, as it is now, meaningful for owner-managers who could shape their jobs as they pleased; however, for the others work was a task to be performed as directed. The situation was summarized by Erich Fromm[2] (1941):

> As the number of journeymen under one master increased . . . more capital was needed to become a master, and the more guilds assumed a monopolistic and exclusive character, the less were the opportunities of journeymen. The deterioration of their economic and social position was shown by their growing dissatisfaction, the formation of organizations of their own, by strikes and even violent insurrections. (pp. 73-74)

Although dissatisfied workers discovered their strength in numbers, they did not have enough influence to prevent the labor-management dichotomy that developed in the late fifteenth century. These social and economic injustices gradually brought into question the theology of the Catholic church. Churchgoers were taught that they had equal status with their fellow human beings in the eyes and love of God and that, though they shared in original sin, if they worked diligently to atone, they could be assured by the church of a place in heaven. The fact that the capitalists were reaping rewards at the expense of the working class suggested to some that the church represented a religion of the rich, and workers began developing an awareness of their own insignificance and powerlessness before the church hierarchy and the capitalists.

Luther, Calvin, and Horatio Alger

The time was ripe for the Protestant theologies of Luther and Calvin. Both the working class and the middle class were ready to attack the authority and power of the wealthy merchants and the established church. Many of Luther's followers believed that the way to heaven

---

[2] *Escape from Freedom* by Erich Fromm. Copyright 1941, © 1969 by Erich Fromm. New York: Henry Holt. Used by permission.

was through good work and success on earth. Calvin taught that salvation and damnation were predetermined, but that success in life through moral and effortful living indicated that an individual was among the elect and predestined for heaven. Their theological views produced an attitude of self-reliance among their followers. Adherents to Protestantism felt responsible for their own salvation. In their eyes human beings became the guardians of their own individual destinies; the church could no longer lift the burden from their shoulders. The work ethic was born, along with what later became Horatio Alger's rags-to-riches theme. According to Fromm[3] (1941):

> This new attitude towards effort and work as an aim in itself may be assumed to be the most important psychological change which has happened to man since the end of the Middle Ages. . . . What was new in modern society was that men came to be driven to work not so much by external pressure, but by an internal compulsion which made them work as only a very strict master could have made people do in other societies. The inner compulsion was more effective in harnessing all energies to work than any outer compulsion can ever be. Against external compulsion there is always a certain amount of rebelliousness which hampers the effectiveness of work or makes people unfit for any differentiated task requiring intelligence, initiative and responsibility. The compulsion to work by which man was turned into his own slave driver did not hamper these qualities. Undoubtedly, capitalism could not have been developed had not the greatest part of man's energy been channeled in the direction of work. There is no other period in history in which free men have given their energy so completely for the one purpose: work. (pp. 112-114)

The Industrial Revolution

As a result of religious and political oppression in western Europe, many of the industrious rebels of the Reformation transferred their efforts to improve their lot to America. Firmly believing that God helps those who help themselves, members of the Protestant faith became associated with the rising commercial class, both in the

---

[3] *Escape from Freedom* by Erich Fromm. Copyright 1941, © 1969 by Erich Fromm. New York: Henry Holt. Used by permission.

colonies and in Europe. In a remarkably short time, they and their descendants had helped to bring about the Industrial Revolution.

Because of its impact on the economy and the people, perhaps the most far-reaching effect of the Industrial Revolution was the development of large industrial organizations. Stimulated initially by the evolution of iron and steel and nurtured by the railroads and entrepreneurs, big businesses were built across the country. The growth of industry was accompanied by the development of mass markets and mass-production techniques, including the standardization of parts and processes, the division of labor, the repetitive production of standard items, the manufacturing of interchangeable parts, and the assembly of parts into finished products.

As big businesses mushroomed, many small businesses disappeared, their owner-managers forced to work for nothing more than wages. Trapped by specialization, division of labor, wage systems, and pyramidal, authoritarian companies, American workers formally joined forces by organizing the National Labor Union in the 1860s and the Knights of Labor in the 1870s in an unsuccessful attempt to regain some of their former status as owners of enterprise. The wage system became permanent, however, in spite of efforts to destroy it. Accepting this fact, in 1886 workers formed a new labor organization, the American Federation of Labor (AFL) to help workers improve their position within the system. Organized on the basis of trades and inspired by Samuel Gompers, the AFL differed from previous unions in that it assumed an inherent conflict of interest between labor and management and foresaw the permanent exclusion of most employees from the ranks of management.

Early Attempts at Scientific Management

Threatened by the aggressive role of labor and the continuing need for new responses to industrialism, managers of business and industrial organizations sought better management techniques—not for altruistic reasons, but for increased efficiency and productivity. They were influenced first by Max Weber's concept of bureaucracy, introduced in 1900. Opposed to loosely organized companies run by whim, Weber proposed highly structured companies conducted by rules. Although these bureaucracies were understandable as a reaction to disorder, they proved to be inefficient and cumbersome in an environment of rapidly changing technology.

More attractive to management at that time was Frederick W. Taylor's concept of scientific management (Taylor, 1911), which placed more emphasis on efficiency and productivity. Believing that the nature of work had gradually evolved from an art to a science, Taylor recommended that each job should be fractionated, analyzed for efficiency techniques, and given to high-aptitude employees trained for one specific task. To maximize efficiency, Taylor further recommended that employees be motivated through piecework-incentive systems of pay, by which the most productive would earn the highest wages. Taylor's research, coupled with that of his successor, Frank B. Gilbreth (Maynard, 1971) is now often known as time-and-motion study.

Taylorism and expressions of that philosophy linger in many of today's organizations as engineered labor standards, time-and-motion study, piecework incentive, paid-suggestion plans, and other hybrid systems. These manipulative programs became known as *attitude surveys, merit ratings, zero-defects, communication, motivation,* and *recognition.* Although such plans might yield sporadic short-term gains, their ultimate impact, because of the way they were designed and administered, was usually alienation and net loss.

In 1927 at Western Electric's Hawthorne Plant, Elton Mayo surprised many managers with his discovery that workers are motivated by incentives other than wages, hours, and working conditions. It seemed that positive recognition and even attention itself, particularly in a culture of cohesive groups, resulted in attitude changes that could profoundly affect productivity.

The resultant shift in emphasis away from engineered efficiency toward an interest in human relations and improved group processes created a new strategy for implementing mass production and automation. However, as machines and processes became increasingly complex, workers who monitored the machines experienced diminishing demands on their intellect, initiative, and creativity. Recognizing that automation was making people into extensions of machines, Charles Walker (1965), former director of the Yale Technology Project, advocated the return of the machine to its proper role as an appendage of people. Attempts to remedy the stultifying relationship between workers and machines initiated the concepts of human engineering and job enrichment, whereby machines are designed to meet the abilities and limitations of human beings and humans are taught to amplify the efficiency of machines.

Emergence of Formalized Job Enrichment

Realizing that the components of a job exceed the conventional formula of wages, hours, and working conditions, Walker cites several other dimensions that can be used as analytic tools in determining productivity and job satisfaction:

1. Knowledge and skill requirements;

2. Pacing or rate of performance;

3. Degree of repetitiveness or variety;

4. Relation to the total product or process;

5. Relationships with people as individuals or as groups;

6. Style of supervision and of managerial controls;

7. Degree of worker's autonomy in determining work methods;

8. Relation of work to personal development.

To the extent that these dimensions are known about a job and improved in accordance with technological and psychological changes, there is a potential for putting meaning back into work. As employers recognize the need to design machines for human beings, they also see the importance of designing jobs to meet human needs. Peter Vaill (1966) concluded, on the basis of research on the working lives of factory employees, that jobs are more meaningful when they (1) offer the worker continuous opportunity to learn; (2) encourage quality work; (3) allow the workers to set their own standards and goals; (4) are experienced by the workers as psychologically whole; and (5) show the relationship between the goals of a particular jobholder and the company goals.

Regarding the link between the design of a job and the working environment of the jobholder, Vaill concluded that there is an inverse relationship between the degree of concern with wages, hours, and working conditions and interest in job challenge and complexity. He found that when job design enabled people to take an active role in the organization, they were more likely to demonstrate increased commitment and self-confidence. Although empowerment and self-reliance are critical to job satisfaction, throughout history job satisfaction has been limited by workers' dependence on powers beyond their control.

Mason Haire (1969) traces the evolution of power through several stages. Primeval people lived in a bewildering and overwhelming world in which their survival depended on their wariness and their ability to react to unpredictable and sometimes uninterpretable threats. *Fear of the unknown* was the major source of power to the caveman. In medieval times the *state*, often identical with the official religious organization, was the source of power. Conformity and servility were keys to acceptance. The late Middle Ages ushered in entrepreneurial activity, with *ownership* or equity as the source of power. Loyalty and industriousness were keys to success. The Industrial Revolution placed a premium on production, and *production technology*, coupled with the Protestant attitude toward industriousness, was the source of power.

The mid-twentieth-century emphasis on professional management and staff expertise has made *professional managers and their systems* a velvet-gloved source of power. Success in modern companies was usually measured in terms of professional competence and advancement in the organization. However, there is not room for all to succeed on these terms, and large numbers of employees at the lower levels resort to emotional disengagement, if only to maintain their sanity.

Managers in modern world-class organizations shun the use of authority and organize physical resources and manpower to enable human talent at all levels to find expression in solving problems and achieving goals. Empowerment, then, is through *human competence*, applied toward the synergistic achievement of the goals of the organization and its members. Only under conditions of responsible self-direction and self-control can escape from outer-directed domination be achieved.

STAGES OF LABOR RELATIONS

Capitalism began in the Middle Ages, flourished during the Industrial Revolution, and hit a peak in the twentieth century. Late in the nineteenth century Samuel Gompers, William Haywood, and other union leaders, seeking to defend workers against exploitative entrepreneurs, made explicit an adversarial relationship that had been evolving since the Middle Ages. From a historical perspective, beginning with the days of Samuel Gompers, one can identify three distinct stages of labor relations: Stage 1, win-lose adversary; Stage 2, collaborative adversary; and Stage 3, organizational teamwork. These three stages are portrayed on a continuum in Figure 7-1.

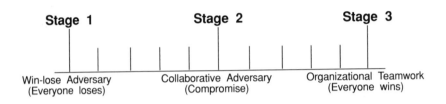

Figure 7-1. Stages of Labor Relations

Stage 1: Win-Lose Adversary

Win-lose adversary relationships are common in unionized organizations but are also found in some nonunion situations. Unionism was started according to this model by leaders who explicitly articulated the gap between management and labor. Samuel Gompers, who founded the AFL, wrote, "We recognize the solidarity of the whole working class to work harmoniously against their common enemy—the capitalists . . . United we are a power to be respected; divided we are slaves of the capitalists" (Gompers, 1925).

The constitution of the Industrial Workers of the World (IWW), organized in 1905 by William Haywood, reads as follows:

> The working class and the employing class have nothing in common. . . . Between these two classes a struggle must go on until the workers of the world organize as a class, take possession of the earth and the machinery of production, and abolish the wage system. . . . It is the historic mission of the working class to do away with capitalism.

Early union leaders encountered fierce opposition to the union movement from employers, government officials, and other conservative defenders of the free-enterprise system. Early unions were attacked as socialistic and anti-American by ruthless capitalists who used the power of laws, economics, politics, and violence to crush the unions. Unions countered, of course, with similar tactics; and with the help of counterbalancing legislation, after a bitter struggle spanning several decades, unions established a power base for per-petuating a hostile adversary relationship in circumstances that in many cases no longer justify them. Union leaders under this model feel compelled from time to time to foment a crisis or issue that enables them to exercise their clout and demonstrate their value to their constituency.

The strike by the United Auto Workers (UAW) of General Motors in 1970 was not wanted by most of the 180,000 strikers from the ninety-six plants affected, nor could many of the workers explain the reasons for the walkout. However, the international union leadership appeared to have a need to demonstrate that it had the power to bring the company to its knees. Actually, the whole demonstration was a wasteful sham in which the company ultimately collaborated by lending money to the union to help tide the workers over their period of unemployment. The episode was a vivid illustration of the extent to which top executives in the company and union shamelessly acquiesced to the tradition of win-lose gamesmanship, at the expense of the workers and the total society.

The consequences of the 1970 strike were assessed by William Serrin (1973) in terms of a variety of far-reaching impacts. General Motors lost more than $1 billion in profits and the production of 1.5 million cars and trucks. Dividends dropped from the usual $5 to $2.09 per share—a gap of $600 million. The union paid out $160 million in strike benefits, had to mortgage its Black Lake recreation and education center, and paid $2.5 million in interest on loans. More than 300,000 people, in addition to strikers and layoffs, were on reduced hours. The government lost $1 billion in taxes, the nation lost hundreds of millions of dollars in retail sales, and taxpayers paid $30 million in welfare benefits.

Most courses in collective bargaining, whether conducted for company or union, are customarily based on Stage 1 win-lose adversary assumptions. Bargainers are taught the fine points and loopholes of the law, briefed on trends and precedents established in other bargaining situations, refreshed on the motivating principles underlying their adversary's strategies, updated on the company's financial status and the results of compensation surveys, and encouraged to share and exchange their strategies for winning.

Under the philosophy engendered by Stage 1, people who otherwise would harbor no malice toward one another are pressured by tradition to become identified as either management or labor and are often required by the adversary system to role play hostility or mistrust in their company-union relationships. In these circumstances affiliation usually takes precedence over ethics.

Stage 2: Collaborative Adversary

Collaborative adversary relationships are typified by the case studies of company-union relationships completed in 1953 under the auspices of the National Planning Association (Golden & Parker, 1955). This project focused on twelve major companies chosen because of their peaceful company-union relationships. Although the presence of a collaborative relationship was the primary criterion by which companies were selected for the study, in most cases the two parties operated from separate and admittedly conflicting charters:

> The employer represents, and is concerned primarily with, a property interest which, in turn, is directly related to the financial interests of a limited number of stockholders or owners. The interest of the employees' organization or union is primarily that of people—a greater number in most cases—and is concerned with their material, as well as their spiritual and psychological, interest and needs. . . The two parties coexist, with each retaining its institutional sovereignty, working together in reasonable harmony in a climate of mutual respect and confidence. (pp. 7-8)

Although the companies and unions described in these case studies operated from different charters, their ability to sustain industrial peace stemmed largely from their attitudes toward each other. Management accepted the collective-bargaining process and unionism as an institution and considered a strong, democratic, and responsible union as an asset to the company. At the same time, the union respected the private ownership of industry and recognized the dependence of its members on the successful operation of business. These attitudes promoted the prompt, mutually trustful resolution of conflict and widespread, informal sharing of information.

With a few noteworthy exceptions, collaborative efforts between companies and unions represent a condition of détente based on the division of issues into two categories: those that are "safe" for collaborative effort and those reserved for adversary collective bargaining. Vice president of UAW Irving Bluestone (1977), listed a number of topics suitable for joint company-union effort, including alcoholism, drug addiction, emotional problems, preretirement programs, disciplinary counseling, and health and safety programs. He also cited issues that were specifically job related, such as the movement of work and workers, job design, the subcontracting of work, the decision-making process, production scheduling, the introduction of technological innovations, and the assignment of overtime. However, he pointed out that while this collaboration is going on, "the parties remain adversaries with regard to subjects that lend themselves more naturally to the hard business of confrontation collective bargaining [such as] wages, fringe benefits, and job security."

In no case are all issues of mutual concern to company and union open to democratic co-determination. Although the list of topics for collaborative effort has grown progressively, the union has clung tenaciously to wages, benefits, and job security as issues to be negotiated through the traditional adversary process. This continuing wish to exclude a few issues from democratic resolution and administration suggests that not many union officials are comfortable in the role of teamwork facilitator. Some of them look on collaborative activities as a transitory fad and still regard the diminishing realm of confrontation as their justification for existence. For example, when quality of working life was intermingled as a topic with bread-and-butter issues during the introduction of Scanlon plans to the Dana Corporation, the internal union's initial assessment of the program was less than enthusiastic (Work in America Institute, 1977). Although the union's local constituency welcomed the opportunity to help improve productivity and the quality of work life, the international union protested on the grounds that the program allegedly placed excessive emphasis on productivity and plant performance. However, the workers themselves did not object to this emphasis.

A former director of the Federal Mediation and Conciliation Service, James Scearce (1977), wrote that cooperation cannot be seen as a threat to the collective bargaining mechanism. In his view this kind of cooperation simply requires that negotiation be achieved through collective bargaining and within existing company-union relationships. If cooperative efforts are perceived as a threat that might undermine the union's structure or if they become a political threat to the established leadership, those efforts will not even get off the ground. Scearce suggests that Stage 3 organizational teamwork might evolve if union and industry management could view the traditional values of American industrial society as merely an evolutionary, transitional process in the collaborative march toward new patterns of management: "American industrial society has its own values and traditions. If we operate through existing institutions, however, with patience and solid programs, people will begin to open their minds to new approaches" (p.47). Searce's predictions are being validated through developments in Harley-Davidson and other unionized companies where JIT/VAM principles are being implemented.

Stage 3: Organizational Teamwork

To many people now embroiled in win-lose adversary relationships, organizational teamwork is merely an ideal; they view it as pure fantasy and completely contrary to human nature. Organizational democracy is based not on the perpetuation of a two-class system, but on an organizational model akin to that of the free society that exists outside the factory gates. Stage 3 is not a condition of détente between friendly and cooperative adversaries, but a matrix of egalitarian conditions in the workplace by which all members of the work force can participate in democratic processes. Through these processes employees create wealth, establish systems for equitable sharing, change the climate of their organization, and take charge of their own careers.

Organizational teamwork is in no way a form of socialism or communism nor is it synonymous with Stage 2 industrial democracy found in Scandinavia and Germany. It is a set of conditions that promote expression of the entrepreneurial spirit through which responsible, creative, and productive individuals and groups reap higher rewards than do the less effective members of the organization. Moreover, these conditions result in competitive advantages in the business sector and cost effectiveness in the public sector.

As discussed in Chapter 4, the culture of a workplace is strongly influenced by interpersonal relationships within the organization. However, when people change their behavior from one style of leadership to another, the organization usually retains much of its previous flavor as a result of the inertia created by systems installed under the preceding regime. Even when the systems are altered, changes in attitudes and perceptions take place slowly as people evolve through the stages of awareness, understanding, conviction, and new habit formation.

A variety of major and minor systems affect the climate of an organization, each carrying with it a positive or negative valence. Few of these systems, functioning alone, would have a major influence on employee attitudes. However, if most of the subsystems in an organization produce a small positive valence, the net impact in terms of employee attitudes is positive. If most of the systems produce a small negative effect, the net valence is negative. Moreover, the interactive force of these predominantly positive or predominantly negative factors tends to amplify their importance.

Attempts to identify a single major cause of sour attitudes are invariably thwarted. If a seemingly causal factor is isolated, attempts to introduce gimmicks to neutralize or reverse its negative valence are usually futile. For instance, job enrichment, when introduced by itself as a strategy for improving job attitudes, often fails because it represents only one of a vast collage of systems in the organization. Thus, attempts to restructure jobs to make every employee a manager will not be well received by hourly employees as long as they continue to be set apart from the management class by the color of hard hats, the use of time clocks, discriminatory parking privileges, signal bells, paycheck distribution schedules, and myriad subtle symbols of the two-class system.

Sometimes a system is damaging to all members of the organization because of its intrinsic reductive design. This is true, for example, of the traditional authority-oriented performance-review system, which causes supervisors to talk down to their subordinates. However, even if the system is transformed into a goal-setting developmental process, it may still be damaging if it is not available to all members of the organization. When a goal-oriented performance-review system is applied only to supervisory personnel, it accentuates the cleft between management and labor and can be even more divisive than a uniformly applied authority-oriented system. The following discussion on meaningful work puts greater emphasis on jobs held by hourly workers than on management jobs. The emphasis exists because it is important not only to make hourly jobs more interesting but also to eliminate practices that symbolically put people into two classes.

MEANINGFUL WORK

Meaning is given or restored to work through job enrichment or job enlargement. Most often benefits resulting from job enrichment include lowered costs, higher yields, decreased scrap, accelerated learning time, fewer complaints and trips to the health center, reduced anxiety, improved attitudes and team efforts, and increased profits.

Most reports on job enrichment are situational descriptions that offer little guidance for applications in dissimilar circumstances. Slavish emulation of inappropriate examples usually leads to failure. Principles and techniques of job enrichment are useful only as guidelines, and each job must be studied in terms of the opportunities and constraints surrounding it. Jobs may be improved through horizontal or vertical job enlargement or through a combination of both, as illustrated in Figure 7-2. Horizontal job enlargement increases the variety of functions performed at a given level. As an intermediate step, it serves to reduce boredom and broaden the perspective of employees, thereby preparing them for vertical job enlargement. Vertically enlarged jobs enable employees to take part in the planning and control functions customarily restricted to people in supervisory and staff functions. Both types of enrichment improve employee versatility and the monetary and nonmonetary rewards that go with it.

Management-Labor Dichotomy

The functions of management (illustrated in Figure 7-3) are commonly defined in business-school terminology as planning, organizing, leading, and controlling. Management functions are descriptive of the job of a manager, but not of the job of a worker. For example, the managers in an automobile assembly plant might describe their own jobs in terms of planning, organizing, leading, and controlling but would see their fifty supervisors as concerned primarily with leading and controlling. As reflected in Figure 7-4, the main responsibility of the supervisors is overseeing the two thousand workers on the assembly line who are doing the work.

This management point of view, still found in backward organizations, excludes employees from the realm of management and creates, unwittingly if not deliberately, a dichotomy of people at

Horizontal

1. Each assembler on a transformer assembly line performs a single operation as the assembly moves by on the conveyor belt. Jobs are enlarged horizontally by setting up work stations to permit each operator to assemble the entire unit. Operations now performed by each operator include cabling, upending, winding, soldering, laminating, and symbolizing.

2. A similar transformer assembly line introduces horizontal job enlargement when assemblers are taught how to perform all operations and are rotated to different operations periodically, or as permitted by peer and supervisory consensus.

Vertical

3. Assemblers on a radar assembly line are given information on customer-contract commitments in terms of price, quality specifications, and delivery schedules. They are also given company data on materiel and personnel costs, break-even performance, and potential profit margins. Assemblers and engineers work together in methods and design improvements. Assemblers inspect, adjust, and repair their own work, help test completed units, and receive copies of customer inspection reports.

4. Operators involved in the assembly of disk drives receive training in JIT principles and techniques and are encouraged to take the initiative in suggesting improved manufacturing and quality-assurance processes. Natural work groups of five to twelve operators each elect a team captain for a term of six months. In addition to performing regular operations, the team captain collects work-improvement ideas from members of the team, describes the suggestions on a standard form, credits the suggesters, presents the recommendations to the supervisor and staff support personnel at the end of the week, and gives the team feedback on idea utilization. Sometimes the whole team is involved in the reporting process. Vertical job enlargement is achieved by providing increased opportunities for planning, reorganizing, and controlling the work.

Horizontal Plus Vertical

5. Jobs are enlarged horizontally in a clad-metal-rolling mill by qualifying operators to work interchangeably on breakdown rolling, finishing rolling, and slitter, pickler, and abrader operations. After operators are given training in methods improvement and basic metallurgy, jobs are enlarged vertically by involving the workers with engineering and supervisory personnel in problem-solving, statistical process control, and goal-setting.

6. Jobs in a large company's employee-insurance section are enlarged horizontally by qualifying insurance clerks to work interchangeably in filing claims, mailing checks, enrolling and orienting new employees, checking premium and enrollment reports, adjusting payroll deductions, and interpreting policies to employees. Vertical enlargement involves clerks in insurance-program planning meetings with personnel directors and carrier representatives and authorizes them to sign disbursement requests, to attend a paperwork systems conference, to recommend equipment replacements, and to rearrange their work layout.

Figure 7-2. Examples of Horizontal and Vertical Job Enlargement

1. **Planning.** Objectives, goals, strategies, programs, systems, policies, forecasts.
2. **Organizing.** Manpower, money, machines, materials, methods.
3. **Leading.** Communicating, motivating, instructing, delegating, mediating.
4. **Controlling.** Auditing, measuring, evaluating, correcting.

Figure 7-3. The Functions of Management

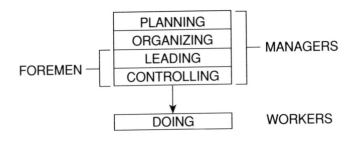

Figure 7-4. The Manager's Traditional Perception of Jobs

work: workers as drones or troublemakers dependent on the direction and control of intelligent and responsible managers. The consequences of this viewpoint are illustrated in Figure 7-5, which points out the social distance and alienation gap between management and labor in organizations that cling to this traditional model.

Although the gap between the employer and the employed has a long heritage and, to some, seems inevitable, it has become broader and more formalized through the efforts of labor unions whose charters seem to demand that workers view management as a natural enemy. The union, while pressuring the company to share profits and the managers to relinquish prerogatives, has at the same time clearly defined the interests of laborers as being separate from, and in conflict with, those of management. Managers typically and naturally align themselves with the goals of the company, but wage

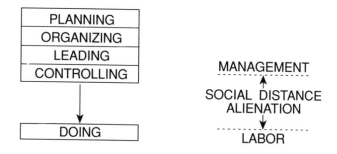

Figure 7-5. The Management-Labor Dichotomy

earners have dual allegiance to the union and the company, often with closer ties to the union.

Autocratic management, tradition, and labor-union strategy collectively perpetuate the two-class concept, but there are forces in America that are reducing it. One is the improving socioeconomic status and the consequent rising aspirations of the less-privileged, accelerated by legislated equality in an increasingly enlightened and affluent society. The second force is a growing awareness by managers of the inevitability of democracy as the pattern for successful competition in world commerce and their acceptance of their role in initiating and supporting it. This chapter focuses on the second of these forces and presents a concept of meaningful work that can guide tomorrow's managers in redefining working conditions and the roles of job incumbents.

Changing Needs

The hierarchy-of-needs theory of Abraham Maslow (1968) helps to explain the consequences of increasing affluence. Primeval man's efforts were directed primarily toward survival needs—safety, food, and shelter—leaving little time or energy for preoccupation with latent higher-order needs. As survival needs were satisfied, people became sensitized to social and status needs. Finally, in the affluence of recent decades, these lower-order or maintenance needs were satisfied to the point that people were ready to realize their potential in terms of growth, achievement, responsibility, and recognition.

Management and unions have both contributed to the readiness of workers for self-actualization. Efficiency engineers of the Industrial Revolution simplified tasks and created mass-production technology. Jobs were fractionated to allow efficiency in training, to eliminate management's dependency on prima donna journeymen, and to satisfy the implicit assumption that employees would be happy and efficient doing easy work for high pay. Although mass-production technology made people the appendages of machines and destroyed their pride and autonomy, it eventually helped to price automobiles, washing machines, refrigerators, and other consumer products within reach. These and other effects of the mass-production economy accelerated the satisfaction of people's basic needs and opened the way for the pursuit of higher-order goals.

The role of unions was just as vital in readying workers for self-actualization, because it forced managers to share company profits with the wage earners, thereby narrowing the economic gap between the manager and the worker, further enabling people to buy the products of mass production. However, the union, for reasons of self-preservation, sharpened the workers' identity as members of labor rather than as members of management—preserving the social gap that might otherwise have been reduced through economic improvement.

When Work Is Meaningless

For many people work is a necessary evil, a form of punishment. It is uninteresting, demeaning, oppressive, and generally unrelated to or in conflict with their personal goals. However, it is an activity that they endure and take in stride to get money for the goods and services that reflect their personal goals. The income itself, however, is not the sole motive for working. Apart from the needs satisfied through income earned on the job, work itself, however dull and menial, can satisfy a wide variety of other requirements, as explained in the following paragraphs.

Work reduces role ambiguity. Work establishes the worker's identity; although the self-image of a worker may not be a desirable one, for most people it is better than an undefined role. Erich Fromm (1941) maintained that work could also be an escape from too much freedom and that such an escape was necessary for people who were culturally conditioned to associate security with roles prescribed by authority.

Work offers socializing opportunities. Close and sustained association with others having similar goals, socioeconomic backgrounds, and interests promotes social interaction. However, social relationships, in the absence of a unifying organizational goal, can be disruptive to productivity. Broad-scale group cohesiveness and social interaction sometimes occur among the members of a work force who are united to defy an oppressive management.

Work increases solidarity. The performance of similar tasks, however routine, is a shared ritual that provides a basis for equality and role acceptance. Misery loves company only because of the solidarity created by shared misery. "Solidarity Forever" has been the theme song of organized labor for many decades. The individual who is promoted or transferred from a unifying, circumscribed role becomes an outsider whose solidarity needs must be satisfied elsewhere.

Work bolsters security feelings. In addition to providing job security, work can foster the feelings of stability that are derived from social and official approval. Authority-oriented people, particularly when performing humdrum tasks, require large amounts of positive feedback from supervisors to satisfy their achievement-related security needs.

Work is a substitute for unrealized potential. "Keeping busy" channels energy or thwarted intellectual capability and helps to obscure the reality of unfulfilled potential (most workaholics are not realizing their potential). Although work in this instance is an escape mechanism, at least it is less destructive than alcoholism or other negative addictions. Employment helps to buy freedom and opportunities off the job that give better expression to talent. Furthermore, a tired body from an honest day's work evokes social approval.

Work is an escape from the home environment. Employment is a culturally acceptable escape mechanism. Aside from the need to satisfy economic demands, people may want to get away from home because of domestic conflict, neighborhood friction, unattractive home facilities, and loneliness.

Work reduces feelings of guilt and worthlessness. In an achieving society, in which dignity and pride are earned through the traits of ambition, initiative, industriousness, and perseverance, idleness violates deep-seated values; and work for work's sake is a virtue. According to the Protestant work ethic or the standards of Horatio Alger, idleness is the equivalent of stealing, and a strong conscience is a key motive for staying on the job.

Meaningless work, as defined above, while satisfying certain personal needs, is not usually constructively aligned with company goals. Such jobs may also thwart long-range personal goals if the work increases dependency relationships and discourages the development of talent. However, this kind of work can be redesigned to lead to the satisfaction of both long-range personal and organizational goals.

Many jobs are already meaningful. For example, a manager's job is usually challenging, related to company goals, and generally aligned with long-range personal goals. The difference in job attitude between manager and worker is usually ascribed to the immaturity of the worker, overlooking the fact that maturity is developed when people are given an opportunity to be responsible.

Most managers manage their jobs, while most workers are managed by their jobs. Workers are frequently only appendages of machines or links between them—doing what is necessary to keep pace with uninspiring, inflexible, and demanding systems.

Dimensions of Meaningful Work

As noted in Chapter 3, meaningful work gives people ownership of their production processes in an egalitarian culture. The function of each worker must include planning and controlling, as well as doing (see Figure 7-6).

The *plan* phase of the work model includes the planning and organizing functions of work: problem solving; goal setting; and planning the use of the labor force, materiel, and systems. Planning is a dimension of work that makes it more meaningful by aligning it with goals. The *do* phase represents the implementation of the plan, ideally involving the coordinated expenditure of physical and mental effort and the utilization of aptitudes and special skills. *Control* includes measurement, evaluation, and correction—the feedback process for assessing achievements against goals. Feedback, to an even greater extent than planning, gives work its meaning; and the

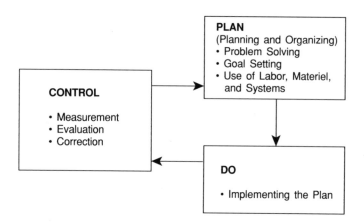

Figure 7-6. Meaningful Work Model

absence of feedback is a common cause of job dissatisfaction. People who are self-employed generally have meaningful work in terms of a cycle of planning, doing, and controlling.

Self-employed farmers, for example, plan and organize in terms of market evaluation, crop rotation, seed selection, utilization of land, purchase of equipment, and the employment of labor. They typically have a major role in implementing their plans: planting, cultivating, irrigating, harvesting, and marketing. Finally, they measure, evaluate, and correct their programs as necessary to provide for a better future cycle. An analogous pattern may be defined for other self-employed entrepreneurs.

The Meaningful Work of Managers

Managers in industry, though seldom having as much autonomy as self-employed entrepreneurs, typically have jobs with ample *plan*, *do*, and *control* phases, particularly at the higher levels. Figure 7-7 shows the job of a manufacturing manager to be relatively rich in the meaningful aspects of work. Although the job depicted is narrower in scope than the division manager's position, two levels above, it nevertheless offers abundant opportunities for planning, doing, and controlling. A company rarely encounters a lack of commitment at or above this managerial level.

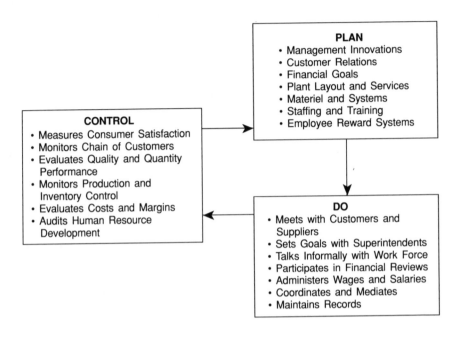

Figure 7-7. Meaningful Work for a Manufacturing Manager

Where Meaningful Work Usually Stops

Even the job of a supervisor, two levels below that of the manufacturing manager, may be rich in terms of the ingredients of meaningful work. Figure 7-8 indicates that the supervisor's job, though narrower in scope than the manufacturing manager's, offers considerable latitude for the management of work. This example depicts the duties of a traditional authority-oriented supervisor.

Although the job of this supervisor includes a complete *plan-do-control* cycle, it is not fully satisfactory, because its authority orientation does not permit the delegation of a similar cycle of responsibility to the operator. Under this supervisor the operator lives in a world circumscribed by pressure to follow instructions, work harder, obey rules, get along with people, and be loyal to the supervisor and the company. This role quashes the potential satisfaction that work itself might offer. The operator is treated no differently than machines and materials by insensitive bosses exercising their management prerog-

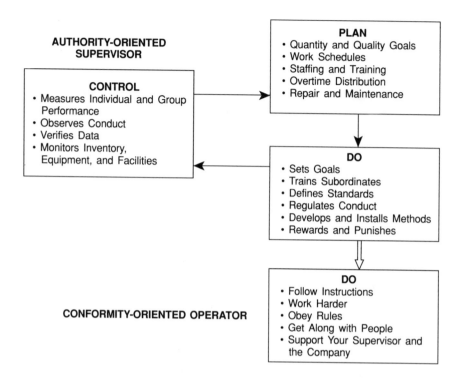

Figure 7-8. Authority-Oriented Relationship Between Supervisor and Operator

atives, as kings once exercised their divine rights. Conformity-oriented workers tend to behave like adolescent children responding to the punishments and rewards of authoritarian parents. Any rights these workers may have were wrested from management through collective bargaining and are seldom aligned with company goals.

The Impact of Supervisory Style

Job enrichment sometimes results naturally from the intuitive practices of goal-oriented, emotionally mature leaders who evoke commitment through a language of action that grants freedom and reflects respect, confidence, and high expectations. Unfortunately, such leadership is rare, and many managers still see job enlargement as a form of benevolent autocracy. Job-enrichment attempts by reductive, authority-oriented managers usually fail to inspire the enthusiasm and commitment achieved by goal-oriented managers. Their transparent motives and their language of action comes across as manipulation and exploitation rather than as acts of trust, confidence, and respect.

Hence, job enrichment depends on style of supervision as well as job design and is not simply a matter of emulating the patterns of work and relationships found to be successful elsewhere. Involvement of supervisors in the enrichment process is necessary for two reasons: they are usually the people most familiar with the work to be done, and their leadership practices are pivotal to its success. Their participation in the job-enrichment process often leads to redefinition of their own roles and self-initiated changes in their managerial style.

Job Enrichment Processes

Job enrichment is a never-ending process. In large organizations attempts to improve all jobs can be disruptive to productivity, and getting started presents a dilemma. A realistic kickoff is to involve all supervisors at least once in a formal way, so that they can take the initiative in testing and implementing enrichment techniques with other jobs under their supervision.

Sometimes job enrichment is best achieved by piecemeal chipping away at existing jobs. This approach is least threatening and disruptive to job incumbents, particularly when they are fully involved in the change process. The next step might involve the collapsing or merging of several allied jobs. In such cases, it is helpful to itemize the planning and control functions of higher jobs, which can then be pulled down to make lower jobs more complete. When possible, routine functions are eliminated, perhaps through automation, or made more bearable by combining them with more interesting functions.

One approach to making work more meaningful is to assign finite modules of work to individuals. For example, in a study at American Telephone and Telegraph a group of ten employees was responsible for mailing out toll billings on staggered dates throughout the month. All bills for telephone prefixes starting with 392 were due out on the first of the month, all 395 prefixes on the fifth, 397 on the thirteenth, and so on. Working as a team, employees would finish

392 and then start 395 under the scheduling and direction of the supervisor. However, productivity was low, due dates were missed, and overtime costs were high. Recognizing each block of billings as a natural module of work, managers assigned responsibility for each module to a specific employee. One person was responsible for getting out 392 prefixes, another for 395, and so on. Each individual was responsible for the *plan, do,* and *control* functions necessary to meet deadlines. The employees made their own decisions and formed mutually supportive relationships with one another. Each employee could succeed or fail, but each controlled his or her own performance and fate. Results were dramatically good: schedules were met, overtime was eliminated, and job satisfaction increased.

In most instances job enrichment is best accomplished with the active involvement of the job incumbent. For example, a group of employees are given an opportunity to examine and evaluate their own jobs and co-workers' jobs. Such an analysis is usually preceded by an educational process that gives them a framework for making their evaluation. If they conclude, as they usually do, that their jobs could be improved, they are given an opportunity to recommend the inclusion of responsibilities that would make their jobs more whole.

For example, employees might be shown a list of their supervisor's responsibilities with the question, "Is there anything in your boss's job that you could handle and would like to handle?" In addition, they might be asked the same question about the responsibilities of staff support people from engineering, inspection, and maintenance. The usual consequence of such an opportunity is that employees tend to overload their own jobs. The overload can be adjusted subsequently by involving job incumbents whose jobs were plundered during the enrichment process.

If the process were to terminate with the enrichment of jobs at the lowest level, the people whose jobs were partially annexed would feel threatened. Therefore, it is usually desirable to move the process successively upward. First-level supervisors may be shown the superintendent's list of job responsibilities with the same question: "Is there anything in your boss's job that you could handle and would like to handle?" This process, continued upward through superintendent, manufacturing manager, and department head, ultimately reaches the plant manager, who customarily retains too much work for himself or herself. The most important consequence of this process is to shorten communication channels by eliminating unnecessary levels of management (see the example cited in Chapter 3).

If such a bottom-up process is to be initiated, managers who will be affected must be briefed on the rationale for the process and given the opportunity to assume a leadership role in the change process. Otherwise, managers may feel threatened by what might appear to them as an erosion of their managerial prerogatives and a threat to their job security.

Improving a person's relationship to his or her job is not limited to the techniques of job enrichment mentioned here. The empowerment of employees through the JIT/VAM applications described in Chapter 3 is perhaps the most effective approach to job enrichment for people at all levels of the organization. Such a process includes most of the nonmonetary reward systems described in Chapter 2. Empowering a chain of customers to take charge of a mission can lead naturally to the transformation of a conformity-oriented work force into creative, goal-oriented individuals and teams.

Enrichment is in the eyes of the jobholder. People who are free to select the job they prefer have in effect enriched their jobs. Job posting, described in Chapter 5, allows dissatisfied job incumbents to seek out, perhaps by trial and error, the job most compatible with their values and skills. Many routine jobs that appear to require enrichment are merely waiting for the right employee. If people are allowed to migrate throughout the company, the spurned jobs may be filled by individuals who prefer them.

Sometimes a routine job is made oppressive only by the inability of the job incumbents to escape it. The chronic complaints of people locked into such jobs may be termed the *jailhouse syndrome*. When the gates are opened and employees are free to transfer out, only a few seek to do so. Freedom and choice often dissipate frustration and hostility.

Enrichment is sometimes achieved by job rotation. For example, assemblers working along a conveyor-belt assembly line were allowed to exchange jobs on the condition that the workers who were leaving a post were accountable for the job skills of the people replacing them. In another situation, an undesirable task was assigned on a rotational basis to all members of a work group. Thus, in a six-person work group, each person might be required to perform the task every sixth workday. Under such an arrangement, it is not unusual to find certain individuals volunteering for more than their required quota of the rotated assignment. Finally, it should be noted that work itself is not the only or even the best medium for enriching jobs. A broader concept of life enrichment in the workplace gives equal emphasis to the peripheral systems discussed in the next chapters.

REFERENCES

Bluestone, I. (1977). A changing view of the union-management relationship. In *Breakthroughs in union-management cooperation* (pp.7-12). Scarsdale, NY: Work in America Institute.

Fromm, E. (1941). *Escape from freedom.* New York: Holt, Rinehart & Winston.

Golden, C.S. & Parker, V.D. (Eds.). (1955). *Causes of industrial peace under collective bargaining.* New York: Harper & Row.

Gompers, S. (1925). *Samuel Gompers, seventy years of life and labor: An autobiography.* New York: E.P. Dutton.

Haire, M. (1969, March). Lecture presented to fellows of the Salzburg Seminar in American Management Dynamics, Salzburg, Austria.

Maslow, A.H. (1968). *Toward a psychology of being* (2nd ed.). New York: Van Nostrand.

Maynard, H.B. (1971). *Industrial engineering handbook* (3rd ed.). New York: McGraw-Hill.

Scearce, J. (1977). Labor-management cooperation: Myth or reality? In *Breakthroughs in Union-Management Cooperation* (p. 47). Scarsdale, NY: Work in America Institute.

Serrin, W. (1973). *The company and the union.* New York: Alfred A. Knopf.

Taylor, F.W. (1911). *The principles of scientific management.* New York: Harper & Bros.

Vaill, P.B. (1966, May). *Industrial engineering and socio-technical systems.* Paper presented before the American Institute of Industrial Engineers, San Francisco, CA.

Walker, C.R. (1965). *Changing character of human work under the impact of technological change.* Multilith working paper, Wellfleet, MA.

Work in America Institute. (1977). The Scanlon Plan at the Dana Corporation. *Breakthroughs in Union-Management Cooperation,* pp. 17-29. Author.

8

Peripheral Systems

In every organization there are small and large systems peripheral to the work itself that influence the ambience of the workplace. Such systems do not usually appear in job descriptions; however, they may serve a variety of functions that influence job incumbents directly and indirectly. Illustrative of these systems are parking facilities, timekeeping methods, charity drives, company newspapers, paycheck-distribution practices, lunchrooms, attitude surveys, safety committees, and conflict-resolution procedures.

Peripheral systems are generally associated with maintenance factors and have little motivational potential. However, many of these systems can be administered in such a way that they become media for satisfying motivation needs. Such potential is illustrated in the following example, which describes the quality of work efforts in one of the plants of the Eaton Corporation.

THE EATON STORY

The Eaton Corporation is composed of more than 150 plants deployed worldwide, engaged primarily in the manufacturing of precision parts such as axles and transmissions. Although many jobs at Eaton require highly developed skills and technical competence, life in the typical Eaton factory was once characterized by boredom, disengagement, and counterproductive behavior. As in most organizations, personnel problems were more bothersome among factory workers than among members of the office staff.

In 1968 the company planners saw an opportunity to revise their traditional approach to labor relations. They were planning the expansion of company operations through the opening of new plants and sought to take advantage of the fact that it is easier to introduce new personnel practices in a start-up situation than it is to revise practices in an established operation. Start-up operations are less inhibited by the crystallized attitudes and systems that often characterize established organizations.

Noting that office staff members had responded positively to personnel practices based on Theory Y assumptions, the planners speculated that shop personnel, who were typically governed by more reductive practices, might also respond better to a Theory Y philosophy. Office personnel usually enjoyed the same freedom as the managers with whom they worked, sharing flexible work rules, egalitarian practices, and informal communications. Shop workers were regulated by the more restrictive atmosphere of a labor-management dichotomy; they were governed by posted work rules, which circumscribed their job roles and personal freedoms. The reductive practices in the shop were obviously not bringing about the desired results and tended only to provoke creative counterproductive behavior.

Eaton managers envisioned and planned for the opening of a new plant in Kearney, Nebraska, in which the traditional practices of discriminating between shop and office would be avoided. Toward that end they established a quality-of-work-life committee composed of both union and management personnel to refine the details of the new strategy.

The implementation of these plans was effective enough to prompt its extension to other start-up operations. Within a decade, fifteen new plants were operating under the new theory with varying degrees of success. This new philosophy was not orchestrated by corporate edict; rather, plant managers were encouraged to involve their own employees in the development of blueprints for applying the new philosophy in their respective plants. In practice, a lot of cross-fertilization took place as managers voluntarily visited one another's operations and exchanged information.

Don Scobel (1981) cites the following examples as expressions of the evolving Eaton philosophy. These applications are not focused on job design or job enlargement, but on factors peripheral to work itself.

1. Special invitation to regular meetings. On an ad hoc basis, people who do not ordinarily attend are invited to sit in on meetings that deal with issues such as production control, supplier appraisal, engineering processes, and sales planning. A nonsupervisory factory or office worker, a union official, or a foreperson might be invited.

2. Departmental meetings. The head of a department or operation holds periodic meetings with employees to discuss issues other than immediate job projects. Meetings are participative or are led by one or more of those present; sometimes a guest speaker is invited.

3. Manager's round table. The manager of a facility periodically meets with people randomly selected from various levels and functions (operations represented are usually selected on a rotating basis) to discuss matters of importance to those attending.

4. Supervisor's meetings. Meetings are held involving supervisors from various functions, including both office and factory divisions, to share information and to coordinate the administration of personnel practices.

5. Newspaper publication. Volunteer reporters and editors publish the plant newspaper. Sometimes several volunteers form an editorial board, which, within specific financial limits, has the full responsibility for the house publication.

6. Hiring process. Groups of applicants for nonsupervisory jobs are invited to informal meetings (often spouses are also invited) to discuss the purpose of the plant. Applicants meet and talk with their future peers, supervisors, and union representatives. They are given a tour of the factory and the offices and later participate in a similarly conducted orientation process.

7. Tour guides. Tours for community groups, guests, job applicants, and current employees are conducted by volunteers from the offices and the factory. Plant tours for families and friends may be planned entirely by the employees themselves.

8. Social-service training. In conjunction with local professional specialists and/or members of social-service agencies, groups of supervisors, union representatives, and other interested employees are jointly trained to spot employee problems and to arrange for appropriate professional counsel.

9. Educational committee. A committee of volunteer supervisors from office and factory analyzes educational resources in the community and recommends courses to meet employee needs.

10. Departmental safety teams. Each factory foreman and two or three division employees (chosen on a rotating basis) form a departmental safety team with responsibility for safety training, accident investigation, statistical reporting, and periodic inspections. Where a plantwide safety committee exists, these local teams serve as grass-roots adjuncts to the plant committee.

11. Recreation committee. This committee, made up of volunteers from every level of the organization, is given specific financial resources and entrusted with the design and implementation of recreational programs.

12. Quality circles. Special task forces find ways to improve quality, to remove errors, and to reduce operating expenses.

13. Process-improvement team. A team composed of engineering, factory-management, office, and factory personnel encourages and reviews process-improvement ideas and plans. This committee solicits such ideas from the entire work force, focusing particularly on the viewpoints of the people who would be affected by changes proposed by professional systems designers.

14. Improvement-sharing plans. The process-improvement team may also provide leadership in the design of a gainsharing plan for all employees. Such sharing plans usually provide earnings adjustments based on gains in the sales/labor ratio resulting from operational improvements.

15. Open-floor policy. The open-floor policy designates a factory worker's area as a legitimate place to conduct small talk and office-type business when it is effective to do so. The plan encourages office personnel to make the open floor their natural habitat during coffee breaks, lunch periods, and routine visitations.

16. Time recording. Mechanical time clocks are replaced by a time-accounting report that is completed by job incumbents.

17. Work schedules. Work groups participate in planning regular and overtime work schedules and the use of flextime.

18. Absence from job. People from all levels and functions may have paid sick leave and paid time off for personal business, provided arrangements are made (usually through self-managed teams) to cover the responsibilities of absent workers.

19. Job evaluation. A permanent part-time task force made up of representatives from various levels and functions in the organization evaluates jobs and responds to requests for clarification of job-evaluation issues.

20. Evaluation of supervisors. Factory and office supervisors have the option of allowing their employees to complete anonymous supervisory-effectiveness rating forms.

21. Food-service committee. A committee of volunteers administers food-service activities within a prescribed budget.

22. Disciplinary counseling. Instead of using formal *Parent-Child* disciplinary warnings and suspensions, supervisors are taught a more *Adult-Adult* counseling process for modifying behavior.

23. Supervisor selection. Employees have an opportunity to influence the supervisor-selection process and the selection of their own supervisor.

24. Community-service activities. Community-service activities such as bond drives, Red Cross blood programs, and the United Fund are directed and coordinated by volunteers from throughout the organization.

25. Bells and buzzers. Unnecessary and undesired sound signals to regiment employee behavior may be evaluated and discontinued.

26. Automobile parking. First-come, first-served parking for everyone, except for physically handicapped, employees on company business, ride-pools, visitors, and customers.

27. Attitude survey. Employees take part in formulating the topics to be covered by the survey, refining the questionnaire, completing the poll, analyzing the appraisal results, and formulating remedial action programs.

None of the foregoing processes, viewed singly, would substantially alter the culture or effectiveness of the organization. However, each process carries with it the potential for a small positive valence for most of the people affected by it. Collectively and interactively the effect of such processes is compounded to make Eaton plants where these ideas have been implemented better places to work.

Don Scobel stresses the point that these processes are not standardized or uniformly applied in all Eaton situations. His advice to managers in public seminars is as follows: "You have to make your own road maps on where you want to go and how to get there; and you may have to modify your approaches as you go along to satisfy the different and changing needs of the participants." Much of the value of these processes derives from the fact that they are systems shaped by the systems' users, and as such, they carry with them the proprietary involvement of the members of the work force. These are not management programs or union programs, but people programs. [1]

ORGANIZATIONAL CLIMATE

Every organization can be said to have a climate that colors the perceptions and feelings of people within the work environment. A company's climate is influenced by peripheral systems illustrated above and by innumerable factors such as its size; the nature of its business; its age; its location; the composition of its work force; its management policies, rules, and regulations; and its leadership practices. The climate in Eaton plants, as described in the preceding pages, is uniquely influenced by various peripheral systems purposely designed to foster egalitarianism and initiative. Some climate factors are dynamic and interactive, resulting in constant flux, or even chaos. Other factors remain relatively constant, tending to stabilize the organization.

Growth Rate

In a rapidly expanding organization, the sense of urgency and the increased speed of change create rich opportunities for individual growth, achievement, responsibility, and recognition. Domineering supervisors who would seem oppressive in a stable organization are tolerated in the growth climate, perhaps because their roles are seen as transitory. Furthermore, the sheer pressure of expanding respon-

---

[1] A more complete list of peripheral systems is presented in Figure A-2 (see Appendix A). The collective impact of these systems has the potential to change the climate of a workplace. Their success is strongly influenced by leadership practices in the organization.

sibility reduces the authoritarian manager's ability to maintain tight controls; delegation does occur, if only by default.

In the stabilized or retrenching organization, a condition that often occurs with economic downturns, managers frequently resort to reductive supervisory practices. Delegation is curtailed, and growth opportunities are interrupted or deferred; the more talented members of the work force become impatient and discouraged. Eager to forge ahead, they seek greener pastures and gradually abandon the organization to those who are less able to revive the company or to find new jobs. The loss of top talent to competitor organizations further handicaps the stalled company. Hence, growth itself helps to retain the talented personnel on whom the continuing success of the organization depends.

This is not to say that perpetual growth is necessary to retain talented employees. The self-renewing organization, through the management of innovation (processes described in Chapter 12), provides conditions attractive to high achievers, even during retrenchment.

Freedom to Act

Freedom to act in an organization is a function of style of supervision and organizational structure. Goal-oriented managers delegate naturally and willingly—particularly when they themselves are the recipients of delegated authority. Authority-oriented managers, in contrast, tend to create organizational constraints and to restrict subordinates with command-and-control tactics.

Businesses organized around decentralized, semiautonomous product-customer centers foster delegation better than functionally layered organizations. Functional layering is commonly found in government bureaucracies and public utilities that have little concern for competition. For example, a manager of manufacturing in a functionally layered organization might direct manufacturing in five plants but would have limited freedom to influence other resources related to engineering and sales. Each of these two silos would have separate silo managers. In contrast, a plant manager who has the threefold responsibility of creating, making, and marketing products or income-producing services has more entrepreneurial flexibility; these managers can manage all resources and maintain a chain of customers necessary for organizational success.

Innovation

Innovation exists in abundance in every organization, but it is not always beneficial. In a democratic company in which people at all levels have the opportunity to receive information, solve problems, and set goals, innovation finds positive expression. In organizations characterized by restrictive supervision, inflexible rules, engineered labor standards, and other authority-oriented controls, creativity is usually counterproductive. The tighter the controls, the more innovative the attempts at circumvention become. Organizations must do more than merely foster innovation; they must also provide outlets that allow creativity to find positive expression.

Constructive innovation is dependent on both leadership style and facilitative systems. The hierarchy of objectives, strategies, and tactical action programs described in Chapter 12 is a framework to encourage companywide work groups and task forces to be creative in achieving organizational goals. Work simplification, also described in Chapter 12, and JIT/VAM, discussed in Chapter 3, teach the problem-solving/goal-setting techniques that encourage creativity at all levels of an organization. The task-force analysis of attitude-survey results, described in Chapter 12, is a system for utilizing constructive talent at all levels of a company. A climate of innovation is also enhanced by avoiding authority-based systems such as engineered labor standards, chain-of-command communication, defensive expense reporting, and elaborate rank-oriented status symbols.

Use of Authority

The reductive use of authority described in Chapter 4 does not mean that authority itself is bad. Authority is freedom to act and is necessary to every member of the organization. Operators who have ownership over their production systems have the authority (and the obligation) to serve their customers. However, employees who perform their jobs in blind obedience to orders from the boss do not have the authority they need to serve their customers.

Unless a conscious effort is made, growing organizations drift inexorably toward conformity and an authority-dominated climate. Authority creates company parking-lot rules and requires employees to punch time clocks. Supervisors tell employees what their jobs are, and union stewards tell them what their jobs are not. Industrial engineers tell them how to do their jobs, and signal bells authorize coffee breaks and lunch periods. Company information is dispensed by authority figures through the public-address system, official notices, the company newspaper, and bulletin boards. The United Fund and savings-bond drives, which are ostensibly voluntary, are administered through a subtle use of authority that makes nonparticipation unacceptable. Hence there is nothing wrong with authority as long as every person has the requisite amount to manage his or her job. Delegators need to remember that "authority delegated" and "authority reserved" are mutually exclusive.

Goal Orientation

Goal orientation is the motivation force that gives direction to the systems and relationships that make broad organizational goals comprehensible and that facilitate the formation of supportive subgoals. It allows access to information and freedom to act so that individual initiative finds expression in setting goals and measuring achievements. Goal-oriented employees manage their own jobs, in contrast to employees in an authority-oriented company, who feel that their jobs manage them. Goal orientation depends on an integrated balance of meaningful goals, helpful systems, and compatible people, as detailed in Chapters 4, 5, and 6.

Deliberate and systematic attempts are made in goal-oriented organizations to minimize barriers to communication, especially rank-oriented status symbols. Dining facilities are shared by all; first-name employee identification badges do not reflect rank; parking privileges, office space, and furnishings are assigned on the basis of functional criteria not necessarily related to job grade or organizational level. Mode of attire is not regimented and tends to be informal. People customarily address one another on a first-name basis and usually communicate through the informal and fluid grapevine that exists in every organization. The unwritten but widely understood ground rule governing vertical as well as horizontal relationships is that individuals treat one another with the mutual respect and informality of social peers. The influence of supervisors is not a manifestation of arbitrary direction and control but a reflection of their role as advisers, consultants, and coordinators. The net effect of such a system enables people to relate to one another on the basis of competence and to work together in the voluntary pursuit of common goals.

Status Factors

Status may be considered as official or unofficial. Official status is established by the bestowal of a job title and responsibility, with commensurate authority, job grade, salary, and privileges. Increased official status is an incentive to personal and professional growth for those who have the talent and desire to move up the organizational hierarchy. However, not every employee receives or wants a higher job grade or the position of supervisor or plant manager.

Unofficial status is a function of an individual's role in his or her work group and is influenced by factors such as skill with tools and equipment, knowledge of processes and technology, and the achievement of production goals. Individuals are also valued for their generosity, their ability to make others laugh, their contagious enthusiasm, their roles as sympathetic listeners, or their willingness to accept unpleasant tasks. The advantage of unofficial status is that it can be applied to everyone; respect for a machinist does not detract from respect for a secretary, an engineer, or an assembler. Nor does respect for one assembler preclude respect for another; each earns respect on the basis of unique competence factors.

Unofficial status stemming from genuine excellence leads to less rivalry and more satisfaction than does official status based on power or wealth. Official status is more vulnerable to the influence of political winds and happenstance and is at the mercy of higher authority. Unofficial status is more intrinsic to the individual, is earned through personal achievements and attributes, and tends to accompany a worker from company to company, granting lasting esteem. Furthermore, the perpetuation of unofficial status is not dependent on authority-oriented prestige symbols. For the mature and accepted member of the work group, earned status (official or unofficial) is its own reward and needs no visible signs. The flaunting of symbols, particularly official reminders of inequality, is symptomatic of immaturity and serves only to undermine feelings of dignity and worth in people who have lower official status—people on whom those more advanced in the hierarchy depend for their continuing success.

Most people like to be proud of their group and to be valued for their role in it. Pride of membership offers an opportunity and an advantage for the organization with a favorable company or product image. Attractive grounds and buildings and prestigious products are often symbols of status in a community and a source of pride at all levels of the organization. The PACCAR employee exclaims with pride when a giant Peterbilt truck barrels down the highway, "I built that truck!"

The attitude of the individual toward his or her work group offers the key to filling jobs that would otherwise have low status— the key to retaining people who perform the less attractive duties. More important than the status of the work itself is the self-image of the group who performs the job. Physicians and nurses, for example, have to do things that would disgust unskilled workers who did not see these actions in a professional context; yet the status of people in medicine is generally high. The prestige of physicians themselves and the overall value of their contributions make the unattractive tasks acceptable. However, prestige is not limited to highly esteemed professions. The janitors described in Chapter 6 enhanced their own self-esteem and the status of their company through creative and responsive behavior. When people feel solidarity with their work groups, they can usually take in stride the more unpleasant aspects of their work.

Communications

As discussed in Chapter 4, communications occur through three languages: words, behavior, and systems. Communications at their best are informal, fluid, and spontaneous; successful communication takes place when each of these languages conveys the same message, removing any possibility of ambiguity. This kind of communication is illustrated in Chapter 3 in the description of the plant at Normandale-South.

The type and quality of communications within an organization are usually determined by the size of the organization and its predominant managerial style. One consequence of the growth of an organization is the tendency to formalize communications. In a small organization informal face-to-face communication usually occurs naturally, and managers who do not actively prevent this kind of discourse have the benefit of a well-informed work force. However, as the organization expands and ages, relationships become more formalized, and communications begin to lag.

A typical bureaucratic response to the breakdown of communications is the creation of the AVO system (avoid verbal orders) and other formalized reporting processes. These systems require that all communications be committed to paper. Although the plans seem harmless at first, traffic in interoffice memos expands exponentially. Memo writers routinely prepare copies for their supervisors, for the recipient's supervisor, and for others whose responsibilities are, at best, remotely related to the issue at hand. These memos and their copies evoke responses in an ever-increasing volume, until eventually employees find themselves working in the proverbial paper mill. The formalized communication process tends to reinforce an authority-oriented chain of command, quashing the spontaneous interactive process natural to small organizations and necessary for the functioning of a goal-oriented, cohesive work force.

Furthermore, as organizations become more complex, computer technology is expanded; and a greater number of management systems are applied. The flow of memos, forms, and computer printouts increases, jamming in-baskets, filling file cabinets, and gradually encumbering the administrative process. The conformity demanded by these formalized systems takes its toll on freedom of action, administrative flexibility, and the constructive expression of talent. As informal communications continue to fail, formalized communications increase in volume, only to increase the likelihood of further breakdown.

Communications may also become inefficient when they are being used as a defense against reductive managerial styles. If employees do not trust one another, they write official memos to provide instruction, obtain compliance, request approval, justify actions, and report progress. Informal oral commitment is no longer adequate; rejected or unheard viewpoints find expression in the form of letters to the file, which are intended as protection against the vagaries of the future. This massive flow of protective paperwork is known as the *paper umbrella*.

Printed media seldom solve communication problems. No matter how formalized the organization, people rely on both formal and informal communication for job information. An increase in printed communications tends to reduce the total percentage of information assimilated. In addition, the formalized management of information evokes reactive behavior and fosters the development of cynical and hostile messages along the company grapevine.

Stability

Organizational stability is a key climate factor, particularly when it relates to employee security needs. Stability has many ramifications; for employees it is freedom from the ups and downs of business. It is the knowledge that jobs will be available for those who do good work, the confidence that workers will have advance knowledge of changes that may affect them. The ability to cope with change is often a function of a person's role in the unstable situation. Unexpected or misunderstood changes may contribute to an atmosphere of uncertainty; but the same changes, when developed with the active participation of those who will be affected by the change, can enhance feelings of security.

So vital are employment stability to the image of an organization and job security to the self-esteem of its members, that a company realizes a substantial return on investment by maintaining its equilibrium despite business fluctuations. Yet corporate leaders rarely plan strategies for maintaining a stable work force. Instead, they focus strategic planning efforts on research, production, and marketing. When business setbacks occur, management will, as a last-ditch effort, pare expense, capital, and labor budgets. In labor-intensive organizations people are usually seen as a buffer for absorbing the adverse impacts of business cycles.

The long-term costs of threatened job security in terms of unfavorable public relations and employee alienation are considerable, but the cost of developing preventive strategies is relatively minor. Strategies built around an imaginative combination of processes listed in Figure 8-1 can often eliminate or at least ameliorate the impact of business reversals.

When business turndowns seem imminent, a moratorium can be declared on hiring. Eventually normal turnover, consolidated operations, and reassignments will begin a natural retrenchment process. Although turnover rates vary substantially from one organization to another and generally decrease during recessions, annual turnover generally averages 20 to 25 percent. In practice, a hiring moratorium will usually yield a 20-percent reduction in personnel in one year and a 40-percent reduction in two years.

1. Suspended hiring	8. Part-time	17. Reclassification
2. Normal turnover	employment	18. Reduced hours
3. Consolidated	9. Subcontracting	19. Loan-outs
operations	10. Advance warning	20. Outplacement
4. Reassignment	11. Problem solving	21. New Business
5. Early/detection	12. Budget revision	
system	13. Vacation	
6. Temporary	scheduling	
employment	14. Educational leave	
7. Temporary	15. Early retirement	
overtime	16. Retraining	

Figure 8-1. Processes for Maintaining a Stable Work Force

Ideally, management should maintain an early-detection system to forecast business trends. In the face of uncertain forecasts, production demands may be satisfied by the use of temporary and part-time help, through overtime, and through the subcontracting of temporary workloads. The cutback of temporary and part-time help during periods of recession, like the reduction of overtime, though painful, does not undermine the security of the permanent full-time employees. It is important that temporary and part-time personnel be told at the time of hiring that their jobs are tenuous.

Advance warning to the work force will often yield an abnormal flow of departures as people seek new employment to escape the crunch. Employees can be involved in task-force efforts to brainstorm cost-reduction strategies pertaining to expense, capital, and personnel budgets. Temporary financial gain can sometimes be realized through revised bookkeeping, amortization, and taxation procedures.

Forewarned employees can adapt to rescheduled vacations; a few may crystallize educational-leave plans, and others may opt for early retirement. Personnel transferred to fill essential positions may require retraining and reclassification. Although some reclassifications may entail promotions, most will be lateral; under severe conditions some may necessitate temporary demotions.

If further personnel budget reductions become inevitable in spite of the foregoing measures, reductions in hours across the board may be more widely accepted than layoffs that destroy part of the permanent work force. Employees who are given adequate advance warning and who are made to understand the causal economic factors are more likely to accept the cutbacks.

Other last-ditch efforts to cope with economic stress include loans of surplus personnel across department lines or to outside organizations. This measure is more feasible in an industry-restricted slump than in a general economic recession. Some organizations give employees special training and time off for job hunting in order to bridge the transition to a new employer. One large Canadian tobacco company avoided retrenchment by diversifying into new product lines that would absorb the slack in the tobacco business caused by new competitors and reductions in tobacco consumption.

No one of these tactics alone will maintain stability and employee job security during severe business recessions. However, various combinations of these strategies, creatively and aggressively employed, can do much to sustain a favorable company image in the eyes of employees and the community.

Although not all people can necessarily be kept on the payroll during business recessions, if they and others in the community feel that employees are being treated fairly and that their chances for survival are justly related to their performance, those who are laid off can retain their dignity; and the company can maintain an image in the work force and in the community as a good place to work. Moreover, if retrenchment squeezes people off the payroll, they leave without hostility toward the organization and can rejoin it without rancor or loss of pride when business conditions improve.

REFERENCES

Scobel, D.N. (1981). *Creative worklife*. Houston, TX: Gulf.

9

Supervisors as Leaders

Chapter 7 described how to bridge the management-labor gap and how to give substance to the slogan "Every employee a manager." A manager is defined in this context as one who manages a job. A self-managed job is one that enables an employee to take charge of the *plan-do-control* phases of the assignment. Although many jobs in their present forms cannot be fully enriched, most can be improved; some can be eliminated, combined with others, or more uniquely matched with employee aptitudes. Whether the supervisor's mission is to modify the job or to match it to the right people, the goal is most successfully achieved by involving the people he or she supervises. Moreover, supervisors must determine which of their customary roles should be modified or discontinued. Because they are human, role changes can be unsettling or threatening, particularly if those changes are opposed by high-status role models within the company. The dilemma is less painful when supervisors themselves are in charge of the change process.

PERFORMANCE MANAGEMENT

Daniels and Rosen (1988) have provided helpful guidance on the use of positive reinforcement to help a supervisor make the transition from boss to facilitator/consultant/adviser. They define four supervisory interventions for modifying behavior:

1. Positive Reinforcement: providing something that employees want, such as recognition for perfect attendance;

2. Facilitative Reinforcement: allowing employees to avoid something they do not want, such as excusing high achievers from punching time clocks;

3. Punishment: giving employees something they do not want, such as reprimands for chronic tardiness;

4. Extinction: taking away something employees want, such as withholding desired overtime because of late start-ups.

Positive and facilitative reinforcements increase desirable behavior, whereas punishment and extinction decrease undesirable behavior. Positive and facilitative reinforcements are usually superior to the other two methods, because most workplace problems are motivational. Punishment and extinction are sometimes warranted, but positive and facilitative reinforcements should be used at least four times as often as the other two.

Reinforcers may be tangible (money, furnishings, equipment, promotions) or social (praise, letters of commendation, thanks, smiles, pats on the back). Social reinforcers are more effective because they are free, more powerful than tangible rewards, readily available, and controllable by the reinforcer; furthermore, they can be used frequently. Tangible reinforcers can be effective when employed under the following conditions: if they are used in conjunction with social acknowledgments; if they are visible reminders of accomplishment; and if they are under the control of the reinforcer. Reinforcing before the employee has performed is a form of bribery and should be avoided.

Contests have little to offer in terms of positive reinforcement, because they usually generate more losers than winners, represent a form of bribery before performance, and often deteriorate over time. Contests work best when initiated by the contestants and when each participant is competing against himself or herself or against achievement standards. Competitions can have some negative side effects when people are pitted against one another.

Positive and facilitative reinforcements should be preceded by pinpointing specific behavior (what people are doing) and specific results (what people have done). Behavior or results are measurable either by counting or by a judging process. Continuous feedback is essential; tangible messages in the form of graphs are most effective.

A potential danger in using positive reinforcement is that inexperienced or autocratic supervisors might positively reinforce the wrong behavior, such as obedience and conformity, thereby stifling initiative and creativity. It is important that supervisors operate from a power base of competence rather than authority.

Self-Imposed Role Ambiguity

When production supervisors at Texas Instruments (see Chapter 6) began applying problem-solving/goal-setting processes, they reached production goals in a number of areas: improving quality, implementing methods that were more cost effective, registering fewer complaints, and reducing absenteeism and tardiness. In some cases, they found commitment so high that it became essential to remind employees to take the legally required rest periods in midmorning and midafternoon.

Enjoying increased freedom and involved in managing their own efforts, operators began working directly with the engineers on methods improvement, value analysis, and rearranging the workplace. Supervisors permitted these new operator work roles primarily because the new tasks resulted in improved performance. However, the operators' activities did not always involve the supervisors, who became uncomfortable with the resultant ambiguity of their own roles. One supervisor's anxiety reached a high when a problem-solving group told him that he was free to leave the meeting to attend to other matters—that they would keep him posted on their progress. This role ambiguity led the supervisors to consult their division training director, who helped them to define their new positions.

Role Redefinition

The essence of the redefinition of leadership roles at Texas Instruments is reflected in Figure 9-1. Initial efforts to remove role ambiguity produced the traditional authority-oriented stance detailed in the left column. Upon evaluating and rejecting these traditional descriptors as inaccurate definitions of their emerging roles, supervisors redefined their responsibilities along the lines stated in the goal-oriented column.

Although most of the items in the left-hand column of Figure 9-1 were acceptable according to traditional views, their collective effect reinforces the authority-oriented relationship depicted in the diagram at the foot of the column. In this type of relationship people are expected to conform to the *plan-lead-control* directives issued by supervisors. Items in the goal-oriented column do not differ completely from those in the authority-oriented column; however, their

Authority-Oriented	Goal-Oriented
Sets goals for subordinates.	Leads group in goal setting.
Solves job problems.	Leads group in problem solving.
Lets them know who's boss.	Treats them as equals.
Gives them job descriptions.	Allows them to write own job descriptions.
Listens superficially.	Listens actively.
Applies close supervision.	Advises/facilitates/consults.
Defines rules and penalties.	Defines constraints.
Catches them doing wrong.	Catches them doing right.
Finds someone to blame.	Helps diagnose cause of failure.
Penalizes them for failures.	Helps them learn from failure.
Motivates with power.	Motivates through empowerment.
Develops and installs new methods.	Teaches them improvement techniques.
Tolerates marginal performers.	Improves or removes marginal performers.
Uses paternalistic career guidance.	Helps them take charge of own careers.
Uses negative reinforcement.	Uses positive reinforcement.

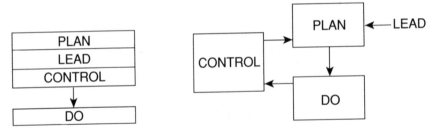

Figure 9-1. Redefinition of Leadership Roles at Texas Instruments

net effect offers more opportunity for workers to manage the *plan-do-control* phases of their work. In this model supervisors view themselves as a resource and concentrate on the following activities: (1) giving visibility to organizational goals; (2) providing resources and defining constraints; (3) mediating conflict; and (4) staying out of the way to let people manage their own work.

Giving visibility to company goals means enabling all members of the group to see a problem essentially as the supervisor sees it and allowing them access to the information they need to achieve the goals. The key to this transfer of power is the recognition that everyone has a client or a customer. Whether this customer is the ultimate consumer (who purchases the product) or another work station or department within the company is irrelevant; individual and group goals are set to satisfy customer needs.

The empowerment of employees requires leadership to provide resources and define constraints; it does not mean that a company must finance every improvement or capital investment suggested by the operators. Leaders arrange for a meeting area, present budgets, and solicit the involvement of support personnel. As part of the effort to define goals and constraints, leaders share with group members the rationale behind a given budget and, if a capital investment is suggested, must explain the amortization process and explore with the group its application to a suggested expenditure. When members of a team can assess a proposed investment in new equipment in terms of increased efficiency, duration of the project, changes in quality, and so on, they can decide themselves whether or not it is a sound economic investment. As a result, operators see the decision to buy or not to buy as a matter of logic rather than as an arbitrary decision by the boss.

The mediation of conflict is an ongoing and often misunderstood role of supervision. Conflict always exists; however, the nature of conflict varies. In an environment of meaningless work and arbitrary supervision, conflict is often a symptom of displaced aggression or of unbearable monotony. In an environment of interesting work and facilitative supervision, conflict may arise as a result of spirited competition and the challenge of achieving individual and group goals. This type of conflict is not harmful, as long as the pervading organizational climate enables group members to cope with it. Facilitative supervisors do not avoid or suppress conflict but encourage its constructive expression.

Staying out of the way to let people manage their work does not mean abandoning the group and heading for the golf course. It does mean being sensitive to the needs of individuals who wish to be responsible for the planning and control functions of their jobs. When delegation is successful, people are not subjected to arbitrary and rigid constraints but have the freedom to pursue goals they helped to define. To achieve these goals, operators seek assistance from any source, including the supervisor if he or she has earned their respect and is perceived as having organizational information or technical competence.

Goals Replace Conformity

Figure 9-2 portrays a supervisory model designed to enable people to manage their own work. In contrast to paradigms that are oriented toward authority on the part of the supervisor and conformity on the part of the operator (see figure 7-7), this model describes a goal-oriented relationship in which the revised *do* phase of the supervisor and *plan* phase of the operator mark the point of interface between the two workers. Figures 9-1 and 9-2 both show the goal-oriented leader to be a resource person whose involvement is activated primarily at the initiative of the operator.

This model, described here as a relationship between supervisor and operator, can be used as a paradigm for relationships at any level of an organization and serves to make leaders out of employees at all tiers. The model is also useful because enriching the operator's job often changes higher-level jobs, in some cases making it possible to reduce the number of levels in the management hierarchy. In the case of Normandale-South, described in Chapter 3, only three levels exist in the plant. Supervisors who are freed of many detailed maintenance and surveillance functions have more time to be involved with higher-level planning functions and are more available to serve as advisers, counselors, and facilitators when needed by their natural work groups.

Meaningful jobs increase profitability, cost reduction, cash flow, share of the market, and return on investment. Empowered employees offer a company other rewards as well: more productive use of employee talent, increased customer loyalty, more responsible civic and home relationships, and the self-renewing growth of the organization.

Responsibility Replaces Prerogatives

Management prerogatives are self-defeating illusions. By definition, management rights are exclusive rights based on authority. Insistence on management prerogatives evokes a counterbalancing demand for labor prerogatives; and evaluation of labor prerogatives

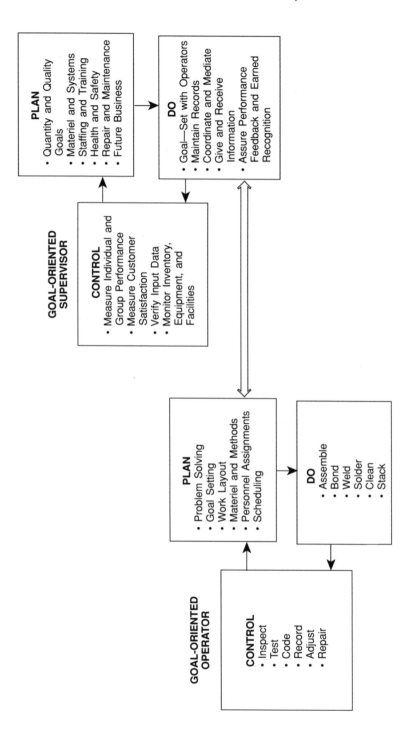

GOAL-ORIENTED SUPERVISOR

PLAN
- Quantity and Quality Goals
- Materiel and Systems
- Staffing and Training
- Health and Safety
- Repair and Maintenance
- Future Business

DO
- Goal—Set with Operators
- Maintain Records
- Coordinate and Mediate
- Give and Receive Information
- Assure Performance Feedback and Earned Recognition

CONTROL
- Measure Individual and Group Performance
- Measure Customer Satisfaction
- Verify Input Data
- Monitor Inventory, Equipment, and Facilities

GOAL-ORIENTED OPERATOR

PLAN
- Problem Solving
- Goal Setting
- Work Layout
- Materiel and Methods
- Personnel Assignments
- Scheduling

DO
- Assemble
- Bond
- Weld
- Solder
- Clean
- Stack

CONTROL
- Inspect
- Test
- Code
- Record
- Adjust
- Repair

Figure 9-2. Goal-Oriented Relationship Between Supervisor and Operator

shows them to be unaligned with, or contradictory to, company goals. Management privileges quash initiative and result in alienation and unachieved goals. The price is much too high for all but those with a pathological need for power and domination.

Prerogatives must be replaced by responsibilities—obligations to customers, shareholders, employees, and the community. From the customer's point of view, the manager is responsible for delivering a superior product or service at minimum cost. To the shareholder or owner the manager is responsible for maximizing return on investment. To the employee he or she is responsible for providing career opportunities.

This new view of leadership and responsibility affects the community, because people emulate in their homes the leadership patterns they learn on the job. The leadership styles of democratic or autocratic managers are usually formed in democratic or autocratic homes under parents whose styles of leadership were influenced by role models in the job situation. Hence, the workplace becomes a potent medium for influencing the behavior of a society.

Competence Replaces Authority

Leaders still need power; however, it is not the clout of official supervisory authority that they need but the influence of people empowered to apply their competence in pursuit of mutual goals. Both kinds of power exist in all organizations, and the manager's leadership style determines and indicates which is predominant. An excessive amount of official authority evokes a counterbalancing expression of people power—as demonstrated in Iran, South Africa, China, Russia, and Eastern Bloc countries.

For practical purposes, what really matters in industry is not whether or not supervisors have official authority but whether they are accepted by the people who depend on their leadership. The supervisors whose behavior has earned the acceptance and respect of their work groups have, in effect, transformed their official authority to unofficial acceptance. They become both the formal and the informal leaders of their groups; and they succeed as leaders not by virtue of authority from above but through the willing acceptance of those who are influenced by their contributions to organizational success.

Leadership is not a psychological trait but a function of the circumstances and the nature of the group. In a given situation, the effective leader is the person most fitted to take charge. Effective group leaders who are officially appointed will try to see to it that they are accepted because they are perceived as appropriate leaders in the particular situation—not because of their official authority. Regardless of how technically correct and logically insightful the direction given by a leader, his or her style of dispensing information and influencing the group will be a key determinant of success. Effective leaders know how to organize their materiel and manpower in ways that allow free expression of talent in defining problems, setting goals, and managing resources for achieving these goals.

A new supervisory role is not always accepted easily. Some managers think that to allow workers to help solve management problems is an expression of weakness that will undermine the respect of subordinates. These managers oppose worker involvement, viewing it as capitulation or as abandonment of managerial prerogatives. Reactions of this type are commonplace because authority-oriented relationships fostered in homes, schools, military organizations, and other institutions often find spontaneous expression in job situations. Supervisors do not switch their leadership styles as a result of a policy statement or as an immediate consequence of reading a book or hearing an inspiring speech. An intellectual message may sensitize them to their problem, but each person must work through the process of self-evaluation, self-acceptance, adjustment of values, and change of behavior at his or her own pace, in his or her own way, and in a climate conducive to change and tolerant of mistakes. The pressure of an edict to "be democratic" may only force these individuals to regress to familiar authority-oriented patterns, from which stance they will obediently recite the official intellectual message.

Supervisory effectiveness results from job enrichment as a circular phenomenon. First of all, job enrichment requires action (or discontinuation of previous action) on the part of the supervisor to provide conditions conducive to empowerment. Positive results from this endeavor reinforce it and encourage its emulation by others. Subtle changes occur in the perceptions, practices, habits, and, finally, values of the people involved, so that in a gradual branching and multiplying process a new way of life at work is put into motion. Thus, in a subtle way the supervisor is the originator and medium for change—providing conditions for the development of others, and thereby bringing about his or her own self-development.

AVOIDANCE OF OBSOLESCENCE

The manager is both an agent and a victim of the accelerated rate of change taking place in society. In industry this accelerated change is shortening the life span of technologies and jobs, placing an unprecedented demand on employees in all functions and levels to adapt to new roles and new job demands. Figure 9-3 presents two career curves: one for the leader who continues to adapt to, cope with, and master change; and the other for the "rainbow curve" of the manager who surrenders to change and progressively disengages from the challenges of a changing world. Although actual careers do not follow such smooth patterns, these two curves reflect a common dilemma in industry.

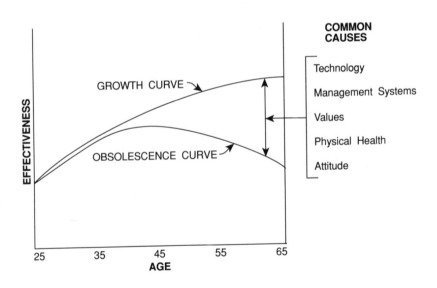

Figure 9-3. Growth and Obsolescence of Managers

The widening gap between effective and ineffective managers usually cannot be attributed to a single cause but can be explained by various combinations of the following factors:

1. Keeping up with product technology;

2. Keeping up with systems technology;

3. Adapting to changing values;

4. Maintaining physical fitness;

5. Overcoming folklore of aging.

Intimate knowledge of product technology is not always a requirement for effective leadership. In fact, the compulsive pursuit of such competence may even sidetrack managers away from their leadership responsibilities. In some cases, ignorance of technology, coupled with leadership competence, may result in more effective delegation and better development of a group's potential.

Management-systems technology is an increasingly important ingredient of the professional manager's repertoire. Certainly, for production managers, knowledge of systems described in Chapters 3 and 6 is vital.

Changing values and expectations are natural consequences of the knowledge explosion. Gorbachev's changes in leadership style are an example of successful adaptation to the changing values of his Soviet constituency and the balance of the free world. The challenge is to relinquish the command-and-control philosophy while retaining time-honored moral and ethical standards.

Physical fitness has a cause-and-effect relationship to leadership effectiveness and obsolescence. Busy executives, in their pursuit of career goals, often overcommit themselves, working long hours, eating irregular and unbalanced meals, getting insufficient exercise, and developing a middle-aged spread when only halfway through their 40-year professional careers. As physical neglect takes its toll, leaders find themselves the unwilling and premature victims of physical obsolescence, which forces them to adjust their aspirations and work habits. Their usual self-confidence give way to anxiety and feelings of powerlessness. Although preventive maintenance in the form of exercise, adequate rest, and balanced diet can avoid this pitfall, most people prior to physical breakdown have little incentive to change long-term living habits. Pritikin (1979) and others have provided evidence that physical health can be retrieved and perpetuated by radically changed and rigorously followed living patterns, but few people seem willing to pay that price.

People's attitudes, as shaped by the folklore of aging, are often the explanation for obsolescence. Many managers seem to accept the cliché "You can't teach an old dog new tricks" and abandon hope in middle age on the assumption that they are too old to learn. Actually, old dogs can be taught new tricks, but not if the old dogs think they can't. A forty-five-year-old manager who believes himself or herself incapable of learning is on the way to obsolescence.

The attitudinal factor is key for two reasons. First, it is essential that people see the feasibility of avoiding obsolescence, know how it is caused, and understand how to take preventive measures. Perhaps more importantly, leaders must understand how their attitudes influence the obsolescence or growth of people under their supervision. If older employees are bypassed when challenging assignments are being distributed, the bypassed workers take this language of action as a signal that their boss believes they are "over the hill." Employees in this situation begin to doubt their own continuing effectiveness, thereby activating a self-fulfilling prophecy. In their anxiety to prove themselves in their narrowed areas of responsibility, they may strive harder to give visibility to their own achievements. In a circular fashion, their random and ineffective efforts cause their responsibilities to be narrowed further. Anxieties are increased, evoking more random and nonproductive behavior and amplifying and reinforcing the image of ineffectiveness.

However, when aging employees receive challenging responsibilities, the assignments represent a vote of confidence—bolstering self-esteem, allaying subconscious doubts, and providing the opportunity for achievement and continuing growth. Sustained opportunity for success through challenging assignments is a potent antidote to obsolescence.

The causes and effects of obsolescence enumerated above are not exhaustive, nor can they be assigned relative importance. They tend to be situational and dependent on the individual, the job, the organization, or a combination of these and other factors.

REFERENCES

Daniels, A.C., & Rosen, T.A. (1988). *Performance management: Improving quality and productivity through positive reinforcement.* Tucker, GA: Performance Management Publications.

Pritikin, N. (1979). *The Pritikin program for diet and exercise.* New York: Grosset & Dunlap.

10

Personnel and Labor Relations

Thoughtful students of organization theory occasionally advance the provocative opinion that the ideal organization would have no personnel department—that personnel administration is the responsibility of the people who manage the mainstream functions of the organization. Proponents of this viewpoint believe that managers who rely on the personnel department for staff administration are neglecting their duties. Such a viewpoint is often a reaction against personnel departments that have evolved into functional silos unaligned with organizational goals.

Personnel departments have assumed a variety of roles over the years. Although somewhat evolutionary, all of these roles have tended to persevere and to find recurrent expression in contemporary organizations: [1]

1. *Counterbalancing influence.* The personnel department counterbalances line management's emphasis on production with an emphasis on human relations.

2. *Authority-directed experts.* Personnel experts exercise authority over line workers on personnel matters.

3. *Bureaucratic control.* Personnel systems and policies guide line management in personnel matters.

---

[1] This historical review of the personnel function is adapted from a working paper by John Paré, written in 1968 when he was vice president for personnel at Steinberg's Limited in Montreal, Canada.

4. *Missionaries for participation.* Personnel emphasizes participation as the goal of the organization.

5. *Change agent.* Personnel specialists interact with line managers to define conditions in which both individual and organizational goals can be achieved.

The role of change agent is gradually evolving as an ideal model for the personnel specialist. However, the other roles are being perpetuated through the conditions and assumptions that brought them into existence. All of these roles are discussed below in terms of the forces that brought them into existence and their impact on the organization.

The Counterbalancing Influence

The counterbalancing function of the personnel department arose when line management neglected or abandoned certain responsibilities. Line managers typically considered personnel problems as less important than, and not clearly related to, the primary job of getting out production. These managers appeared to divide management problems into two distinct areas of responsibility, and they assigned the responsibilities as follows:

Production problems. Line management is responsible for the planning and controlling of materiel and systems—making the decisions, giving orders, assigning responsibilities, and seeing to it that people get the job done.

People problems. Personnel is responsible for handling complaints, grievances, and discipline; negotiating labor agreements; administering salary and benefit programs; training supervisors; establishing work rules; and building employee morale.

This division of management responsibility reflects an assumption that the needs of people and the needs of production are mutually exclusive. This viewpoint holds that operations are more efficient when interference from human factors is minimized. The personnel representative, reacting to the line manager's apparent insensitivity to the needs of employees, emphasizes human relations, often with little regard for production goals.

Authority-Directed Experts

Traditional organization theory holds that authority must be commensurate with responsibility. When line management relinquished its responsibility for human resource problems, personnel departments began asking for, and obtaining, authority over the line in these matters. Because authority was seen as the primary means of influencing behavior, this development was only logical: an individual cannot be held responsible for things that he or she cannot control. Thus, use of authority by the personnel department crept into the line-staff relationship, widening the emerging split between the two management functions. Personnel assumed responsibility for recruiting, hiring, placing, and training line people; handling grievances and labor negotiations; and administering wages, salaries, and supplemental benefits.

This split in jurisdictions not only creates a major cleavage in the line-staff relationship but is also impractical; it is impossible, for example, to separate the function of assigning work from the function of processing grievances that arise from the work assignment.

In the ensuing struggle for power, line managers came to regard the personnel function as a burden and a threat rather than as a source of help. Instead of coping with this conflict, line managers typically severed contact with the personnel department, leaving the staff experts out of touch with operations. As a consequence, personnel experts became preoccupied with their narrow specialties, appeared unconcerned with the welfare of the business as a whole, and were often ignored by other departments. Under these conditions, personnel programs and procedures become less useful in solving line problems.

Bureaucratic Control

Line management, reacting to the authority exerted by personnel over human resource activities, began to reconsider the line-staff relationship. It was apparent that another tenet of traditional management theory, the principle of *unity of command*, was being violated: every individual must have only one boss.

Line managers were faced with a dilemma. They lacked the insights and skills necessary to resolve increasingly complex human resource problems but resented their own dependence on the personnel experts, whose specialties made them essential to the organization.

The solution was to set up the personnel department as a coordinative rather than a controlling function. The policies set by the personnel department were then expressed through job descriptions and evaluations, organization charts, policies, programs, manuals, rules and regulations, and a variety of formalized procedures for detailing personnel activities. Line management had final authority for adopting or rejecting the policies and programs formulated by personnel—but personnel was responsible for obtaining line conformity once the policies and programs had been adopted. In effect, the role of coordination proved to be merely camouflaged authority. From the line manager's point of view, personnel representatives exercise as much authority under the bureaucratic form of personnel administration as they do in the authority-oriented system.

Missionaries for Participation

The policing roles of the personnel department under authority-directed or bureaucratic modes caused personnel to be regarded by lower- and middle-line management as a source of arbitrary, though sometimes candy-coated, authority. Mutual distrust, if not open hostility, characterized line-staff relations; and both groups began to question the use of authority as the exclusive means of managerial control. The influence of partially understood behavioral theory led managers to abandon the principle of authority and to adopt the principle of participation. Influenced by the assumption that people support only what they help to create, personnel representatives sought ways to involve line people more and more in problem-solving activities.

The fundamental error of this approach is that participation is seen as the goal rather than as a means for achieving goals. Decision making then becomes stalemated by reluctance on the part of both line and staff members to reach any decision until the full support of the line is assured.

Change Agents

In their most recent role, personnel departments provide change agents that help to achieve organizational objectives through the soundest use of human resources. This approach is based on an underlying assumption that people can achieve their personal goals through attainment of company goals. The plan also depends on the widespread understanding of company goals and the collaborative commitment of individuals and groups to achieve them. It requires empowerment of the members of the organization to identify and remove barriers to organizational effectiveness.

The personnel department, in this role, provides specialists, advisers, consultants, trainers, counselors, and researchers to support a goal-oriented philosophy that calls for a reunification of the two categories of management (production and human relations) under the line manager. A deep concern for excellence of production and the quality of decisions must be fused with an equal concern for people. The proper fusing of these two concerns brings about not only a better use of talent but also a significantly different relationship between line management and human resource facilitators (this phenomenon is described in the JIT/VAM model in Chapter 3). Many of the responsibilities that the personnel department acquired over the years are being returned to the line. In many cases, such as wage and salary administrations, personnel still provides a staff support role. However, the dynamic nonmonetary components of reward systems, as described in Chapter 2, are clearly line responsibilities.

LABOR RELATIONS

The administration of labor relations is traditionally based on the assumption that the goals of the organization, as represented by upper-level managers, are in conflict with the needs of the employees at the lower levels of the organization. The labor portion of the work force is usually made up of hourly paid personnel in production, maintenance, and administration, whose jobs (in the United States) are not exempt from the restrictions of the Fair Labor Standards Act. These workers comprise about 80 percent of the work force in private industry and government bureaucracies; however, less than 20 percent of them are members of labor unions.

People at the top of the organization are usually identified as *management*; but people in the middle ranks are often uncertain whether they should identify with management or labor, even though most of them are exempt from the requirements of the Fair Labor Standards Act. Although these employees are usually assured they are members of management, they feel at times as though they are being treated like labor. Some of them overtly espouse management viewpoints while covertly identifying with labor. Until recently, management and labor have represented two enemy camps whose conflicting goals were the basis for ongoing warfare moderated through collective bargaining. Although the role of unions is diminishing as enlightened employees become aware of their own interest in organizational success, the win-lose adversary relationship still prevails in some organizations.[2]

Formalizing the Management-Labor Gap

Most formal agreements between management and labor reflect an implied conflict of interest between the two parties. Figure 10-1, excerpted from an agreement between a large firm in the Southwest and a major national union, illustrates some typical prerogatives of management and labor. The time-honored rights of management stem from authority derived from ownership. The implicit assumption underlying these rights is that management must protect the organization from the insatiable and irresponsible demands of labor. In a climate of mistrust, workers feel threatened by management's power to hire, classify, promote, transfer, suspend, discipline, discharge, and lay off employees. The establishment of labor prerogatives is an understandable consequence of this mistrust.

Managers accustomed to nonunion work forces believe that union rights represent a startling degree of capitulation by management and a serious limitation on the manager's freedom to manage. However, these rights are protected, or even required by law in union plants, where they are also perpetuated as unquestioned long-standing traditions.

When a union is recognized as the exclusive representative of employees, there is an implied assumption that people need a protector against management and that the goals of the employees are different from the goals of the organization. Moreover, the union's

---

[2] The basis for the management-labor dichotomy is illustrated in Figure 7-5. For a detailed description of the win-lose adversary relationship see Chapter 7.

Rights of Management

The management of the plant and the direction of the working force is vested exclusively in the company. This shall include and not be limited to the right to hire, classify, promote, transfer, suspend, discipline, discharge for cause, lay off, or release employees for lack of work, provided these rights shall not conflict with this agreement.

Rights of Labor

1. The company recognizes the union as the exclusive representative of all employees.

2. The company agrees to deduct the initiation fee and monthly union dues from the pay of employees who authorize such deductions.

3. Stewards are privileged to handle grievances in the plant during working hours without loss of compensation.

4. The company will maintain a bulletin board for the use of the union.

5. The company shall provide the group insurance program as outlined in Appendix B of this agreement.

6. The retirement plan shall remain in effect as specified in this agreement.

7. Overtime records shall be kept by the company for the purpose of distributing overtime work as equally as possible.

8. When terminating employment, an employee shall be paid for each day of earned sick leave not used.

9. An employee who works on a day considered a holiday shall receive holiday pay plus double his regular rate for all hours worked on the holiday.

10. The maintenance-electrician job includes installation and maintenance of electrical systems and equipment and electronic controls and tape-making equipment used on machine tools; and installation, maintenance, repair, servicing, and alteration of air-conditioning and refrigeration systems.

11. The maintenance-electrician job excludes electrical assembly and maintenance work on airplanes and their component parts.

12. All job classifications and their descriptions as listed in Appendix A shall remain in effect for the duration of this agreement.

Figure 10-1. Some Traditional Prerogatives of Management and Labor

initiative in demanding bulletin boards, group insurance, retirement plans, equitable distribution of overtime, and other conditions suggests that management is derelict in meeting these reasonable requirements. When the union has established itself as the people's protector, enlightened as well as unsophisticated managers often find themselves in the position of opposing programs that, in reality, they approve. In turn, the union, with single-minded determination, directs more effort toward combating management than toward supporting the health of the organization.

Although management may only be trying to keep the organization in financial equilibrium, managers often acquire the image of penurious exploiters. The union, in its unrelenting drive to support its membership, unwittingly impairs management's ability to invest in the future and remain competitive and unwittingly plants the seeds of indolence, dependency, and disaffection among workers. For example, at some firms sick leave has become more than a cushion against the burden of illness; it is time off with pay—time that can be used as the job incumbent sees fit or exchanged for unearned income. Triple pay for holidays makes holiday work attractive to the worker and undesirable to management, but either alternative—holiday pay or holiday closure—is harmful to the organization and ultimately to its members. Union rules that circumscribe jobs reduce the flexibility, versatility, and job satisfaction generally required for a creative and viable work force. Union leadership, while paying lip service to the long-range growth needs of the organization, usually applies pressure for a share of any short-term gain, thereby undermining long-range growth strategies and encouraging defensive financial reporting by the company.

Symptoms of Management Failure

Management brought the problem of unions on itself by earlier exploitation, paternalism, and manipulation. Much of management's failure was incurred by promoting into supervision people whose primary credentials were unrelated to leadership. Although managers trained in human resource development are penetrating organizations in increasing numbers, they are plagued by two obstacles.

One problem is a work force of maintenance seekers—the older ones jaded by long confinement to meaningless work, and the younger ones rebelling against conformity pressures imposed by the company, the union, and the work itself. Initial or cursory attempts to treat people as responsible adults typically evoke suspicion, hostility, or disengagement; and few managers have the courage, capability, and perseverance to undertake the reprograming of the mentality of such a work force.

The second, and often the greater, obstacle is command-and-control management—people who are conditioned to mistrust the enemy below. The development of a responsible and committed work force requires a long-range strategy involving the risk of short-run setbacks. Unbending tradition often stands in the way of aspiring innovators, who eventually capitulate and perpetuate the status quo. They may justify their capitulation with the rationale that it is better to survive today in order to win the grand battle tomorrow. All but the very courageous take on the protective coloring of the world about them and become inadvertent perpetuators of a philosophy that they know intellectually and feel intuitively to be destructive. These people find themselves rationalizing: "All organizations are equally handicapped by the same bad management practices, and at least we are not so bad as most of them."

Win-lose strategies and stalemates between unions and management are understandable in the light of history. Nineteenth-century managers flagrantly exercised their presumed rights to motivate people through fear, threats, manipulation, and paternalism. Influenced by the accepted practices of their time, these owners and supervisors often instituted practices without awareness of their long-term consequences.

Wage earners living at bare subsistence levels responded well to the security of uninterrupted employment. When Henry Ford opened an automated assembly line in 1914 and doubled his workers' pay to five dollars a day, his plant prospered; the workers were both happy and motivated. Although his management innovations satisfied many needs of that era, they introduced two practices that became the foundation for latter-day labor problems. One innovation was the simplification of tasks, forerunner of a trend described in a study of an automobile assembly plant (Walker & Guest, 1952) showing 83 percent of the jobs to have fewer than ten operations and 32 percent but a single operation. The average time cycle for these jobs was three minutes, and the learning time ranged from a few hours to a week.

As jobs became more impoverished, pay rates continued upward, maintaining the automotive industry's leadership in providing higher-than-average wages and benefits. The maintenance needs of workers were satisfied better, but their talents were utilized no better, or even less well. In the era of thwarted maintenance needs, automotive workers with steady jobs counted their blessings and tolerated the monotony of the automated assembly line. However, as society achieved greater affluence, improved maintenance factors lost their relative importance in the wage earner's hierarchy of values. Furthermore, opportunities abounded elsewhere for satisfying maintenance needs, and the security of workers was not jeopardized by changing jobs. The union had successfully protected employees against the arbitrariness of management and had given them adequate recreational time and discretionary income to buy goods and services previously beyond their aspirations. A lack of meaning and motivation rather than a lack of income became the source of worker frustration.[3]

Attacking the Symptoms

People who experience need frustration are not always able to pinpoint the cause of their distress. This phenomenon held true for factory workers culturally conditioned to gain satisfaction by improving wages, hours, and working conditions. Union-led victories were valued less for the benefits they yielded than for the opportunity for successful conquest they represented. Conflicts between opposing management and labor forces share some of the characteristics of team sports such as baseball, football, or hockey. The sides are competitively matched by the terms of their agreement and are refereed by the National Labor Relations Board. Workers are vicariously aligned with the union team, and management with the company team. The issues are of relatively less importance than the satisfaction of winning the battle; the more bitter the relationship between parties, the sweeter the victory. The winning and

---

[3] For an illustration of motivation needs and maintenance factors see Figure A-2 in Appendix A.

losing of battles provides an outlet for frustrations that otherwise have little chance of dissipation.

Rebellion against the status quo in America, particularly after World War II, became more frequent and demanding. Korea, during its industrial build-up in the 1980s, experienced the same type of rebellion. In the United States whole industries were paralyzed by strikes and other forms of reactive behavior, occasionally directed toward union leadership, which, in some cases, had become no less a source of oppression to its members than the company management. In frantic attempts to perpetuate their jurisdiction and to demonstrate their clout, unions in the United States bargained indiscriminately for continuing improvements in wages, hours, and working conditions, baffled by their members' lack of gratitude for hard-won battles. The worker, the union, and the company were all victims of a mutual failure to understand the real causes of worker frustration and alienation.

A Gradual Awakening

Allegations of deterioration of worker loyalty and loss of pride in work reached consensus proportions. Only gradually, and among an enlightened few, was an awareness developed of the real causes of disaffection. Discovery of the key to revived human effectiveness stimulated enthusiastic, though often misdirected, efforts to return responsibility and challenge to the job. As the concepts and techniques of job enrichment led to the redefinition of the supervisor's role, as discussed earlier, labor-relations specialists became aware of a dilemma. They found themselves administering a strategy based on the use of power, authority, and cunning to satisfy maintenance needs, in the face of an emerging philosophy based on the influence of mutual respect and competence and the pursuit of self-actualization. "Labor skates" or "labor hacks," accustomed to the use of compromise, deception, and coercion, began to realize that they had been dealing primarily with symptoms of problems—and that real and lasting peace could be obtained only by curing the causes. The insights of the behavioral sciences were needed, and labor-relations specialists had a choice of acquiring these insights or becoming vocationally obsolete.

The Intermediate Goal

Labor-relations strategies must adapt to the unique qualities of each organization. Nonunion organizations require an approach based on the assumption that people are not divided into classes. In the unionized organization an intermediate goal may be to make peace with the union—to reach a collaborate adversary relationship, as described in Chapter 7. This is not an easy accomplishment because in most union-management relationships any act initiated by one party arouses the suspicion and resistance of the other. The first step is some type of intervention process to get the two parties to listen to each other.

An intermediate goal—for some the ultimate goal—of labor relations is the harmonious coexistence and active cooperation of the company and the union in the attainment of their mutual aims. For many managers and employees the ultimate achievement is the synergizing of individual and organizational goals to the point that union intervention is unnecessary. However, pursuit of the intermediate goal, constructive coexistence, offers the best platform for launching a program of union-company realignment. Charles A. Myers listed some conditions for the constructive coexistence of companies and unions, based on a review of thirteen case studies sponsored by the National Planning Association (Myers, 1955).[4] Although these case studies date back to the 1950s, they are still valid descriptors of company-union Stage 2 relationships:[5]

- There is full acceptance by management of the collective-bargaining process and of unionism as an institution. The company considers a strong union an asset to management.

- The union fully accepts private ownership and operation of the industry; it recognizes that the welfare of union members depends on the successful operation of the business.

- The union is strong, responsible, and democratic.

---

[4] From *Causes of Industrial Peace Under Collective Bargaining* by Clinton S. Golden and Virginia Parker. Copyright © 1955 by Harper & Row, Publishers, Inc. Reprinted by permission of Harper Collins Publishers.

[5] For a view of the stages in labor relations see Figure 7-1.

- The company stays out of the union's internal affairs; it does not seek to change the workers' allegiance to their union.

- Mutual trust and confidence exist between the parties. There have been no serious ideological incompatibilities.

- Neither party to the bargaining has adopted a legalistic approach to the solution of problems in the relationship.

- Negotiations are problem-centered: more time is spent on day-to-day problems than on defining abstract principles.

- There is widespread union-management consultation and highly developed information sharing.

- Grievances are settled promptly, in the local plant whenever possible. There is flexibility and informality within the procedure. (p. 47)

Under the foregoing conditions, collaborative adversary relationships can exist. Through intervention processes, union and management people participate in joint educational experiences, which become the foundation and building blocks for converting adversarial into collaborative relationships. Under these conditions, union and management can gradually proceed toward Stage 3—organizational teamwork. Collaborative relationships have become more feasible as a result of four changing conditions:

1. Contemporary union members are more enlightened than their counterparts of earlier eras, are more responsive to opportunities for self-actualization, and are less tolerant of command-and-control tactics by companies and unions.

2. Union leaders are also more enlightened and recognize the limitations of wages, hours, and working conditions for satisfying the needs of their more enlightened constituency. Although somewhat uneasy about the increasing ambiguity of their time-honored adversary charter, more union leaders are willing to play a part in achieving organizational teamwork.

3. Company managers are more sophisticated about the principles of motivation and encourage the constructive use of talent as the only viable alternative to counterproductive rebellion. Today's managers have fewer hang-ups, unlike their

predecessors, who needed managerial prerogatives and rank-oriented status symbols.

4. Corporate innovations and trends in legislation encourage the implementation of broader reward systems, as described in Chapter 2. Such reward systems, in combination with team-driven production processes such as JIT/VAM, help to depolarize the management-labor stand-off.

Because unions came into existence primarily as protectors of the less-privileged at the lower levels of the organization, the survival of unions would seem to require continuing conflict between management and labor. However, even when a company and its local unions learn to achieve industrial peace through the cooperative pursuit of common goals, this achievement alone will not automatically cause the dissolution of unions. The inertia of outmoded management practices, legal restrictions, and conditioned dependency relationships between workers and unions, coupled with the active resistance of the parent (sometimes international) union, requires extraordinary initiative on the part of both parties. Unions often continue functioning long after they achieve a level of mutual trust with management that would have precluded the formation of the union in the first place. Their continued life depends on their ability to redefine their role under conditions of organizational teamwork.

The Ultimate Goal

The ultimate goal of labor relations is the same in both nonunion and union companies: the creation of a climate of mutual trust through goal-directed individual and group relationships throughout the organization. This condition, described in detail in Chapter 7 and illustrated in Chapter 3, is described as *organizational teamwork*. The strategy for building such an environment is the central theme of this book and is based on the philosophy of involving all members of the organization in the pursuit of synergistic goals. The driving force behind such a coalition is the influence of competence rather than the application of authority.

If nonunion companies are to withstand attempts at unionization, their members must enjoy economic conditions comparable to those of their unionized counterparts. However, the traditional maintenance factors—wages, hours, and working conditions—are of secondary importance if employees can enhance their careers through the application of their talents in the performance of meaningful work. Managers must be facilitators rather than coercive and manipulative bosses. They must empower employees to take charge of their own jobs and careers. With the fervor of union stewards, leaders must defend the rights of the employees to exercise legitimate roles in the organization and make it possible for them to pursue personal and organizational goals that are synergistic, or at least compatible.

Handling Grievances

Grievance procedures in unionized work forces are inappropriate models for nonunion organizations. These procedures imply and incur the assumptions of a two-class system that precipitated the intervention of unions in the first place. In a typical union plant the grievance procedure moves upward through dual chains of command, engaging the contestants in win-lose conflicts to be resolved sooner or later in fact finding, power pressures, compromise, and mediation. As noted earlier, this process is based on the premise that management and labor have conflicting goals and hence are incapable of voluntary or natural problem resolution. Such a process in the nonunion plant would fail to surface grievances because of the intuitive recognition by the aggrieved employees that their supervisors have the trump card of authority and that there are no safeguards against subtle reprisals. Hence, simply introducing a traditional union grievance procedure in a nonunion plant not only fails to surface and resolve grievances, but more damagingly, it precipitates and increases the management-labor gap and paves the way for unionization of the work force.

Grievances rarely spring into existence as a consequence of a single recent event or cause. More often a grievance is an eruption that releases tensions built up from sustained subjection to petty injustices, oppressive restrictions, monotonous and demeaning work, economic pressures, and, particularly in large organizations, frustrations arising from lack of opportunity to be heard or to obtain wanted information. Emotions displayed in connection with a grievance are often disproportionate to the stated reason for the grievance. However, taken in the context of precipitating factors, the specific complaint of an aggrieved employee can be understood as the final straw that pushed the individual temporarily beyond his or her threshold of self-restraint. Many grievances are filed by people who would normally seek more rational resolutions for their problems. However, having locked themselves into a win-lose conflict during a moment of high emotion, they allow their pride and the lingering pressure of previous frustrations to formalize the grievance for official processing.

Psychologists in the Los Angeles school system, recognizing that adolescent rebellion often has it roots in frustrations arising when teenagers do not have someone trustworthy with whom to discuss their problems, established a telephone hot line through which young people could call for help. Counselors receiving calls listened and gave advice, often referring the callers to other resources. Most importantly, the counselors were immediately available and did not demand that callers identify themselves. Most of the seven thousand calls received in one year dealt with boy-girl relationships and conflict with authority—problems not considered important by many adults. Because the youngsters could find an understanding ear at the right moment, they were able to defuse tensions that might otherwise have found harmful expression.

Similarly, grievances in industry are often precipitated because there is no one who cares enough to listen to employees' problems or to give them information or advice when they need it. Employee frustrations often result from an accumulation of unresolved minor problems and unanswered questions about such matters as benefits, job opportunities, interpersonal conflict, and home problems. Large organizations need a telephone line that can give immediate responses to anonymous requests for information and that can offer help on complaints about real or imagined injustices. This outlet for stress can prevent the ground swell of alienation that infiltrates an organization and ultimately contaminates the vast majority of employees whose attitudes might otherwise be positive or at least neutral.

An appropriate grievance procedure in a nonunion workplace allows aggrieved employees complete freedom to use their judgment in whatever way seems appropriate to them. The procedure does not force them, even informally, to take the matter up with their supervisors as a first step, because the supervisors may be the problem. Employees should be able to consult an anonymous information line, their peers, a personnel representative, a technical specialist, or someone in a position above their supervisors. In other words, workers must have the freedom of citizens in a democratic society to appeal their cases in whatever manner seems appropriate, with confidence that they are not violating rules by doing so and that they will receive a fair hearing. At the same time, sustained circumvention of supervision deprives the supervisor of the feedback necessary for self-correction. The anonymous information line can provide constructive suggestions to supervisors without jeopardizing the anonymity of the complaint system.

If the grievance is not resolved through informal first-step procedures, the second step should permit the supervisor to be involved, perhaps through the mediation services of a mutually acceptable third party. Such a mediation assists in clarifying the problem and working out a satisfactory resolution. Should the grievance become more formalized, the third person and/or the supervisor may assist the complainant in writing the formal grievance. Complaints not resolved at this level to the satisfaction of the individual and the supervisor may be appealed upward to successively higher levels in the organization. If the problem is not resolved through the management hierarchy, a mutually acceptable outsider, in an ombudsman's role, can be asked to mediate an impartial and acceptable resolution.

The Ingersoll machine-tool company in Rockford, Illinois, and the Milliken Company in Spartanburg, South Carolina, defuse grievances through a *twenty-four-hour turnaround* policy. Employees in these organizations who present a grievance to a supervisor are entitled to an answer in twenty-four hours. If the conflict is not satisfactorily resolved in the twenty-four-hour period, the supervisor presents a progress report by the end of the interval, along with another twenty-four-hour commitment to resolve the problem.

Discipline

Tradition has standardized discipline as a four-step process sometimes called *progressive discipline*. It could more appropriately be labeled *regressive discipline* as it is based on the assumption that punishment will correct misbehavior. The first step is a finger-pointing admonition called *oral warning*. If violations are repeated, *written warning, disciplinary layoff*, and *termination* may ensue. In practice, particularly with today's enlightened work force, punishment does not improve performance and is more likely to incur hostility and costly litigation.

Richard Grote (1979) defines more constructive methods for handling discipline. He suggests a four-step process that on the surface appears similar to the steps in the more traditional system. However, the implementation of Grote's plan is based on assumptions that are more likely to evoke commitment than resentment. The four steps of positive discipline are (1) oral reminder; (2) written reminder; (3) decision-making leave; and (4) discharge.

The oral reminder is an Adult-Adult discussion about the problem, rather than an attack on the offender. The aim is to evoke a voluntary commitment on the part of the employee and to produce a plan that will prevent recurrence of the problem. The written reminder is a description of the problem; the explanation is written by the supervisor in phraseology that both people agree is fair and accurate. The violator receives a copy of the statement; another copy is placed in the personnel file with the understanding that it will be removed at some mutually agreed-upon time that is appropriate to the seriousness of the offense and that takes place after the employee has demonstrated success in solving the problem.

Decision-making leave with pay is given to an offender who has not successfully responded to previous corrective attempts. The leave period, which may range from a half-day to a week or more, allows a period of deliberation in which the violator can decide whether to follow the rules and stay with the organization or to resign. The fourth step, termination from the work force, results when the preceding steps fail to correct the problem. When very serious offenses occur, discharge can take place without going through the previous three steps.

Anecdotal testimonials from companies employing positive discipline show it to be effective in modifying employee behavior. Evidence also indicates that this kind of system is, in the long run, less costly to the organization. Needless to say, a positive reaction to decision-making leave could not be expected if the plan were introduced as the first step in a win-lose adversary culture. However, as an organization evolves toward the teamwork model and when the players understand that the price of freedom is responsibility, positive discipline can serve a cause-and-effect role in creating and maintaining a harmonious workplace.

Role of the Labor-Relations Specialist

Labor-relations specialists must focus increasingly on preventive maintenance and less on fire fighting or dealing with problems spun out by inept supervisors. Although labor-relations professionals must continue to handle these problems, their talents are better spent in reorienting supervisors in order to prevent the recurrence of old conflicts. The need for reorientation is not restricted to the lower levels of supervision but is perhaps even more obvious in the nonverbal communications of middle and upper-middle management. The labor-relations representative can help supervisors to understand that employee behavior is a response to the opportunities and restrictions of different jobs and different supervisory styles. In an advisory or educative role the labor-relations representative reinforces supervisors as they relinquish outmoded supervisory tactics and gradually become comfortable with new roles. The labor-relations professional has succeeded when supervisors are able to surface and cope with conflict within their own natural work groups and when those supervisors rely less and less on the help of personnel specialists to bail them out. The ultimate success of labor-relations specialists is reflected in a culture in which there is no labor-management dichotomy.

Labor-relations specialists serve other ongoing functions as well. They take the pulse of the work force and the community in order to anticipate unjustified activity on the part of labor unions and to prepare defensive strategies. They offer legal advice to supervisors, systems designers, and procedure writers to prevent innocent infractions of organizational rules. Finally, they send recommendations to local, state, and federal lawmakers to promote the enactment of sound industrial-relations laws.

REFERENCES

Grote, R.C. (1979). *Positive discipline*. New York: McGraw-Hill.

Myers, C.A. (1955). Conclusions and implications. In C.S. Golden & V.D. Parker (Eds.), *Causes of industrial peace under collective bargaining* (pp. 46-54). New York: Harper & Row.

Walker, C.R., & Guest, R.H. (1952). *The man on the assembly line.* Cambridge, MA: Harvard University Press.

11

Measuring Performance and Finding Talent

This chapter deals with performance appraisals and staffing procedures and with matching people to the right jobs through aptitude measurement.[1] Good leaders know that performance appraisals are supposed to give people feedback as a basis for pay adjustments and self-improvement. However, the manner in which such appraisals are conducted is crucial to the success of the process.

Douglas McGregor (1972) noted that the judgmental aspects of ratings, particularly when administered by command-and-control bosses, tended to undermine the developmental potential of performance reviews. As real human development is self-inspired and self-directed, traditional performance appraisals undermine self-development by fostering conformity, resentment, and dependency relationships. Although some individuals improve their job performance as a result of advice from the supervisor, the value of the improved performance might be outweighed by the conditioned dependency of the individual on the boss for prescriptions for development. Not only are individuals bound to apron strings that relieve them of the responsibility for their own self-development but they also acquire a model for advancement that encourages them to meddle with the self-improvement of the people under their supervision.

This is not to say that performance appraisals are not needed and that supervisors should not have a role in them. Performance

---

[1] The performance-measurement guidelines discussed here should be used along with the measurement criteria examined in Chapter 3 and the leadership principles reviewed in Chapter 9.

appraisals are in process continually, informally if not formally, in terms of both self-appraisal and evaluations by others. The supervisor, as a member of a natural work group, has a key role in the performance-appraisal process. However, this role, if it is to result in personal and professional development, requires the right kind of leadership.

THE PARENT-CHILD APPROACH

The process of appraisal and criticism in industry is a natural extension of command-and-control relationships learned elsewhere: at home, in schools, in the armed forces, and in other companies. Traditional job-performance rating factors, illustrated in Figure 11-1, are similar to school report-card criteria and provide the basis for supervisory judgment and criticism. Studies of the traditional performance-review process show that some people improve as a result of criticism. However, most do not change at all; and a few actually perform less well.

Traditional Rating Factors, Completed by the Supervisor	Goal-Setting Factors, Completed by the Job Incumbent
Quality L———H	Achievements During Past Six Months
Quantity	
Initiative	Six-Month Goals
Loyalty	
Cooperativeness	
Creativity	Long-Range Goals
Stamina	
Dependability	
Potential	

Figure 11-1. A Comparison of Traditional and Goal-Setting Review Forms

Some raters, discovering the ineffectiveness of criticism, conclude that the problem is not so much the fault of criticism itself as of tactless managers. Much effort has been devoted to the definition and application of what is called *constructive criticism*. Attempts to be constructive in applying criticism are usually efforts at sugarcoating and tend only to make people cynical and defensive. For example, the *sandwich technique* is used to sequence a critical comment between two positive comments. Although the practice no doubt takes away some of the sting of disapproval, repeated use of the technique conditions people to become wary of compliments.

Feedback Versus Criticism

If performance reviews are to serve a constructive role, raters must understand the distinction between criticism and feedback. The term *criticism*, as used here, is usually experienced as an attack on the person, and refers to evaluations, advice, warnings, admonitions, threats, and other judgmental information transmitted by someone of higher authority to someone of lower authority. The same information, when requested from peers, may serve a constructive role. However, such judgments from higher-ups evokes defensiveness and seldom creates a climate conducive to candid discussion or uninhibited rebuttal. Bosses are often insensitive to this problem because employees usually mask resentment with artificial smiles and expressions of gratitude.

Successful performance and continuing improvement requires feedback rather than criticism. The term *feedback*, as it is used here, refers to an Adult-Adult process through which individuals can learn how well their behavior matches their intentions.[2] Feedback, at its best, can be described as follows:

1. Timely—usually immediate,

2. Descriptive rather than evaluative,

3. Specific rather than general,

---

[2] For further information on feedback see *Organizational Psychology—An Experiential Approach* by D.A. Kolb, I.M. Rubin, & J.M. McIntyre, 1974, 2d ed., Prentice-Hall, Englewood Cliffs, NJ.

4. Sensitive to the needs of the recipient,

5. Directed toward controllable behavior,

6. Solicited rather than imposed, and

7. Tested for accuracy with the recipient.

Supervisors wishing to convey performance information to someone in their group must decide on timeliness. Should it be immediate, at the next staff meeting, or deferred until the next performance review? In the encounter, the supervisor describes the incident or circumstances in terms that require the receiver to make a self-evaluation of the situation. Further, the supervisor deals with the specifics of the situation rather than generalizing that "the program is a total failure." The supervisor demonstrates sensitivity to the needs of the receiver by thoughtful choice of time and place for the feedback and also by being descriptive and specific rather than evaluative and general. Feedback deals with information that is within the capability of the receiver to remedy. Although the initial input by the supervisor may not be solicited, the manner in which information is shared should make it easy and natural for the receiver to solicit further information. Finally, the supervisor should test how accurately the message has been received by asking the job incumbent to describe his or her understanding of the problem and to propose an action program.

GOAL-SETTING APPROACH

Because job performance changes constantly, performance appraisal must be a continual process. Some critics snipe at periodic performance appraisals on the grounds that six-month or annual reviews are not realistically keyed to the evolving and sporadic nature of work. This is a valid critique if reviews are conducted only occasionally. However, periodic performance appraisals can be a constructive part of a continual feedback process. The Adult-Adult periodic-review process ideally builds on prework by a natural work group. For example, department heads should involve their natural work groups in developing plans for the coming year, perhaps through off-site, two-day workshops for defining departmental goals and strategies. Having reached consensus on the master plan, each member, through choice, negotiation, or assignment, assumes ownership of a portion of the departmental mission. Responsibilities assumed at this stage are tentative, pending ratification of the proposed departmental charter during the upcoming divisional planning conference.

The department head activates the individual performance-review process by distributing to each person in the work group an evaluation form that asks: (1) What were your major achievements during the past six months? (2) What are your goals for the next six months? and (3) What are your long-term goals?

Ideally these three responses are summarized on a single sheet of paper and returned to the immediate supervisor, as illustrated in Figure 11-2.

After reviewing the completed form, the supervisor consults the goal setter regarding a mutually convenient time to hold the performance-review discussion. A supervisor who is sensitive to the symbolism of organizational rank will attempt to hold the meeting away from his or her own office—perhaps in the job incumbent's office or in a nearby conference room. Supervisors holding meetings in their own offices should avoid the throne-behind-the-desk posture and should take measures to assure privacy and to prevent interruptions.

Interviews are more developmental when supervisors are determined to do more listening than talking. The use of feedback, rather than criticism, establishes a climate in which a helpful dialog can take place. Skills and insights gained through transactional analysis and conference leadership are helpful in this encounter. Supervisors should act naturally and should not depart too radically from their everyday style.

After opening the discussion—usually with small talk—the supervisor decides whether to start the business discussion by asking a question or by following a course initiated by the other person. If the supervisor begins the discussion, he or she may acknowledge the employee's enumerated achievements and then ask how he or she feels about them. Supervisors should not be in a rush to get a response; they should be prepared to give the person an opportunity to warm up to the question. Supervisors may wish to follow this initial discussion with another question: "Now that this experience is behind you, if you were doing the project over again, is there anything you would do differently?" Again, the supervisor should

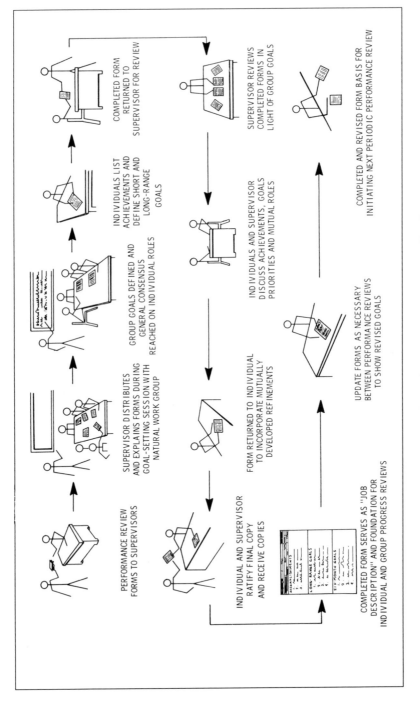

PERFORMANCE REVIEW
FORMS TO SUPERVISORS

SUPERVISOR DISTRIBUTES
AND EXPLAINS FORMS DURING
GOAL-SETTING SESSION WITH
NATURAL WORK GROUP

GROUP GOALS DEFINED AND
GENERAL CONSENSUS
REACHED ON INDIVIDUAL ROLES

INDIVIDUALS LIST
ACHIEVEMENTS AND
DEFINE SHORT AND
LONG-RANGE
GOALS

COMPLETED FORM
RETURNED TO
SUPERVISOR FOR REVIEW

SUPERVISOR REVIEWS
COMPLETED FORMS IN
LIGHT OF GROUP GOALS

INDIVIDUALS AND SUPERVISOR
DISCUSS ACHIEVEMENTS, GOALS
PRIORITIES AND MUTUAL ROLES

FORM RETURNED TO INDIVIDUAL
TO INCORPORATE MUTUALLY
DEVELOPED REFINEMENTS

INDIVIDUAL AND SUPERVISOR
RATIFY FINAL COPY
AND RECEIVE COPIES

COMPLETED FORM SERVES AS "JOB
DESCRIPTION" AND FOUNDATION FOR
INDIVIDUAL AND GROUP PROGRESS REVIEWS

UPDATE FORMS AS NECESSARY
BETWEEN PERFORMANCE REVIEWS
TO SHOW REVISED GOALS

COMPLETED AND REVISED FORM BASIS FOR
INITIATING NEXT PERIODIC PERFORMANCE REVIEW

Figure 11-2. Goal-Setting Performance Review

wait if the employee does not answer immediately. The supervisor might also say, "You had a major hand in opening our new production line. I'll bet you learned a lot from that experience," and then pause for the response. Another question might be "A couple of our employees are going to Charleston to start up operations in our new South Carolina plant. If they asked you for advice, what would you say?" The employee then has a chance to give a revealing and productive answer: "It's funny you should ask that question, because if I were doing it over, I would do three things differently." The person then details a better approach to the accomplishments of the past six months.

The primary role of the supervisor in this situation is to help job incumbents to assume responsibility for reviewing and evaluating their own accomplishments. If job incumbents are under the false illusion that they have accomplished their goals adequately, the misconception may be a function of supervisory failure to give timely and valid feedback. Or it could result from a supervisor's failure to help job incumbents establish well-defined goals and acceptable criteria by which they can assess their own performances.

Having reviewed achievements and the lessons learned, supervisors and team members can then discuss goals. Together they can establish short- and long-range priorities and strategies for achieving them. The two can also define their individual and mutual roles in attaining and measuring accomplishments. Supervisors must not override goal setters' opinions with official authority. However, supervisors do share information with job incumbents regarding budgetary constraints, schedules, policies, laws, and customer commitments. Thus, operating from the same data base, the incumbent and supervisor can arrive at decisions through consensus in an Adult-Adult style. When agreement is reached, the meeting is adjourned; the job incumbent takes the performance-appraisal form to modify it according to their agreement. The employee makes any necessary changes, duplicates the form, gives one to the supervisor, and retains a copy to use as a foundation for his or her six-month charter.

After completing a one-on-one meeting with each individual in the group, the supervisor convenes them for a joint session. Each person reports to the group his or her goals and strategies as a basis for planning collaborative efforts and avoiding conflicts and redundancies.

Although the periodic performance review establishes a six-month charter, the plan usually needs interim updating. After the forms are completed and discussed, the supervisors may consult the group and choose monthly two-hour meeting dates for interim reviews. During these monthly meetings each person reports on his or her achievements, obstacles, breakthroughs, assignments, setbacks, problems, and opportunities. These meetings keep the group updated and allow individuals to modify their charters and to help one another through suggestions and collaborative effort.

Thus, when the next review period arrives, there are no surprises. Under this system all employees are continuously responsible for their own goals and achievements and the measurement of their own performances. If the performance review is the occasion for awarding discretionary bonuses or merit increases, or for giving notice of termination, such actions come as no surprise. To the extent that the individual and the supervisor are working from the same data base, allegations of favoritism, unfairness, and arbitrariness are less likely to be made.

When performance reviews are not taken seriously at lower job-grade levels, it is usually because the reviews are not appropriately initiated and supported at the higher levels. Vice presidents may protest that their missions are established at the annual planning conferences and that they see no need to go through the performance-review procedures used at lower levels. People at the top often fail to realize that the primary purpose of using the performance-review process at upper levels is not to establish charters but to initiate and validate a system that will be used throughout the organization. When the vice president distributes review forms to the department heads, he or she is saying through the language of action, "Performance reviews are important." Moreover, successfully conducted performance reviews at the upper levels serve as models to be emulated by people at lower levels.

Goal-oriented performance appraisals customarily are not used for hourly paid employees. The reasoning supporting this tradition is that wage-roll people are paid to carry out orders—not to set goals. Moreover, the responsibilities of employees at this level are presumed to be determined by standard job descriptions set through union-management negotiations. Because of such assumptions, performance reviews for the hourly work force tend to be Parent-Child processes. However, perceptive managers are finding that traditional practices provide inappropriate guidelines for dealing with enlightened employees and are beginning to innovate Adult-Adult performance-review systems appropriate for wage-roll people.

Such a goal-oriented performance review can be adapted to lower-level employees if appropriately keyed to their job constraints. When people are interdependent members of a work team, it may be appropriate to administer the system to them as a group. The first-level supervisor may convene the work group in a conference room, distribute the forms to them, and lead them through the goal-setting process. Using a flip chart or chalkboard, the supervisor involves the group in compiling a list of their six-month achievements. The list may be narrowed to the most important achievements, which each member then records on his or her performance-review form. In a similar manner, following the principles of problem solving and goal setting described in Chapter 4, the supervisor involves the group in defining goals. Thus, each person ends up with a form listing the group's achievements and goals.

The group process paves the way for involving each person in a one-on-one discussion. The supervisor arranges for a private meeting with each member of the group, asking each person to bring the completed form to the meeting. To adapt the process to employees who do not like to exercise initiative, as well as to those who do, the supervisor might say, "Bring this completed form to the meeting because it will be the basis for much of our discussion. By the way, if you wish to add some of your personal achievements or goals to those we have listed as a group, feel free to do so. I'll be glad to discuss them with you."

In the ensuing one-on-one discussions, supervisors should listen more than they talk, apply the Adult-Adult process of feedback, and avoid Parent-Child criticism, condescension, and instruction. Furthermore, as in the case of managerial reviews, the supervisor should schedule interim periodic meetings to keep members of the group updated, to involve them in the changes that invariably occur in a workplace, and to enable them to keep their goals updated.

Controversy continues to rage over whether or not performance reviews should include a discussion of pay. The traditional Parent-Child viewpoint holds that performance review and pay should be discussed separately because money is an emotion-arousing subject that could impair the logical and deliberate process of goal setting. The assumption behind this viewpoint is that a disappointing pay adjustment would activate counterproductive attitudes and behavior.

The Adult-Adult position is that mature people like to understand the relationship between their accomplishments and the reward systems of the organization. Pay, being one of the more tangible forms of feedback from the supervisor, is an integral part of the performance review. Needless to say, the better individuals understand the criteria by which they are appraised and the better they understand the technicalities of the reward system, the less likely they are to be surprised or disappointed when pay issues are included in the performance-review discussion. To use the analogy of the baseball game, Adult players do not blame the umpire when they strike out, nor do they expect the umpire to give them special consideration because other players are more talented. In contrast, immature players often try to blame the umpire or others for their failures. A paternalistic umpire who attempted to assume a helping role would perpetuate this immaturity and violate the accepted ground rules in doing so. People are more likely to act like adults when they are treated like adults. In summary, performance review at its worst tends to promote resentment, intimidation, and disengagement. At its best, performance review is an Adult feedback process that helps people to take charge of their own careers and job responsibilities.

STAFFING

The purpose of staffing is to find, attract, and utilize qualified people in such a way that talent will find expression in the successful pursuit of organizational and personal goals. Traditional staffing practice reflects the following assumptions:

1. The richest source of talent is outside the organization.

2. The company is responsible for matching individuals to jobs.

3. Staffing is a responsibility of the personnel department.

The premise of this discussion is that both organizational and individual goals are better achieved when staffing is based on a different set of suppositions:
1. The richest source of talent is inside the organization.

2. Individuals should be permitted to pursue and move into growth opportunities.

3. Staffing is a line responsibility.

External Versus Internal Staffing

All organizations are composed of members brought in originally from the outside. However, an organization can be said to be staffed internally when most job openings above entry job grades are filled through a process of upward mobility from within. A company is staffed externally when job openings above the lowest levels are filled primarily by newly hired employees.

Proponents of external staffing hold that the injection of new blood is needed at all levels and that staffing from within is a type of inbreeding that results in excessive conformity and technological obsolescence. Moreover, they reason that hiring in outsiders at upper levels attracts stalemated high achievers from other organizations.

Advocates of internal staffing counter with the view that external staffing fills jobs with people who, in a broad sense, failed to make adequate adjustments in other organizations. According to this perspective, managers who hire outsiders are often hiring other organizations' rejects. Moreover, external staffing, by not offering upward mobility, stifles initiative and results in stagnation, frustration, and a higher rate of voluntary separations by high achievers. Internal staffing, in contrast, stimulates hope and ambition; encourages self-development; and leads to realized potential, personal commitment, and reduced turnover. More important, a sound promotion-from-within practice makes it possible to retain impatient high achievers who might otherwise look elsewhere for growth opportunities.

External staffing, as a primary strategy, is a costly and wasteful circular process. At a conservatively estimated rate of 20 percent turnover per year, an organization loses the equivalent of 100 percent of its work force in five years. Those who leave are replaced by people who (except for entry-level applicants) were separated from other organizations. Thus, companies are often the victims of an insidious and expensive process of exchanging misfits.

Although many managers tend to see recruited replacements as superior to employees who have left the organization, the real beneficiaries of external hiring are the job hoppers. Some individuals, in fact, have found that the only way to improve their job status in their own organizations is to move temporarily to another company and then to return with the cachet of a newly hired employee. All organizations and, hence, society in general, lose by this process, which accelerates inflation and undermines the competitive ability of companies.

The merits of internal staffing generally outweigh those of external staffing, but the relative effectiveness of one strategy over another is a function of the uniqueness of each organization. Neither strategy is pure, nor should it be. Good organizations attract good people, who bring in fresh viewpoints. Failing organizations are sometimes saved by the influx of new talent. The exceptions that enable or require organizations to attract and hire limited numbers of high-level, talented outsiders do not vitiate the principle of internal staffing, provided insiders have first choice of promotional opportunities.

A company that promotes from within is more likely to retain high achievers on the company work force. The hiring of key managers from the outside is no less damaging to the morale and ambitions of an organizational work force than exporting managers into multinational subsidiaries to direct indigenous personnel. In both cases, the newcomers are seen as outsiders who are insensitive to the needs of the local people and who are taking jobs that rightfully belong to natives.

An ideal system for internal staffing is one that duplicates as nearly as possible the process people use when they go job hunting. Openings must be visible; employees must be able to apply for the positions without fear of reprisal; and applicants must encounter no difficulty in cutting across job classifications and departmental lines in order to fill jobs for which they qualify.

Management Values Reflected in Staffing

The staffing of an organization is governed by the prevailing management philosophy, which attracts and retains individuals who, in a circular fashion, reinforce and perpetuate that philosophy. Some people are attracted to command-and-control organizations with procedure-manual mentalities. Conformity in such a culture is rewarded by job security and peer acceptance. Others are attracted to the less formal organization that encourages initiative and risk taking. Although freedom can result in failure, it also creates an exhilarating environment for high achievers. As these two types adapt to their differing organizations and progress upward to positions of administrative influence, they develop relationships, systems, and policies that perpetuate their own values and practices. They tend to hire people whose values match or reinforce their own and promote and reward those who fit in best.

Although conformists tend to hire conformists, it does not naturally follow that individualists always hire individualists. Uncommon men and women sometimes inadvertently surround themselves with bright but unassertive personalities who become satisfied with implementing their mentor's innovations. Brilliant and forceful innovators may unintentionally quash creativity in less forceful people. Therefore, all organizations run a greater risk of attracting and developing too many conformists than they do of fostering too much individuality.

The orientation of personnel recruiters usually mirrors the management philosophy of their organizations. Particularly in the larger organizations the hiring function is often delegated to professional recruiters who tend to select candidates whose values match their own or match their perceptions of the requisitioning supervisor's values. However, even when the requisitioning supervisor is achievement oriented, personnel people tend to be maintenance oriented as a result of the maintenance problems unloaded by line managers. As a result, personnel people are more prone to focus on the wrong factors when hiring high achievers.

For example, professional recruiters may advertise jobs as stimulating and challenging but emphasize as major attractions generous pay, supplemental benefits, and a congenial environment. During the screening interview these peripheral factors are usually stressed, along with detailed descriptions of the compensation system, the retirement and group-insurance plans, the recreation program, and other benefits. Candidates are invited to the company on an all-expenses-paid visit, are taken on a whirlwind tour that steers them away from the less attractive sectors of the organization, are entertained at an expensive restaurant, and are made to feel like temporary royalty.

However, when the recruit reports to work, he or she may find that reality differs from the recruiting publicity. Confronted with long hours, the ambiguity and pressure of multiple assignments, too much or too little guidance, and pressure from demanding supervisors, the new employee feels deceived. He or she may rise to such a challenge and thrive or may recoil and withdraw in disenchantment. Disenchanted people often leave the organization in search of the nonexistent job described during the employment interview. They are branded by the organization as chronic complainers who are too preoccupied with maintenance factors; however, it is the organization's recruiting strategy that fosters the wrong expectations.

A far better recruiting strategy is to advertise the difficulty of the challenge and the opportunity to learn; the long hours should be stressed and the value of the maintenance factors understated. During the company visit the candidate should be shown the workplace, goals to be achieved, and jobs to be done; but off-site entertainment should be de-emphasized. An informal dinner meeting at the end of the visit with informed company representatives provides an opportunity to discuss career possibilities and to answer questions that determine the candidate's fitness for and interest in the organization. Although such a strategy might eliminate more candidates, those hired are better prepared for the realities of the new job. Moreover, the new employee's first encounter with the organization would not be an act of deception.

Internal staffing, to a greater extent than external staffing, increases human effectiveness within an organization and activates a more achievement-oriented recruiting strategy. Internal staffing offers growth opportunities and rewards talent, effort, and demonstrated achievements; external staffing tends to lure opportunists looking for ready-made opportunities. However, the success of either staffing strategy depends heavily on the systems through which it is implemented. The key factor here is whether the staffing system is managed by someone above the user (a company-managed system) or by the people who use the system to do the staffing (a user-managed system).

Company-Managed Staffing System

Company-managed staffing systems are usually designed to keep management in control of staffing decisions. For example, the personnel inventory is a company-managed system designed to enable management to match employee talent with job opportunities. Computers store and retrieve information about educational achievements, job experience, aspirations, and special skills or achievements such as foreign-language fluency, patents, publications, and honors. Job openings are matched against inventory descriptors, and the records of potential candidates are referred to the hiring supervisor.

Although occasionally useful for locating rare skills, personnel inventories are found in practice to have several fundamental flaws that actually impair employee development. For one, the files rarely keep pace with the membership of the work force, let alone with the changing skills and aspirations of company employees. Second, the sensitivity and accuracy of the system are limited because personnel data are translated into machine language and subsequently retranslated when candidates are being considered for a new position. Third, qualified candidates are often by-passed because supervisors are reluctant to release them for reassignment. Fourth, the system, particularly when managed through big-company bureaucracy, seldom tells employees when opportunities will be available, when reviews will be held, or whether they are actually being considered for new positions.

Perhaps the most harmful characteristic of the personnel inventory is its use as a management control system for limiting enterprising action on the part of employees. The system casts employees as passive, dependent individuals, waiting for management to take the initiative, administer the system, and find the candidates when they are needed. Systems of this type do little to inspire employees to assume responsibility for their own career opportunities. Misled by an assumption that paternalistic management has their interests at heart and is looking out for their welfare, they may drift into obsolescence or retirement waiting for the company to point the way.

User-Managed Staffing System

The consequences of a user-managed system are quite different. A user-managed system meets the criteria of an effective system as discussed in Chapter 6: the employee must understand and agree with the purpose of the system, must know how to use it, must be in control of it, and must be able to influence its revision and receive timely feedback from it. The user activates the system to satisfy a personal goal; therefore, he or she must be assured that there is no risk in doing so. The Texas Instruments job-posting plan described in Chapter 6 is an example of an effective user-managed staffing system.

The TI system is based on an assumption that individuals are responsible for their own development. However, a philosophy of self-development can be a platitude and an excuse for company dereliction if realistic opportunities are not provided to enable members to meet this responsibility.

Texas Instruments' system gives employees advantages over outsiders. For example, current employees have one week's opportunity to apply for a new position before outside applicants are considered. Job requirements are defined according to the grade and location of the position and in terms of the education, skill, and experience expected of the applicants. Biweekly listings of all job openings up to the level of vice president are published, distributed, and posted and are made available at all work sites.

Any employee can activate the system by completing a form noting his or her interest in a posted job and by submitting a bid to the personnel department. At their option applicants may also inform their current supervisors of the bid.

Bids are screened by the personnel department along with those of outside applicants and, if not eliminated, are referred to the requesting supervisor who considers, interviews, and selects a candidate (or decides to consider outside candidates). A selected candidate who accepts an offer then notifies his or her own supervisor. The requesting supervisor initiates the personnel-transfer paperwork, and the individual is released to the new job within three weeks from the date of acceptance. During this period the releasing supervisor posts the vacated job and attempts to select and train a replacement. In practice, vacated jobs are often filled immediately from a reservoir of qualified bidders on file from previous bids. Hence, several bidders may be released simultaneously for their new assignments.

Job posting is effective for surfacing hidden talent. Individuals in quest of career opportunities are far more sensitive and perceptive as search mechanisms than any programmed computer could ever be. More important, when this system is used, individuals are responsible for their own growth opportunities and can initiate self-development plans suggested by job-posting specifications and bidding rejects. For example, participation in TI's educational-assistance program increased approximately 80 percent after installation of the job-posting system.

This system synergistically serves the users and the organization. Employees find outlets for their talents through voluntary promotions, transfers, and reassignments. Although personnel mobility causes some short-term inconvenience, long-term gains are made when talented transferees are retained. Job posting takes the sting out of work-force reductions by transferring surplus personnel; it helps place people who have acquired new skills, increases the incentive to learn new skills, accommodates employees returning from leave, and facilitates the application of equal-opportunity employment.

Although equal-opportunity programs are commonly monitored and administered by the personnel department, equal-opportunity practices are more successfully implemented by line management. In addition, job posting reduces dependency relationships between job incumbents and their supervisors, increases employee versatility, fosters improved morale, rewards leadership practices that retain and attract star performers, and promotes greater community stability.

Job posting helps the other staffing procedures at an organization to become more user oriented. Training programs, for example, become more focused on the needs of specific job incumbents and more reflective of the real job opportunities available in the company. Employees no longer view training as a duty but as an opportunity by which they can attain personal goals. Without job posting, training programs sometimes appear to be merely management-prescribed obligations that do not have a realistic relationship to job opportunities or employee aspirations.

Similarly, aptitude testing—long perceived by workers as a threatening tool by which managers select and reject candidates for jobs and training programs—can become an aid to employees, particularly when used in conjunction with job postings. With the insights offered by aptitude tests, people have a better understanding of their potential and limitations and can direct their aspirations and learning activities and assume greater responsibility for their own self-development. Aptitude tests are sometimes limited by inappropriate validation and legislative restrictions; however, despite these limitations, they can be potent tools for furthering self-development.

APTITUDE MEASUREMENT

The use of aptitude tests improves the probability of selecting qualified job candidates. However, tests are not perfect predictors of job success and occasionally eliminate qualified applicants who perform poorly on tests; sometimes the system may select unqualified applicants who perform well on exams. Unfortunately for the society that stresses equal opportunity as a cornerstone of its philosophy, tests tend to eliminate larger percentages of minority groups. In some cases the selecting out of minority-group candidates is a result of not having included these groups in the test validation studies, in which case the tests are valid predictors of job success only for candidates from within the culture for which the tests were validated. Even when tests are properly validated as predictors of job success for all groups, it is sometimes reasoned that minority members should be exempt from standardized predictors on the basis that these individuals are innocent victims of social injustice, which handicaps them both in test performance and job performance. In any event, aptitude tests, regardless of their validity, are not widely used as a selection device.

Paradoxically, part of the problem of aptitude testing is that the tests are too potent as predictors. The apparent ability of psychologists to predict behavior from tests often leads managers to disregard interview impressions, biographical data, and job histories. Overreliance on psychologists stems in part from the esoteric language they use in describing the characteristics, interest patterns, skills, and intelligence of the candidate. Not fully understanding the jargon, managers often capitulate and permit the psychologists to make selection decisions. This practice makes managers into users of a system they do not fully understand. Aptitude testing becomes a crutch, displacing other proven predictors and common judgment in matters of personnel selection and evaluation.

Much of the mystery can be removed from testing if the user realizes that all aptitude tests, regardless of their labels, can be grouped into four families of human characteristics: capacity, achievement, interest, and temperament.

Capacity Tests. There are two kinds of capacity tests—mental and physical. Mental capacity is measured by various intelligence tests that evaluate factors such as verbal fluency, numerical facility, inductive and deductive reasoning, detail perception, reasoning speed, and ability to comprehend spatial relationships. Physical capacity refers to capabilities such as eye-hand coordination, manual dexterity, hand steadiness, sense of balance, visual acuity, depth perception, and color vision.

Achievement Tests. Achievement tests are measures of knowledge and skill. Knowledge achievement tests may rate mastery of mathematics, economics, geography, grammar, electronics, or principles of leadership. Skill achievement tests measure a candidate's capacity to perform tasks such as typing and shorthand and may evaluate his or her ability to operate a desk calculator, write a computer program, lead a conference, or operate a lathe.

Interest Tests. Interest tests measure vocational or avocational interests, usually through multiple-choice questionnaires or inventories. Vocational-interest measures may describe a person's preference for job activities (such as computational, persuasive, scientific, or mechanical tasks) or may evaluate the candidate's aptitude for specific vocations (mechanical engineer, chemist, editor, business manager, or athlete). Avocational-interest questionnaires measure preferences for off-the-job pastimes such as playing a musical instrument, reading, oil painting, flying, coin collecting, bird watching, engaging in sports, or following politics.

Temperament Tests. Temperament tests, depending on the degree of sophistication and the competence of the administrator, measure surface or subconscious personality traits. Surface personality traits are usually determined from responses to questions about such topics as parents, siblings, friends, enemies, teachers, supervisors, sex, religion, social situations, dishonesty, fears, and aspirations. This kind of test is often transparent and may evoke responses that are deliberately faked or that the individual erroneously believes to be correct or desirable. Even when the respondent attempts to be completely candid or honest, the questionnaire may tap only his or her conscious personality. As a measure of surface personality, such a test might be valid. For example, the test might accurately describe one person as an optimistic extrovert and another as a depressive introvert. In terms of everyday observations, and under normal conditions, these may be valid descriptions. However, a test that measures subconscious personalities might offer quite different results. The subconscious measure is more subtle, perhaps inducing respondents to project their personalities into the interpretation of ambiguous pictures and patterns, thereby giving expression to subconscious feelings. Such a test, coupled with an in-depth interview by a competent psychologist, might show, for example, that the happy-go-lucky extrovert is really using a facade to conceal sadness and despair stemming from alienation and misfortune. The facade makes everyday living bearable to these people and becomes the pattern by which their acquaintances may know them. Depressive introverts might harbor a subconscious need to be in the limelight or to be empire builders, and their behavior might also be imposed by an overdeveloped conscience or a reaction to despair. The paradoxical swing from depression to euphoria (or from joy to melancholy) when inhibitions are lowered with alcohol or other drugs is sometimes an expression of this phenomenon. It does not logically follow, of course, that surface personalities are always in conflict with subconscious personalities; usually they are not.

None of the tests described above should be administered or interpreted by untrained personnel. All are subject to misinterpretation, especially in the hands of untrained professionals, particularly the measures of mental capacity and temperament. When adequate safeguards are provided against the pitfalls noted above and when tests are properly validated, administered, and interpreted within the balanced context of other predictors, they represent one of the most effective and democratic systems for uncovering hidden talent. People in manual occupations, for example, may have talents untapped by previous jobs. Self-discovery through aptitude tests may provide the necessary spark of inspiration and encouragement needed to lift talent from dormancy or to transform it from reactive to constructive expression. Aptitude tests can also perform the merciful mission of redirecting unrealistic aspirations, enabling individuals to recognize and accept reality, thereby preventing the later trauma of vocational failure.

Aptitude tests should not be used to label people as successes or failures but, instead, should support the concept that all people have an aptitude to succeed—but in different roles. Some have a greater variety of aptitudes than others, but opportunities exist for all to succeed. Particularly in a tight labor market or during implementation of a promotion-from-within policy, tests offer a valuable key to the location of submerged talent and a stimulus to self-development.

Aptitude tests, when administered under the direction and control of management authority, can hinder self-development. No matter how accurately tests are interpreted by management, they increase the dependency relationships of individuals to those above them and represent one more bureaucratic inhibition to self-discovery and initiative.

However, when an employee initiates the aptitude test, the assessment process can become a developmental, personal experience. When organizations provide access to, and refund the cost of, aptitude testing, much in the same spirit and for the same sound business reasons that educational assistance is offered, the use and control of test scores should be proprietary with the individual. The psychology consultant should release aptitude data only by voluntary authorization of the examinee. Thus, test scores become constructive aids to self-understanding and development and are optionally withheld or released as the examinee chooses when applying for promotional opportunities.

REFERENCES

McGregor, D. (1972). An uneasy look at performance appraisal. *Harvard Business Review, 50*,(5) 133-138.

12

Managing Innovation

All management is the management of innovation. People who simply perpetuate the status quo are not managers but puppets or automatons who are replaceable by programmable machines.

Creativity is a form of spontaneity that can find productive expression in a climate of freedom. Creativity also finds expression in a climate of oppression, but usually in rebellious or counterproductive ways. Therefore, an effective organization provides an environment in which its members assert themselves constructively. However, freedom without focus can result in anarchy. Therefore, the effective organization provides a balance of opportunities and constraints guided by a vision that inspires individuals to unite in the pursuit of common goals.

People who work for themselves understand the opportunities and constraints of self-employment. Creativity can flourish in such circumstances. Unfortunately, when self-employed people prosper and hire additional workers, the bosses usually fail to provide their employees with the same conditions that inspired their own success. The key to organizational leadership is to provide a data base and reward systems that unite all members of a group in support of a common cause.

In his autobiography Alfred P. Sloan (1964) described how the application of innovation in research and engineering, manufacturing, corporate finance, marketing, and distribution led to the emergence of General Motors (GM) as the largest corporation in America. However, innovation in GM was restricted largely to the salaried, exempt people in management and technology. Two-thirds of the work force—people classified as hourly, nonexempt workers—were not part of the innovative process. Sloan referred to the labor problems that plagued the company after World War II as though they were the imponderable and inescapable consequences of running a company. The only applications of innovation directly affecting the workers were attempts to automate production to limit the role of wage earners or to reduce their numbers. In fairness to Sloan, it should be noted that he endowed the Sloan School of Management at the Massachusetts Institute of Technology, and in doing so acknowledged the need for better insights into the management of human resources.

Sloan was not alone in his perception of innovation as the exclusive realm of the managerial class. Many of his contemporaries and successors did not envision the involvement of workers in industrial engineering, quality control, and other management processes. Wasteful as this oversight was during the post-World War II era, it is exponentially more counterproductive now. Today's enlightened workers expect and accept involvement as a right and respond counterproductively with anger, indignation, frustration, and disengagement to constraints that inhibit their participation.

Even in organizations that attempt to motivate their workers, traditional reward systems remain a major shortcoming. Only the most progressive companies use the three-dimensional reward systems described in Chapter 2.

Like Sloan, most people associate the management of innovation with managerial and professional employees. Hourly paid workers, traditionally referred to as *hired hands,* usually exercise their initiative and creativity in unofficial and informal ways, often to the detriment of the organization. If constructive creativity is latent in all individuals, then manual workers represent the greatest reservoir of untapped resources, because in most cultures these workers outnumber the salaried staff by at least two to one.

WORK SIMPLIFICATION

In the 1930s Allan H. Mogensen, in the traditional role of industrial engineer, took a clipboard and a stopwatch and approached workers in order to study and improve work methods and to establish standards for incentive pay. He found workers to be creative in thwarting his efforts. When not under surveillance, they would change work methods to increase their pay. Reasoning that this creativity could be legitimized and harnessed in more constructive ways, he developed a curriculum and methodology now widely known as *work simplification*.[1]

In practice, work simplification puts the management of change into the hands of job incumbents—a responsibility previously restricted largely to industrial engineers. Many employees would like to improve job methods but fail to do so simply because they lack the skills for developing their ideas. In other cases, where workers can and do recommend improvements, they are often discouraged by supervisory apathy or hostility. Traditional union leaders sometimes oppose methods improvement if they perceive it as "pro-management."

Employees usually learn work simplification through standardized company programs prescribed by Mogensen and his disciples. Because industrial engineers sometimes oppose this intrusion into their territory, many companies put them in charge of teaching work simplification to operators. Thus not only is the engineer's responsibility for methods improvement left intact but it is also broadened to facilitate method improvements by others. Similarly, union leaders who might otherwise oppose work simplification are receptive if they are involved in its planning and implementation when it is being introduced into the organization.

Company training programs are usually taught in two-hour blocks for a total of approximately twenty to thirty hours. Course content includes principles and techniques of motion-and-time economy, flow-process charting, cost analysis, and teamwork and entails on-the-job projects for applying newly learned techniques. Projects may be undertaken by individuals or groups; training takes place under the guidance of either a trained line worker or a staff person.

---

[1] *Work simplification* is now applied under a variety of names, including *job management, operation improvement, deliberate methods change, methods-change programs,* and *team-improvement programs.* Whatever the label, many companies, including Texas Instruments, Detroit Edison, IBM, Dow Chemical Company, Canadian Industries Limited, Procter & Gamble, and Goodyear Tire and Rubber Company, are applying the principles and techniques of work simplification in furthering the management of innovation. Many of the techniques and underlying theories of JIT/VAM had their origin in Mogensen's principles of work simplification.

An Application of Work Simplification

A creative amalgamation of behavioral theory and technique was developed by Irving Borwick (1969) and his associates in Steinberg's Limited, a major food chain headquartered in Montreal. Their plan uniquely offered management-development training to rank-and-file employees in order to give substance to the concept "every employee a manager." The system introduced at Steinberg's is probably one of the best early examples of a plan that enables wage earners to assume managerial responsibility for their jobs. Although the empowerment of employees illustrated in Borwick's program is more commonplace today under JIT/VAM, it is still a viable model for emulation.

Borwick's team-improvement laboratory (TIL), described below, was based on Mogensen's principles of work simplification and incorporated concepts from Blake and Mouton's managerial grid. [2] Although subsequent applications in more than a hundred stores differed experimentally from the model described here and were implemented under different program names, the same basic principles and techniques were applied.

A typical TIL would involve about twenty people, including the store manager, department managers, cashiers, and clerks. Group activity during lectures and workshops is carefully scheduled to accomplish the following goals:

- Providing an opportunity for people to make use of their capabilities and their creative and imaginative skills in improving the work they are doing;

- Enriching the jobs of the employees and giving them managerial control over their areas of responsibility.

- Unleashing the ideas and know-how of employees to bring about useful improvements in the work situation.

- Bringing about cost savings through improvements made on the job by individual employees.

---

[2] Robert Blake and Jane Mouton (1968) defined organizational effectiveness in terms of two coordinates of a grid, numbered 1 to 9, showing the manager's concern for the human factor and for production. See Figure A-1 in Appendix A.

- Creating an atmosphere conducive to open communication and mutual trust among people at various levels of the organization.

- Fostering an organizational atmosphere and employee attitude that challenges accepted methods of operation and that is conducive to constant change for improvement.

- Building project teams in which employees are best able to work together on planning, controlling, doing, critiquing, and improving their work.

At the beginning of the workshop an hour is set aside during which subgroups reach a consensus on their responses to forty-nine questions concerning concepts of the managerial grid. Teams adjourn to the team room to complete this task and return to the conference room following the session to compare and discuss their results.

This session is followed by a forty-five-minute lecture that introduces the following assumptions, on which work simplification and the TIL are based:

1. People do not resist change; they resist being changed.

2. Every job can be improved.

3. All employees have the ability to improve their jobs.

4. People get satisfaction from improving their work.

5. People like to participate in groups.

6. Improvements are best made by those who perform the job.

7. Employees should be provided with the basic skills for job improvement through an educational program.

8. The role of the supervisor is one of adviser, consultant, and coordinator.

9. The role of the employee is to function as manager of his or her own area of responsibility.

Acceptance of these premises is the foundation for assuming managerial responsibility of a job. The first assumption, "People don't resist change; they resist being changed," emphasizes the need for modifying the system rather than the person. Too often, criticism of an operation is perceived as being directed at the person who does the job rather than at the job itself. It is important to disassociate the two and to objectify the analysis of the job. This objectivity prevents defensive behavior on the part of the operator, who is no longer the butt of adverse criticism and who can then willingly participate in altering the task. Changes introduced by an individual not responsible for performance of the job are not likely to gain the same commitment as changes generated through employee involvement. The participation of workers must be genuine, not a pretense designed to pacify bored or disengaged employees.

Assumption 6, "Improvements are best made by those who perform the job," may be seen as a corollary of Assumption 1. People who perform a job know it best. This is not true in all cases, but it appears to be true more times than not. The person who performs a task usually has in-depth knowledge not readily available to a supervisor or an outsider.

This assumption is tied into two other concepts, "Every job is capable of being improved" and "All employees have the basic ability to improve their jobs." The latter is another case in which the exceptions to the rule are so minimal as to be practically nonexistent. Any employee capable of performing a task has the capability to improve that job. The only exceptions are likely to be jobs in which mentally handicapped individuals perform menial tasks under supervision. These exceptions are rare and do not invalidate the principle. On the other hand, the assumption leads one to the realization that there is a reservoir of untapped intellectual power. This tremendous reserve of people who perform rote tasks and whose energies and abilities are hardly utilized can effect a total revolution in the manner in which business is conducted.

It is important to stress this capability. Many employees, blinded to their own abilities by outmoded managerial practices and inhibited by the authoritarian nature of their primary education, have lost faith in their capacity to alter the world in which they live. Allusions in the lectures and sessions to the work of published authorities reinforce the scientific underpinning on which such assumptions are made and give additional confidence to those small sparks of individuality that are thought to be alive in all people, no matter how limited their managerial background.

To support the premise that every job is capable of being improved, reference is made to work experiences that are familiar to group members. A classic example, frequently quoted, is the case of Procter & Gamble and wooden and paper pallets.

Procter & Gamble used regular wooden pallets to handle its products. Although there was no problem with the efficiency or capability of such pallets, there was a cost factor involved. Procter & Gamble developed the paper pallet to replace the wooden pallet and reduced operational costs while maintaining efficiency. Efficiency was improved further when the "palletless pallet" was developed, a redesigned fork truck with two broad parallel plates that lifted a load by applying pressure from the sides. The innovation eliminated the use of pallets for approximately 90 percent of Procter & Gamble products. This type of case history illustrates three principles of work improvement:

- Every job is capable of being improved.

- Improvement efforts should not be restricted to problem areas. It is sometimes preferable to select jobs that are functioning well. There is no such thing as perfection.

- The ultimate goal in improving a job is to eliminate the task altogether.

Illustrations of this type, which should be selected for their relevance to the areas in which employees work, demonstrate the validity of the concept that every job is capable of being improved. In the same lecture participants are introduced to Mogensen's five-step pattern:

1. Select a job to improve;

2. Get all the facts;

3. Challenge every detail;

4. Develop the preferred method; and

5. Install it and check results.

In conjunction with the five-step pattern, participants are also taught the rudiments of flow-process charting. This technique helps employees to analyze their current jobs in an effort to improve what they are now doing. The teams are given a task to perform in which they apply the five-step pattern. In the case of the flow-chart process, once they have learned the rudiments of analysis, they immediately set to work using the five-step pattern and the charting technique to tackle their projects.

Teaching techniques place emphasis on team participation and direct involvement by participants. Every effort is made to avoid telling the students what to do; emphasis is placed on students' discovering ideas for themselves. The four lectures occupy only two of the thirty-eight hours normally spent in the TIL. The TIL learning sequence takes place as follows:

1. Prereading and activities are assigned for completion before the sessions begin;

2. The task assignment is based on prework, completed first by the individual and then by the team;

3. Results are scored if scoring is appropriate, or a verbal exchange of results takes place between representatives of each team; and

4. Each team offers a critique of the results and the methodology used in achieving these results.

The function of the laboratory leader is to coordinate these activities, to act as a resource for problem situations, and to deliver the four lectures. Most of the learning is done without the leader's intervention.

Films are used during the laboratory sessions to introduce new information not covered in the prereading and are the object of further task assignments. In this laboratory three films are used to teach management styles, the flow-process chart, and one approach to team job improvement.[3]

1. Assumptions and the Five-Step Pattern

2. Managerial Styles

3. Every Employee a Manager

4. How to Manage Improvement

---

[3] Topic 1 is based on theories developed by A.H. Mogensen; Topic 2, on work by R. Blake and J. Mouton; Topic 3, on the views of M.S. Myers; and Topic 4, on the work of L.B. Moore.

At the end of the program the employees, working in teams, establish an improvement program to be implemented upon their return to the work situation. The teams determine objectives, design a strategy for achieving the objectives, and then implement the tactics that will accomplish the goal.

It is made clear to employees during the lecture on change that the task of developing a program for innovation is a team effort and is clearly related to their new roles as managers. Through examination of the managerial functions already outlined in the lecture "Every Employee a Manager," a correlation is made between the management functions (planning, doing, and controlling) and the development of a regular program of planned improvement on a systemic basis. For example, Figure 12-1 illustrates the scope of the management functions for an enriched clerk-packer job in a supermarket.

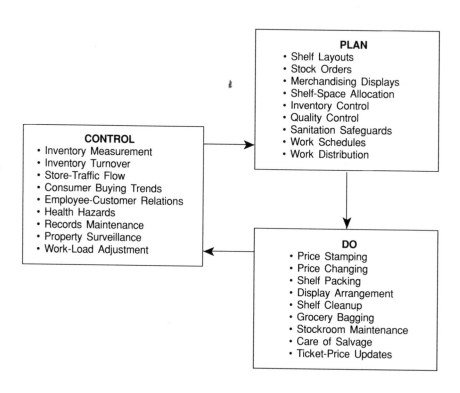

PLAN
• Shelf Layouts
• Stock Orders
• Merchandising Displays
• Shelf-Space Allocation
• Inventory Control
• Quality Control
• Sanitation Safeguards
• Work Schedules
• Work Distribution

CONTROL
• Inventory Measurement
• Inventory Turnover
• Store-Traffic Flow
• Consumer Buying Trends
• Employee-Customer Relations
• Health Hazards
• Records Maintenance
• Property Surveillance
• Work-Load Adjustment

DO
• Price Stamping
• Price Changing
• Shelf Packing
• Display Arrangement
• Shelf Cleanup
• Grocery Bagging
• Stockroom Maintenance
• Care of Salvage
• Ticket-Price Updates

Figure 12-1. Management Functions of Supermarket Clerk-Packer

Change should occur not as the effect of random events on current practice but as a result of planned efforts by managers in control of their own areas of responsibility. To implement this concept, teams are asked to define operations that they would like to improve in their respective work areas. This task follows immediately after people have undergone training in flow-process charting as a technique for analysis. Armed with their new knowledge of managerial responsibility, team activity, problem solving, and analysis, project teams began a determined assault on their projects. Teams spend approximately eight hours working on this task.

There are a number of reasons for devoting so much effort to these projects. In the first place, sufficient time must be allocated for analysis and improvement. Second, the aim of the TIL is to develop every employee as a manager. It is not sufficient to tell employees how to manage. If they are ever to be managers, they must begin to assume managerial responsibility.

Graduates of TIL assume managerial responsibility for assigned areas immediately upon completion of the program. Eventually, individuals and/or teams will be responsible for scheduling, budgeting, controlling, critiquing, and improving their own areas. They will also be provided with sales objectives, margins, product turns, and costs. The initial program has envisaged a slow development of these responsibilities based on a growing demand by trained employees for greater managerial responsibility. Moreover, employees receive additional skill training on the job and off, in order to increase their efficiency and productivity and to enable them to assume greater responsibility.

The final session is designed to allow the employees and their senior supervisor, the store manager, to meet and to work out the details of implementing the TIL in their stores. The store manager, who has been a participant until this point, becomes the discussion leader. Employees know that this program is not a one-shot affair, that following the conclusion of the laboratory, they will continue to meet once a week in the same teams in their respective work areas.

Store personnel have been provided with a model of how the program should work, but every model must be altered to suit the unique circumstances of the store. Details regarding the logistics of future meetings are agreed on before personnel return to the work situation. Together, the entire staff—including department heads, managers, and all employees—plans how the program will operate, when participants will meet, and how projects will be implemented on an ongoing basis.

People who went through the TIL program were excited and actively participating. Employees not yet involved in the program were actively interested and excited by the possibilities. When a TIL meeting was canceled because it conflicted with a union membership meeting, employees asked the union to reschedule its gathering.

Jobs have been enriched, new ideas have been unleashed, and a greater openness of communication has come about. More and more employees influence the management of the operation. Improvements generated through the program include a productivity increase of more than ten dollars in sales per work hour. Although other improvements were realized, it is difficult to measure improvements directly attributable to TIL efforts. For example, although observations indicated that courtesy and concern for the customer increased and that the rise in sales was above normal, it may be premature to assume that the results will be lasting. However, in terms of the intervening variables of improving attitudes, educating employees, developing managerial skills, and introducing the management of change, the program was successful.

The team-improvement laboratory in Steinberg's Limited illustrates how work simplification, broadly applied in all functions and at all levels of an organization, makes every employee a manager. Work simplification utilizes the *plan-do-control* concept described in Chapter 7 and meets the criteria for an effective system discussed in Chapter 6. It is a medium for giving people a psychological and financial stake in the organization, particularly when monetary gains are shared through group monetary and nonmonetary reward systems. Most important, work simplification is a medium for facilitating the professional growth of people whose initiative might otherwise be quashed and whose opportunities were limited by traditional supervisory practices, union constraints, and bureaucratic systems.

NATURAL WORK GROUPS

Natural work groups offer the best opportunity for creativity to find expression. A natural work group generally consists of a group of peers who work together with their common leader. Such groups might range in size from two to fifty members, but more commonly would have six to twelve members. Natural work groups can exist at all levels and functions of any type of organization and might include, for example, the president and vice presidents, a superintendent and his or her supervisors, a supervisor and his or her production operators, a laboratory head and the members of the technical staff, an office manager and the clerical staff, an infantry lieutenant and members of the platoon, a school principal and the teaching staff, or a union president and shop stewards.

A natural work group is potentially a ready-made task force for solving problems and setting goals. (See Chapter 4 for a discussion of the qualities common to all effective teams; these descriptors can serve as guidelines for preparing the members of a group to function together successfully.)

A supervisor usually activates the problem-solving, goal-setting process by convening his or her natural work group in order to deal with specific job-related problems pertaining to quality, costs, schedules, or any other aspect of customer satisfaction. An actual problem need not exist for the supervisor to call such a meeting; the group may be convened to improve on a smoothly functioning process. Any process can be improved, and sometimes the group's anticipatory efforts to reduce costs and improve quality can forestall the encroachment of competitors.

During the first meeting supervisors should attempt to share their managerial perspective with the members of the group. People can think and act like managers only to the extent that they see the problem as managers see it. Hence, regardless of the nature of the organization—whether it is in the private or public sector—members of the group are made to understand that they are convening to devise better ways (both internal and external) of serving their customers. In addition, the supervisor makes sure that the group understands the constraints under which they pursue their mission: for example, budget limitations, delivery schedules, quality standards, legal restrictions, pricing targets, downtime probability, competitor performance, or technical requirements. All goal setting is done within constraints, and realistic goals can be set only when the goal setters understand them. Constraints cannot always be defined in advance of the problem-solving efforts but may be introduced during the idea-evaluation stage before goal setting is completed.

Problem-solving/goal-setting meetings are held during regular working hours when possible, but before or after the work shift (with pay) when necessary. The supervisor begins the meeting by candidly stating the problem, providing detailed information when possible about the history of the project, delivery schedules, overhead costs, material and labor costs, and any other relevant constraints. Applying principles and techniques of transactional analysis and conference leadership, the supervisor encourages members of the group to raise questions and discuss the problems informally. When the leader believes that all members of the group understand the problem, he or she is ready to ask for their suggestions.

Using a flip chart and brainstorming approach, the supervisor records all ideas suggested by the group. Ground rules prohibit criticism, ridicule, and premature evaluation of the merit of any idea. When further ideas are no longer forthcoming, or when time limits are reached, the supervisor begins the evaluation phase.

In reviewing the items, the supervisor avoids statements that evoke defensiveness, such as "Let's go over the items and throw out the half-baked ones," or "Let's review and rank-order the ideas." Instead, the leader might say, "Let's review the items and, without discarding any, pick out a few with which we can all agree." This kind of review will usually produce only a few recommendations that the members of the group consider feasible and worthwhile at that time (perhaps less than 10 percent of the items on the list).

Having narrowed the options, the group is ready for further analysis and goal setting. Occasionally, the most effective role of the supervisor at this stage is to toss the ball to the group by saying, "See what you can come up with; I'll be back in forty minutes," and leaving the room.

Giving the group ownership of the goal-setting process is essential to success. Group members are best qualified to set goals against which they can measure their performance. (See Figure 6-2, which illustrates the accomplishments of a problem-solving/goal-setting team during a series of meetings. The team's efforts reduced the work hours per unit from 138 to 41 in the first year; during the following year the rate declined to 32 per unit.

A problem-solving/goal-setting meeting usually starts with a natural work group but expands to include others who are not members of the natural work group but whose roles as engineers, inspectors, technicians, buyers, or other members of the chain of customers can influence the achievement of the mission. These additional resource people are not usually under the organizational jurisdiction of the supervisor who conducts the problem-solving/goal-setting session. In some cases, they are not even members of the organization. People should be included in the sessions if they have a stake in the outcome of the effort and if they have the ability to contribute to the creative process. For example, when planning problem-solving/goal-setting meetings, a food chain in Canada included supermarket customers; an electronics manufacturing company included vendors; a government service group included welfare recipients; and educators in secondary schools included parents as well as students.

Outsiders to the natural work groups are not usually invited into problem-solving/goal-setting sessions until after the members of the natural work group have become comfortable in their conference-room role, assume ownership of the process, and have begun to discover their own limitations. If work-group members themselves see the need for and recommend the inclusion of an industrial engineer, an inspector, or a customer, these people can be added without usurping and threatening the basic charter of the group. Outsiders should not be allowed to dominate the meeting; it is better for them to be perceived as guests or resources rather than as authority figures.

Guidelines for Problem-solving/Goal-setting

A natural work group at its best is a team that can effectively achieve organizational goals. As an effective team, it will exhibit the descriptors cited in Chapter 4. The supervisor, functioning as leader of the natural work group, plays a key role in expediting the productivity of the group. The suggestions below are provided as a guide by which supervisors can maximize work-team effectiveness.

1. Size of the group. Ideally, a problem-solving group in its initial stages does not contain more than twelve people. Groups as small as two or three can be effective but do not offer the diversity of viewpoints provided by larger groups. A supervisor with a natural work group of more than twelve members may wish to subdivide it into two or more problem-solving teams so that all members can participate. Although beginning groups ideally should not have more than twelve participants, as members become comfortable and skillful with the group process, additional members may be added.

2. *Composition of the group.* All members of a natural work group should participate even though it may be necessary to subdivide the group to make this possible. As members of a natural work group gradually discover their limitations, other resource people (engineers, quality-control professionals, vendors, customers, taxpayers, etc.) may gradually be phased into the work-group meetings. Hence, a beginning group of ten might be expanded to twenty or more. Resource people should be introduced in a style that will not undermine the proprietary responsibility of the natural work group.

3. *When to hold sessions.* To the extent possible, problem-solving/goal-setting sessions are held during regular work hours and on company time. Increasing numbers of supervisors are reserving the last part of the shift for review, critique, and feedback. When work demands do not permit this arrangement, meetings are held on a paid overtime basis on a schedule established through advance consultation with members of the group. On-the-job meetings of this type enable people to develop a new self-image; workers begin to realize that they are valued for their intellectual abilities as well as for their manual skills.

4. *Starting the meeting.* The supervisor starts the meeting with an open, candid, and friendly manner, presenting a customer requirement or organizational problem on which group members can focus their talent. Inexperienced conference leaders can trap themselves in a gripe session by announcing that the meeting is a problem-solving session and by asking participants to enumerate their problems. Although the group may be successful at compiling a list of gripes, and though such an exercise may have a cathartic effect, the discussion will often focus on parking lots, eating facilities, air conditioning, coatracks, coffee breaks, and other maintenance issues. A preoccupation with this kind of complaint makes it difficult for group members to focus on the purpose of the meeting—the better serving of customers.

5. *Defining constraints.* As mentioned earlier, all goal setting is done within constraints, and an important element of the supervisor's role is to enumerate the limitations that apply to the group's situation.

Constraints may include time limits, budgets, technology, laws, customer requirements, union agreements, company policies, skill limitations, and other matters. Although not all constraints can be identified in advance, the rejection of ideas is far more acceptable when caused by insurmountable constraints than when due to the arbitrary use of authority. For instance, a recommendation for the purchase of new equipment can be evaluated by the members themselves by familiarizing them with the amortization procedure on which the purchase decision is based.

6. Need for a goal. The creative problem-identification or brainstorming process typically results in a long list of suggestions and associated ideas. This list has little value until it is translated into one or more goals. When the list is condensed into two or three ideas judged to be workable by all concerned, the group is ready to set quantitative goals and target dates. Targets are to be expressed in tangible terms: quality standards in parts per million, shortened lead time, cost reductions in dollars and cents, on-time deliveries, market shares, and so forth. Sometimes goal setting is less inhibited and more productive if the supervisor leaves the room during the creative process.

7. Importance of feedback. Goals acquire their meaning through feedback. Goals expressed in tangible terms continue to be interesting only if the goal setters receive timely feedback on progress toward the goal. Traditional inspection functions often fail to satisfy this requirement if they delay or distort the feedback. Feedback requirements are best served when operators are in charge of quality-control processes and when they have access to other operational information.

8. Techniques of questioning. The appropriate use of questions serves as a stimulant to group participation. Group leaders are aided by their ability to use four types of questions: (1) overhead, (2) directed, (3) reverse, and (4) relay. The overhead question is directed to the group as a whole: "Does anyone have a suggestion?" The directed question is addressed to a specific person: "What do you think, John?" The reverse question is returned to the questioner: "Before I try to answer your question, Susan, have you thought of a possible solution?" The relay question redirects a query to another person: "Mary, how would you answer Jim's question?" The experienced conference leader also finds that the use of silence can be an effective pump primer. A supervisor who asks an overhead question should be prepared to wait for up to two minutes before interrupting the silence. In practice, such a long wait is not necessary because few people can tolerate the ambiguity of more than thirty seconds of silence.

9. The meeting climate. The principles of transactional analysis, illustrated in Chapter 4, are useful for establishing a climate that fosters constructive spontaneity. Positive strokes nurture freedom of expression; negative strokes create inhibitions. Adult-Adult transactions, with a sprinkling of Child-Child transactions, promote mutual respect, spontaneity, and solidarity; Parent-Child transactions breed *not-O.K.* feelings, conformity, hostility, and dependency relationships. Rather than rejecting an idea through the Parent-Child use of official authority, a facilitative supervisor involves the group in evaluating an idea in terms of relevant criteria. Ideas can be rejected constructively through Adult-Adult consensus if rejections are based on more complete and widely shared information. The meeting climate is further enhanced through ground rules against ridicule or premature evaluation of suggestions. To reduce their authority-figure image, conference leaders can democratize the team effort by bringing additional flip charts into the conference room and by asking for volunteers to help in the idea-recording process. Authentic first-name informality supports a climate of friendliness and mutual respect.

10. Job security. Cost-reduction efforts customarily lead to cutbacks in personnel costs. However, one of the quickest ways to kill creativity on the job is to lay off people made superfluous by their own creativity. Therefore, employees must feel assured of an equivalent or better job if they are displaced from their current assignments. For example, Donnelly Corporation in Holland, Michigan, guarantees employees that they will not lose their jobs because of procedure changes (Donnelly, 1977). If sustained job continuity cannot be assured because of factors unrelated to the creative process, such as a market slump or contract cancellation, it is important that those affected not associate the cutback with the creative process. In some instances group creativity can be used to anticipate and minimize the impact of economic retrenchment.

QUALITY CIRCLES

Quality circles are made up of people who contribute their intelligence and creativity to solving problems affecting their work. Each quality circle is led by a circle leader and is usually composed of small groups of volunteer employees from the same or similar work areas who meet for about an hour a week on paid company time to identify, investigate, analyze, and solve work-related problems. The recent surge in the use of quality circles during the 1980s stems from Japan's reported success at applying them in Japanese companies.

During the rebuilding of Japanese industry after World War II, the Japanese people made a national commitment to improve the quality of their products. W. Edwards Deming and Joseph Juran, quality-control experts from the United States, were invited to teach their methods to Japanese managers. In 1962, Kaoru Ishikawa, head of the Union of Japanese Scientists and Engineers, introduced quality circles in Japan to involve employees at all levels in improving product quality.

Although quality circles are not a key ingredient in the Japanese application of JIT/VAM, they were one of the more visible processes seen by visitors to Japan. As a result, variations of the quality circle were implemented in thousands of companies worldwide. Quality circles require the commitment and active support of people in all levels and functions (see Figure 12-2).

Steering committee. This committee, representing a cross section of the company, is made up of representatives of major plant functions. It is responsible for establishing the operating guidelines under which quality circles function and provides liaison for management support.

Top and middle management. Upper-level managers provide active support by visiting quality-circle meetings, showing interest in the team's activities, and making sure that approved projects are implemented.

Technical support staff. Staff from various functions such as engineering, manufacturing, quality control, materials handling, accounting, purchasing, sales, and personnel, are available on request to serve as resources in facilitating circle processes and implementing circle goals.

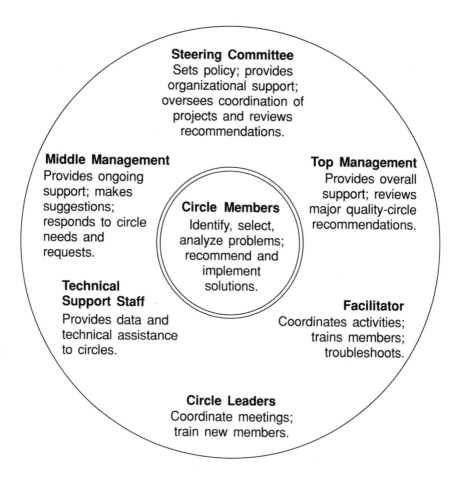

Figure 12-2. Organizational Structure of Quality Circles

Facilitator. The coordinator is responsible for the overall quality-circle program, including circle activities, and ensures that teams receive the necessary training, time, and resources. A facilitator organizes and schedules circle meetings and attends each team meeting.

Circle leader. The chosen leader of the circle, having volunteered or having been selected by circle members, is responsible for the effective functioning of the team, serving as conference leader to involve all members in activities of the meeting.

Circle members. Circle members are employees who volunteer for the department team. On occasion, technical specialists are asked to join the team. In their regular weekly meetings, quality circles focus on solving problems in their own work areas. Each team follows a specific process that begins with problem identification and progresses through implementation.

Quality-Circle Procedures

Problem identification. Team members identify problems within their work area that they would like to solve. Managers and others can make suggestions at this point.

Problem selection. Problems are selected by team members. Better than anyone else, workers know the problems that affect the work they do. Team members may select problems affecting quality, efficiency, cost, equipment, process control, and many other areas. Quality circles do not usually deal with company policies, procedures, or personalities.

Problem analysis. Problems are analyzed by team members, sometimes with the aid of technical specialists invited by the team to act as consultants.

Recommended solution. Team members evaluate proposed solutions to the problem and recommend the best alternative.

Management review. Team members present their recommendation to their managers in a formal presentation. Managers, in turn, review the proposed solution with other appropriate management personnel.

Management decision. After deciding to accept or reject the team's recommended solution, the managers communicate their decision directly back to the circle members. On an average, more than 80 percent of all recommendations are approved by management and are implemented. If a solution cannot be implemented as recommended, the project goes back to the team for further analysis.

Project implementation. Implementation of the approved solution is the responsibility of the quality-circle team.

Initiation of new cycle. When a project has been completed, the team identifies a new problem and repeats the quality-circle procedure. More than one project can be in process at any given time.

Quality-Circle Techniques

All members of a quality circle receive training in a variety of techniques that help them to be more effective in identifying, analyzing, and solving problems. The following techniques are commonly used:

Brainstorming. Brainstorming is a conference-leadership technique that encourages all members of the team to express ideas spontaneously and creatively without fear of censorship or criticism from other members of the group.

Cause-and-effect analysis. Team members use Pareto and Ishikawa (fishbone) charts to analyze and prioritize the causes of production problems.

Data collection. Various measuring techniques for collecting data are used as a basis for analyzing problems.

Management presentation. Circle members present project recommendations to management through the use of charts, slides, and written reports.

Quality circles do not exist in a vacuum. To function successfully, they must be viewed as part of a broader network of change media that includes processes such as JIT/VAM, work simplification, attitude surveys, performance appraisal, open-door/open-floor practices, and three-dimensional reward systems like those described in Chapter 2. When the organizational climate is right, quality circles can be a starting point for organizational change and become an important ingredient in the total process of managing improvement.

ATTITUDE SURVEYS

Attitude surveys are feedback mechanisms traditionally used by management to take the pulse of the organization as a basis for corrective action. However, as noted earlier, actions taken by management can be threatening, particularly if the employees affected by them do not understand them or if they suspect an ulterior motive. Attitude surveys, as traditionally administered, can actually lower the attitudes being measured.

However, it does not have to end up that way. Just as motion-and-time studies by industrial engineers were converted, through work simplification, into a process to enable job incumbents to manage innovation, traditional attitude surveys can be converted to processes to involve a broad cross section of the work force in creative problem solving.

The attitude survey offers four opportunities to tap the creative potential of the work force. The talents of employees can be applied (1) in designing the survey instruments, (2) in answering the questions on the survey form, (3) in analyzing survey results, and (4) in prescribing remedial-action programs. The least effective of these opportunities is the second, yet in most organizations it is the only one used.

Step 1: Designing the Survey Instrument

The subject of a survey is best introduced to the members of an organization through a face-to-face group process such as a department meeting. Department heads in an engineering company of thirteen hundred employees in eight departments introduced the subject by saying, "We believe our organization is a good one but that it can be improved. The best way to improve an organization is through the help of all its members. As a starter, we would like to find out what's right and what's wrong with our company. We need to design a survey questionnaire to get the opinions of everyone in the organization. Would each of you now spend ten or fifteen minutes, working alone or in small groups, in listing topics that you'd like to see covered by such a survey."

When employees are offered such an opportunity without guidelines, they tend to list topics related to maintenance factors such as parking lots, eating facilities, air conditioning, supervision, and coffee breaks. To obtain a better balance of questions in the engineering company, department heads explained to their employees the distinction between maintenance and motivation needs and asked them to list topics related to both maintenance and motivation issues. (See Figure A-2 for examples of maintenance and motivation needs.)

More than two thousand suggestions were collected from the eight departments. These were given to the personnel department to be collated, combined, condensed, and refined into approximately two hundred topics. These were then written in the format of a survey to facilitate rapid response and machine scoring. Figure 12-3 illustrates the format of such a questionnaire.

	Agree	?	Disagree
The hours of work here are OK.	( )	( )	( )
Favoritism is a problem in my area.	( )	( )	( )

Figure 12-3. Attitude-Survey Question

Thirteen hundred copies of the two hundred questions were printed and were distributed to all employees at the next round of department meetings. Department heads explained that the form was preliminary—that it represented an attempt by the personnel department to reduce more than two thousand items to a more manageable number. Workers were asked to review the form for important omissions and to write these oversights in the blank spaces provided. They were instructed not to complete the questionnaire but, rather, in the interest of economy, to designate the items that they would most like to see in the final form.

These preliminary forms were collected and subjected to an item analysis by the personnel department. The form was shortened according to employee preferences, and a final questionnaire of one hundred items printed for administration to the entire work force.

Step 2: Completion of the Survey Form.

At the next department meeting the final forms were distributed to all employees, who were asked to complete them at that time. Workers were told to keep the questionnaire anonymous and to drop the completed form in a slotted box provided for that purpose. Administration instructions specified that participation was voluntary and that any person not wishing to complete the form could simply drop the blank survey in the box, with the assurance that nonrespondents would also be anonymous. The time required to complete the questionnaire ranged from fifteen to twenty-five minutes.

Completed forms were forwarded to data-processing where data-entry operators were instructed to obliterate signatures or any unsolicited identifying information, on the assumption that departure from complete anonymity could ultimately inhibit candor and undermine survey validity.

In some organizations neutral outsiders (college professors or consultants) are chosen to administer the survey on the assumption that presumed neutrality would promote greater candor. Although this observation may hold true for the initial administration, the experience of participating in an anonymous company-administered survey can do much to establish a climate of trust within an organization.

Step 3: Analysis of Survey Results.

Survey results are printed in profile form by attitude category and individual item as shown in Figure 12-4. Separate profiles are shown for the company and for each department. The department profile for the previous annual survey is shown with a broken line. Each department head receives a complete set for his or her department and for the company, in the form of overhead transparencies. Department heads report the results to all employees during department meetings, candidly projecting the profiles on a screen and inviting questions and comments. Comparisons are made between departmental and organizational profiles; when surveys are admin-

istered periodically, time trends may be identified and traced. Although the candid feedback of survey results to all members of the
department is in itself an educational process, it is only a foundation
for the more action-oriented diagnostic process that follows.

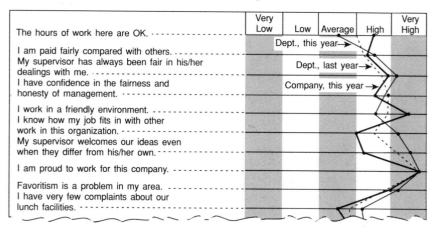

Figure 12-4. Attitude-Survey Profile

Task forces are organized in each department to analyze survey
results and to formulate remedial actions. Task forces may be nom-
inated by peers, selected by lottery, or simply chosen through supervisory judgment or with the help of union leaders. Task forces are
formed with due regard for maintaining uninterrupted productivity
while the task forces are functioning. Task forces vary in size from
two to twelve members, but five or six is usual.

The task force is given a four-point mission: (1) study survey
results and identify problems or obstacles to organizational effectiveness; (2) determine the causes of these problems; (3) prescribe
actions for dealing with these problems; and (4) identify positive
survey results and explain why these favorable conditions exist.

In dealing with the third point, task-force members are asked to
identify with management by asking themselves, "What specifically would I, as a department head, do to resolve these problems
within the constraints imposed by budgets, laws, schedules, market
conditions, quality standards, prices, and manpower availability?"
The fourth point is included to put the complete process in perspective. If the focus is placed exclusively on identifying and dealing with
obstacles and problems, task forces tend to present a negatively

distorted impression of the organization. In addition to offering a more balanced perspective, the identification of positive features in the organization calls attention to the importance of remembering them.

Task-force members have access to any information they need and are encouraged to consult their peers in carrying out their task-force assignments. Because group activities of this type are easily sidetracked and prolonged, the task-force mission is specifically limited to the four points enumerated above and is restricted to a time frame of two to four weeks. In unionized organizations it is usually desirable to sidestep collective-bargaining issues.

When task forces are formed, members are asked to choose a coordinator to schedule and chair meetings and to prepare the written report. Members of such task forces are seldom skilled in participative methods. Hence, some training is needed. Logistics usually do not permit the training of all task-force members; however, special instructions can usually be arranged for group coordinators. A half-day orientation session for task-force coordinators on conference-leadership techniques, transactional analysis, decision making, and the functioning of an effective team usually yields a high return on investment (see the discussion in Chapter 4 on effective teams). The use of the group-feedback form (Figure 4-3) enables task-force members to assess and improve on their own group effectiveness during their assignment.

Attitude-survey task forces vary considerably in terms of the number and duration of meetings required to complete the assignments. An average of five two-hour meetings over a three-week period is normal. The final report may be handwritten but is usually typed by a member of the task force or by typing services provided by the department head. A report is typically eight to ten typewritten pages but may be as long as twenty-five pages or as short as two pages. The quality of the final report is usually a reflection of the task force's proprietary interest in the project, and most such reports are meticulously prepared before submission to the department head.

Step 4: Development of Action Programs

Upon receiving the completed report from the task force, the department head shares it with other managers in his or her department.

Sometimes a managerial group will suggest a tentative action plan to be reviewed and discussed with the task force. In other cases managers and task-force members participate in joint working sessions to develop action plans. The latter approach is usually preferred because it is less likely to create or perpetuate adversarial positions.

When a course of action is agreed on, the department head shares the action plan with the balance of the work force at a department meeting. Although department meetings are typically chaired by the department head, more candid and spontaneous discussion may result if the department head turns the meeting over to the task-force coordinator, who makes the presentation and leads the discussion. The departmental feedback meeting should take place without long delays—ideally within six weeks of the administration of the questionnaire. The feedback report usually covers the following issues:

- The results of the attitude surveys;

- Remedial actions already taken or to be undertaken immediately;

- Actions deferred to some specific date; and

- Recommendations that could not be acted on and the reasons why not.

The engineering company mentioned earlier carried the action-program planning process to the top management of the company. The president scheduled twenty-five one-hour meetings in the boardroom so that each of the twenty-five task forces could have a one-hour review and planning session hosted by the president and vice presidents. Each team was accompanied by its department head as it reviewed survey results and recommended action programs. In preparation for their meetings, task forces were asked to assess each proposed change in terms of anticipated constraints, with particular emphasis on the cost of implementation and return on investment.

During this top-management review, actions were sorted into two categories—those that could be handled at the departmental level and those requiring top-management action. The departmental action programs provided continuing opportunities for operators to be involved in the implementation process.

The most important underlying principle governing the use of an attitude survey is *The survey results are not nearly so important as the process by which the survey system is developed and administered.* After completing a survey like the one just described, every member of the organization understands what an attitude survey is; how it is formulated, refined, and administered; and how the poll results are translated into action programs for improving the organization. In other words, the survey is a medium by which all members of the organization can be given access to the same data base, allowing every employee to think and act like a manager. Companies that bypass their members in the development, refinement, administration, and interpretation of surveys and in the application of resultant action programs probably realize less than 10 percent of the creative potential of the attitude-survey system.

In summary, the attitude-survey procedure, as described above, is more than just a tool for identifying problems that must be resolved or for taking the pulse of the organization. It is a system that unites people from throughout the organization in a democratic process of problem identification and resolution. Members involved in such a process acquire a new perspective on conflict resolution, a view not focused on the management-labor dichotomy or on the use of official management or union authority. Rather, such a survey procedure for sharing information and reaching consensus is but an extension of Mogensen's work-simplification principles, discussed at the beginning of Chapter 12.

INNOVATION STARTS AT THE TOP

Innovation in an organization involves more than techniques or programs: innovation is a way of life that permeates the culture of a workplace. Work-simplification and attitude surveys are merely examples of vehicles through which creativity can find expression. Effective as they are, these programs alone cannot be expected to foster creativity throughout an organization. Innovation is a phenomenon that cannot be engineered mechanically or created by edict. By definition, creativity is spontaneous and fragile. It thrives best in a climate of informality, open communications, trust, mutual respect, stimulation, and high expectations. Unfortunately, the kind of innovation that leads to the growth of giant organizations is usually quashed by the bureaucratic constraints that accompany organizational growth and aging. The secret of preserving creativity in a giant organization is to manage the company in a style that fosters self-renewal—the responsiveness and agility found in small, young organizations.

Business Week (Staff, 1978) cited Texas Instruments (TI) as an organization that was coping well with organizational growth. When TI was under the stewardship of Pat Haggerty during the 1960s and '70s, the company became a classic example of the successful management of innovation. The organization's rapid climb to prominence resulted from a network of systems designed to stimulate and manage creativity.

Under Haggerty, TI programs for managing innovation centered on the OST system (objectives, strategies, and tactical action programs). The OST plan constituted a systematically interrelated hierarchy of goals. Objectives were presented as formal statements of ten-year goals for a dozen business areas (such as materials, exploration, electronic components, and consumer products) or for intracompany staff functions (such as personnel, facilities, and marketing). Objectives were typically pursued through about sixty supporting strategies, which, in turn, were implemented through approximately 250 detailed twelve- to eighteen-month tactical action programs (TAPs). The TAPs were activated through the goal-oriented systems at the lower levels of the organization, and lower-level involvement shaped the TAPs. Strategies and TAPs were used to manage innovation in the various research, development, manufacturing, marketing, and staff-support groups. The OST pyramid created a matrix with TI's operating hierarchy of thirty-some divisions (with annual sales of $50 million to $150 million each) and more than eighty product-customer centers (with sales of $10 million to $100 million each). These divisions were often self-sufficient in that many of them had their own engineering, manufacturing, and marketing units. Each product-customer center defined its long-range mission through formal strategies and, with the participation of lower levels, recommended tactics and reported progress toward the current goal. Reports were submitted on standard TAP forms to top management for review and approval. The ratified TAP thus became a meaningful official charter that could be implemented at all levels.

Reviews of selected strategies and TAPs were presented monthly or quarterly to the office of the president or to the appropriate group or division vice president by strategy and TAP managers; these managers were, in most cases, several organizational levels below the president or reviewing officer. The presentation, which was made directly to company officers, served several vital purposes not usually satisfied in organizations. First, it circumvented the traditional multilayer, upward screening process and presented the president and other senior officers with firsthand progress reports on important projects; the reports were made by the people who were most familiar with the work being done. Second, the presentations kept top management updated on developing technologies. Third, the reports gave the project head immediate feedback, undistorted by the traditional multilayer, downward filtering process, and enabled the project leader to align his or her efforts more directly to the needs of the corporation. Finally, the recognition afforded by this process reinforced the prevailing entrepreneurial spirit at the company.

In short, the OST goal-setting model was a system for managing innovation at all levels and made possible the planning, implementation, and measurement of goals within the framework of a meaningful whole. Moreover, the system itself was an innovative process for bypassing the traditional barriers to communication, decision making, and involvement—impediments that quash innovation and undermine the corporation's ability to compete with smaller and more agile companies.

TI's Annual Planning Conference

The impact of the OST system on members of the organization is best understood by considering the subsystems that comprise it. For example, the annual planning conference at TI was far more than a traditional program for reviewing plans and approving budgets. It was a system that served at least eight important functions:

Sharing information. When two hundred managers from around the world convened at TI corporate headquarters every December, each was prepared to make a presentation lasting from ten to thirty minutes and covering three basic points: goals for the previous year; achievements during the previous year; and plans for the year ahead. This presentation of TAPs and strategies was made with visual aids, most of which reflected standardized measures of financial, technological, manufacturing, marketing, and personnel accomplishments. This information was also shared with about three hundred additional people who filled the remaining seats in the auditorium and was sent through closed-circuit television to other major plant sites. The two hundred managers who made presentations sat through the complete conference, which generally ran from Monday morning till noon on Saturday. The other thousand or so people who attended various portions of the conference provided an ever-changing audience made up of those with a need or wish to hear the presentations and resultant discussions. By the conclusion of the conference each participant had acquired a better understanding of the mosaic that comprised the total organization and appreciated how his or her contribution related to the whole.

Avoiding conflict and overlap. Each manager of a product-customer center or division enjoyed a high degree of autonomy with the understanding that each was to avoid jurisdictional conflict and wasteful overlap. For example, managers from the several plants in the European common market were expected to coordinate their strategies to avoid competing adversely with one another. If a manager activated a new system in his or her operation, the change was made with the understanding that it would not conflict with systems in other operations. During the planning conference, managers were expected to show sensitivity to this concern and to define measures by which they could avoid conflict and wasteful overlap.

Synergizing strategies. One of the greatest benefits of the planning conference was that managers could share information and form programs that were mutually beneficial. For instance, a manager in Holland faced the problem of overproduction but could not reduce his work force because of local laws. A product manager in the United States seized the opportunity to subcontract work to the Dutch manager, simultaneously enabling both to be more cost-effective in achieving their profit goals. Texas Instruments managers were expected to buy equipment and supplies from one another when the materials were available, instead of using outside vendors. If during the conference it became known that outside sources were superior or less costly, the TI source was required to explain why he or she was not competitive with the outside vendor. In addition, to deal with fluctuations in the numbers of workers required at any given time, managers at TI were expected to borrow and lend personnel to the mutual advantage of the employees and the organization. During the planning conference presentations were sometimes interrupted to discuss possible synergistic interactions.

Establishing priorities. Presentations at the planning conference were usually in the form of "decision packages" and were not finalized until all presentations had been made and priority comparisons established. Some decision packages were go/no-go proposals; others involved alternative levels of expenditure for a given project or strategy. Priorities were inevitably tied to the expected return on investment. For instance, scientists proposing a research project to develop a new product or system were expected, as part of their presentations, to indicate the probability or feasibility of making the necessary technological breakthrough; to estimate the time frame and budget required; and to designate the available market should the breakthrough materialize. Hence, the scientists' creativity went beyond the laboratory and found expression in principles of business management.

Legitimizing competition. Many organizations tend to suppress competition on the assumption that it has a divisive effect on its members. Actually, competition cannot and should not be suppressed, particularly among high achievers. An organization that succeeds in stifling competition drives away the high achievers or converts them to docile conformists. The TI planning conference was an arena in which individuals could display initiative, creativity, and accomplishments; moreover, the audience was composed of the officers on whom their careers depended. A manager, standing before the top-management superstructure of the organization, was in effect competing with company standards and with his or her peers. If average company growth is 15 percent, a 12-percent growth goal may not be impressive. On the other hand, a goal of 18 percent growth may appear laudable by company standards but may pale in comparison to a peer's goal of 22 percent. It was well known in the TI culture that the highest achievers were the ones tapped for promotions and were the recipients of higher merit increases and discretionary bonuses. The TI planning conference offered people a legitimate opportunity to compete at empire building, but always with the understanding that they could not run roughshod over their fellow goal setters.

Recognizing accomplishments. Feedback received by job incumbents in many organizations is strongly dependent on the perceptions and managerial style of the supervisor. As a result, these evaluations are not standardized or based on well-understood criteria. In contrast, the TI planning-conference participant was in effect being judged by a panel composed of peers and the top management team. The evaluation was made according to standardized criteria well understood in the company's culture. Because the participant had a major role in establishing goals and criteria of achievement, evaluations were based not only on the judgment of the supervisor but on the goal setter's own statement of accomplishments. When failures were recounted, each presenter could diagnose his or her own problems and prescribe remedial actions rather than be subjected to the indignity of admonitory advice from the boss. When outstanding achievements and examples of innovation were the subject of open discussion, recognition was amplified by the importance attached to them by the large group of high-status people in attendance. Each presenter listed the contributors to the supportive strategies or tactical action program, and because membership on project teams is based on competence, inclusion on such a list was a further form of recognition.

Developing managers. Participants in the planning conference brought to the podium the collective experience and creativity of all the people who had helped to put the company's plans together. Successful managers did not sit between the four walls of their offices and write their plans; instead, they involved their engineering, manufacturing, and marketing personnel (as well as other relevant staff members) in developing the program. After a plan was ratified, or modified and ratified, at the planning conference, the manager could go back to the people who helped put it together and share with them the final strategy, which could then be used as a framework for each department's goals and tactics. Should managers quit their jobs, they would not leave their plants leaderless, because their lieutenants, who had been continually involved, made up a cadre of experienced talent from which replacements could be drawn. Sitting through the planning conference was an educational experience, because it represented, in effect, two hundred lectures in business management. These were not theoretical presentations; they were explanations of the hard facts of managing by individuals who had earned their places at the podium through high achievement. New managers, in particular, benefited because of the experiences shared by the more seasoned presenters. Discussions of unusual circumstances or innovations broadened the perspective of the recently appointed officers. Discussions might center, for example, on the merits and disadvantages of licensing other manufacturers; on the benefits of wholly owned subsidiaries over joint-venture enterprises; on hiring custodial help rather than subcontracting; on the pros and cons of opening a plant in a particular country; on a comparative analysis of union and nonunion operations; or on the reasoning behind the opening of a new product line or the discontinuance of an old one. The planning conference endowed participants with insights not attainable through formal seminars or membership in traditional organizations.

Fostering goal orientation. Planning conferences in many organizations are show-and-tell presentations by individuals operating under an unwritten code or gentlemen's agreement not to harass one another by asking embarrassing questions. Such presentations are occasions for budget gamesmanship by which upper managers, who assume that all requests for funds have been padded, cut all budgets by 15 percent. The presenters, having anticipated this standard practice, protect themselves by padding their budgets by 15 percent. Lower-level managers go through the ritual of acquiescing to budget cuts with groans and protests and usually end up with the budgets that they expected all along. Plans that grow out of such practices are politically motivated or are the result of a preoccupation with issues of authority. The contents of these programs may have little relationship to actual operations and may reflect little sensitivity to the needs of other divisions within the organization. However, if the plans contain the right buzz words and present concepts that are known to reinforce the biases of the reviewers, the outlines will probably be accepted.

The OST system at Texas Instruments made possible a hierarchy of goals to which all presentations were related. Objectives, strategies, and tactical action programs were objectively quantifiable realities, less subject to arbitrary or capricious manipulation. Managers presented goals and strategies in which they had a proprietary interest; and the presentations were made within a framework that the officers had helped to formulate. People pursued their own goals with far more initiative and creativity than they would have given to goals foisted on them by official authority.

Because annual goal setting is a serious business, it can easily degenerate into a somber authority-oriented ritual. Planning conferences at TI, on the other hand, were often laced with levity, practical jokes, and creative humor. For instance, the head of the research laboratory once held an eighteen-inch Stillson wrench in his hand while making remarks about his new insights into motivation; a bald controller made a presentation wearing a dust mop for a wig; the labor-relations director flashed open his coat to reveal a dozen union buttons; the president bet a division director a case of whiskey that the department would not achieve its goal (but it did!); and the president gave a speech during a recession reminding long-faced managers that life at work must be fun. Informal and spontaneous expressions such as these help avoid the humorless, authoritarian orientation that can stifle the creativity of a goal-oriented person.

The TI planning conference at corporate headquarters was not the end of the process—it was the beginning. The information that managers took home from the conference represented charters on which local strategies were built. The problem-solving/goal-setting sessions by production operators, described earlier, were extensions of the charters established at the planning conference. More than 83 percent of all TI employees were organized into what they termed *people-involvement teams* that sought ways to improve their own productivity.

Mindful of the stultifying potential of formal management systems in a giant organization, TI established what they called *IDEA* programs in the early 1970s to circumvent big-company administrative constraints. An employee with an idea for process or product improvements could approach one of the forty IDEA centers and request a grant for developing the concept. If the notion was turned down by one IDEA representative, the employee could take it to another. About one-third of the ideas were accepted and funded with grants of up to $25,000 each, drawn from an annual pool of $1 million. Once a grant was made, it could not be canceled—not even by the president. About half the funded ideas paid off, and some of the big winners were spawned by the IDEA program. The entry of Texas Instruments into the digital-watch business, the subsequent development of an electronic analog watch-face, and the low-cost voice synthesizer leading to Speak & Spell and other voice devices came out of the IDEA program.

Although TI's huge expenditures for research and development and capital improvement were essential to its success, the key was the company's ability to develop a culture that welcomed and fostered innovation. The organization's success rate did much to institutionalize innovation in TI, but the prevailing culture suffered in the late 1970s with the untimely death of Pat Haggerty. The famous Compaq corporation was founded by former TI engineers who struck out on their own because of constraints in effect at the time. The important message here is that the institutionalization of a culture is not complete until it can survive the departure of its architect. However, many of TI's innovative concepts survived the loss of its founder; today several TI plants are implementing the JIT/VAM concepts described in Chapter 3.

Texas Instruments' OST system established a companywide framework on which innovative practices could be built, but it was also a framework for employee development. The following chapter focuses on the development of human resources. Because systems for managing innovation are also media for developing human resources, the management of innovation and the development of human talent are bound in a synergistic cause-and-effect relationship.

REFERENCES

Blake, R. & Mouton, J. (1968). *Corporate excellence through grid organizational development*. Houston, Texas: Gulf.

Borwick, I. (1969). Team improvement laboratory. *Personnel Journal, 48*, 18-24.

Donnelly, J.F. (1977, January-February). Participative management at work. *Harvard Business Review*, pp. 117-127.

Sloan, A.P. (1964). *My years with General Motors*. Garden City, NY: Doubleday.

Staff. (1978, September 18). Texas Instruments shows United States business how to survive in the 1980s. *Business Week*, pp. 66-76.

13

Training and Development

The development of human talent at the workplace cannot be discussed separately from the process of managing an organization. Just as learning in life results from the process of living, employee development results from being a member of an organization. When employees are managers of their own jobs, the opportunities for development are rich. If employees are robots or automatons, little development will occur.

Organizations trying to focus on the importance of people often appoint a vice president for human resources. The appointment may boomerang if the appointee is perceived by self and others as being in charge of personnel development. Overhead is increased by the recruitment of human resource specialists, who may help or hinder the development of people in the organization. If the specialists recognize that development is best accomplished through everyday job roles and relationships at the workplace, they are on the right track. However, if the focus of development is through training programs, job-enrichment projects, and attitude surveys—all administered by the personnel department—employee development may actually be impaired. Such programs have their proper role; however, the takeover by the personnel division can cause managers to assume that someone else is taking care of employee education and growth. Under these circumstances, managers may unwittingly neglect their responsibility and opportunity to enhance employee development.

Human development and organizational development are inseparable. When both are being achieved successfully, they are synergistically related. People are more highly motivated in a financially viable and self-renewing organization. Organizations, in turn, prosper if their members are highly motivated. The effective organization satisfies two basic human conditions: (1) members are free to assert themselves as individuals and (2) all individuals are united in the pursuit of common goals.

As mentioned in Chapter 12, a policy that allows people to be creative benefits both the organization and its innovative members. Thus, managing innovation is also a developmental process. The discussion of training methods later in this chapter illustrates the dual role of media in fostering innovation and personnel development.

For instance, the Texas Instruments OST system described in Chapter 12, though described as a plan for managing innovation, was simultaneously the primary vehicle for managing management development. Customers of TI, investigating the organization's management-development program, would sometimes express concern about the apparent absence of formalized training programs at the company. It was often necessary to clarify for them the uniqueness and efficacy of the TI philosophy and TI management systems and to explain how these processes were used to develop managers. Because the OST system permeated the organization so thoroughly, people in all levels and functions were influenced by it. For example, when the *plan-do-control* concept (which helped to make every employee into a manager) was first presented as part of the meaningful-work strategy at the annual planning conference in 1964, the president was quick to integrate it into the OST system and held all managers responsible for implementing the concept throughout the corporation.

Grains of Sand

The organizational media by which people are influenced, positively or negatively, are figuratively as numerous as grains of sand by the seashore. Rearranging a few granules does not alter the basic characteristics of a beach. However, a hurricane can move enough sand to give the coast a strikingly different appearance. In the same way, the countless systems within an organization give it a distinctive ambience. Rearranging a few systems will not significantly alter the climate of a company. However, if enough of the systems are modified, an organization's climate may be substantially changed—either positively or negatively.

To borrow a term from physics, each small system in an organization carries a small negative or positive *valence*. For example, an unfriendly security guard might be seen as a negative valence; a friendly guard would create a positive valence. Punching a time clock might represent a negative valence, whereas self-recording of attendance could be a positive valence. If a majority of the systems carry a positive valence, the net effect on the climate is positive, allowing people to take the few negative valences in stride. If a preponderance of the systems carry a negative valence, the critical mass is negative, causing people to be oblivious to the few positive valences. Two factors can give a system a positive or negative valence: the design of the system itself and the manner in which it is administered. For instance, time clocks and self-recorded attendance are two different systems that serve the same purpose; the behavior of the two guards illustrates contrasting styles of implementing the same system.

Figure 13-1 lists a variety of systems affecting the attitudes and perceptions of people in the workplace. The shading of the blocks in the figure indicates whether these systems are likely to find expression under each of three stages of labor relations. The labor-relation steps are summarized below and described in greater detail in Chapter 7.

Under Stage 1 conditions, in which management and labor exist as adversaries, workers have little access to systems that treat them as mature, responsible adults; for example, employees in a Stage 1 company rarely plan their own work. Instead, they are involved in systems that exact compliance. Workers at these organizations must follow instructions, perform jobs that are designed by managers, and produce according to engineered labor standards, often without feedback. In a Stage 1 company the negative valences outweigh the positive valences, causing employees to view even constructive experiences through cynical eyes. Most of the systems that give meaning to a job do not exist under Stage 1 conditions.

Under Stage 2 conditions, in which management and labor co-exist as amicable adversaries, workers are occasionally involved in activities that enable them to exercise initiative and judgment, although usually under the watchful eye of a friendly boss. Occasionally employees in Stage 2 companies are permitted to manage their own work, receive merit pay, participate on safety committees, or evaluate working conditions—activities that allow workers to begin

Stage 3—Organizational Teamwork ┐
Stage 2—Collaborative Adversary ┐
Stage 1—Win-Lose Adversary ┐

	Stage 1	Stage 2	Stage 3
Managing One's Job			
Planning	☐	▨	■
Doing	■	■	■
Controlling	☐	▨	■
Performance Review			
Evaluation	■	■	■
Feedback	☐	☐	■
Goal setting	☐	☐	■
Reporting	☐	☐	■
Compensation Systems			
Salaried status	☐	☐	■
Hourly wages	■	■	▨
Automatic pay increases	■	☐	☐
Merit pay increases	☐	▨	■
Piecework incentive	■	☐	☐
Paid suggestion plans	☐	▨	☐
Contributory benefits	☐	▨	■
Noncontributory benefits	■	☐	☐
Discretionary bonuses	☐	▨	■
Sharing plans	☐	▨	■
Co-determination of pay	☐	▨	■
Staffing Systems			
Recruiting	☐	▨	■
Interviewing	☐	☐	■
Selection	☐	☐	■
Orientation	☐	☐	■
Placement	☐	☐	■
Training	☐	▨	▨
Promotions	☐	☐	▨
Discharges	☐	☐	▨
Layoffs	☐	▨	■
Health and Safety			
Attending meetings	▨	■	■
Chairing meetings	☐	☐	■
Establishing standards	☐	☐	▨
Monitoring compliance	☐	▨	■
Investigating hazards	☐	☐	■
Recommending corrections	☐	▨	■
Report statistics	☐	☐	☐
Hosting OSHA inspectors	☐	☐	■
Receiving safety training	☐	☐	▨
Meetings and Task Forces			
Attending department meetings	▨	■	■
Receiving information	■	■	■
Attending group discussions	☐	▨	■
Influencing meeting agendas	☐	☐	■
Chairing meetings	☐	☐	▨
Participating in task forces	☐	▨	■

**Figure 13-1. Employee Roles Under
Three Stages of Labor Relations**

	Stage 1—Win-Lose Adversary	Stage 2—Collaborative Adversary	Stage 3—Organizational Teamwork
Newspapers and Bulletin Boards			
Receiving newspapers	Usually	Usually	Usually
Writing to editors	Seldom	Usually	Usually
Placing ads in newspapers	Seldom	Usually	Usually
Reporting news	Seldom	Seldom	Usually
Editing newspapers	Seldom	Seldom	Usually
Reading bulletin boards	Usually	Usually	Usually
Posting bulletins	Seldom	Seldom	Usually
Attitude Surveys			
Designing surveys	Seldom	Sometimes	Usually
Completing questionnaires	Sometimes	Usually	Usually
Receiving results	Seldom	Usually	Usually
Analyzing results	Seldom	Seldom	Usually
Preparing recommendations	Seldom	Seldom	Usually
Participating in implementation	Seldom	Seldom	Usually
Receiving implementation feedback	Seldom	Seldom	Usually
Rank-Oriented Status Symbols			
Parking	Usually	Sometimes	Seldom
Furnishings	Usually	Sometimes	Seldom
Office location	Usually	Sometimes	Seldom
Dress Code	Usually	Sometimes	Seldom
Signal bells	Usually	Sometimes	Seldom
Time clocks	Usually	Sometimes	Seldom
Pay schedules	Usually	Sometimes	Seldom
Eating facilities	Usually	Sometimes	Seldom
Coffee service	Usually	Sometimes	Seldom
Rank-coded ID badges	Usually	Sometimes	Seldom
Functional Status Symbols			
Product image	Usually	Usually	Usually
Landscaping	Usually	Usually	Usually
Architecture	Usually	Usually	Usually
Facilities maintenance	Usually	Usually	Usually
Noncoded ID badges	Seldom	Sometimes	Usually
Miscellaneous			
Access to telephones	Seldom	Sometimes	Usually
Use of computer terminal	Seldom	Sometimes	Usually
Open door	Seldom	Sometimes	Usually
Open floor	Seldom	Sometimes	Usually
Access to library	Seldom	Sometimes	Usually
PA announcements	Usually	Usually	Usually
Closed-circuit TV	Sometimes	Sometimes	Sometimes
Grievance procedure	Usually	Usually	Usually
Conflict resolution	Seldom	Sometimes	Usually

■ Usually   ▨ Sometimes   □ Seldom

Figure 13-1. Employee Roles Under Three Stages of Labor Relations (Continued)

to think like managers. Negative and positive valences tend to be rather evenly balanced at this stage.

Under Stage 3 conditions management-labor class distinctions are obliterated by a joint concern for organizational effectiveness, and people of various levels and functions pull toward common goals. Employees typically manage their own work but are coordinated by supervisors who act as advisers, consultants, and facilitators. Individuals function as teams and play an active role in influencing certain compensation and staffing systems and in managing safety programs and are seldom set apart by rank-oriented status symbols. Even when people in a Stage 3 environment are subjected to the tedium of uninspiring and restrictive responsibilities, they can take them in stride because these negative valences are outweighed by the more numerous and influential positive valences that characterize a Stage 3 climate.

Systems listed in Figure 13-1 illustrate the high potential of the workplace as a medium for facilitating the development of human resources. Stage 3 conditions provide both the systems and the environment necessary to make every employee a manager.

TRAINING

The term *training* refers to a process that is intrinsically unsound as a strategy for changing people. Most learning and growth result not from training programs but from living itself; people learn best in those life situations directed toward the attainment of personal goals. Individuals are motivated by their personal goals and will take the initiative to acquire the necessary knowledge and skills to attain them. Employees are motivated by organizational goals or other people's goals only if the attainment of those aims will in some way contribute to the satisfaction of their own goals. Beyond the subsistence level, the attainment of most personal goals leads to the satisfaction of needs for growth, achievement, responsibility, and recognition. Training, when viewed in this context, is not something that is done to people; instead, it provides incentives and opportunities to learn.

The Changing Focus of Training

The knowledge explosion, which has accelerated changes in technology and human values, has produced training programs that focus on both new skills and managerial effectiveness. Engineers and technicians, whose technological competence once lasted a lifetime, now must continually update their skills just to stay employable. Large numbers of skilled and semiskilled people are continually rendered temporarily obsolete by product and process evolution.

The philosophical underpinnings of scientific management are also changing in ways that give new meaning to managerial competence. Increasing numbers of people in business organizations react adversely to command and control supervision; these employees seek and expect opportunities to influence organizational goals and to determine methods for achieving them. Consequently, managerial training must now apply to people at every level of the work force. If all employees are to be managers of their jobs, they must be granted much of the knowledge and freedom previously reserved for top-echelon people who formerly hoarded the full burden of organizational responsibility.

A Pitfall of Paternalism

If individuals are to experience sustained growth and maturity, their learning must result from their own initiative. However, over the years, particularly in the public sector and in big industry, people have gradually been conditioned to look to organizations for guidance and support in furthering their careers. It is not uncommon to find massive training programs that routinely schedule people at all levels of the organization, from top management through semiskilled ranks, for participation in courses prescribed by someone in line or staff management.

The fault in these programs lies not so much in the content of the courses as in the source of initiative by which they are undertaken. In essence, the system undermines responsibility by conditioning people to be outer-directed and to wait for directions and cues from authority figures. It leads to dependency relationships and complacency based on the feeling that management knows what is best for employees and will see to it that they are trained and utilized effectively. The duplicity of such a system is discovered by many individuals late in life when they abruptly realize that life has passed them by and that retirement is approaching. Only then do they discover their own dereliction in abandoning responsibility and recognize their company's dereliction in encouraging them to do so. Paternalism, though often initiated through ignorance and good intentions, is an insidious trap that takes the initiative away from the individual but fails to replace it with an alternative that can satisfy long-range goals.

Learning Processes

Activities that cast participants in passive listening roles, such as films and uninterrupted lectures, are less likely to result in change than methods employing active learning techniques, such as those illustrated by the JIT/VAM processes described in Chapter 3. Effective learning opportunities are usually not canned training programs but are processes that encourage development and involve individuals in the pursuit of meaningful goals.

The Planning Process

The TI planning process described in Chapter 12 offered rich opportunities for managerial development. It not only perpetuates the development of upper and middle managers but also involves people at lower levels in defining goals, strategies, and budgets, which prepares them for advancement and determines their candidacy for promotion. Moreover, their participation in the formulation and implementation of higher-level goals provides a model for involving their natural work groups in similar problem-solving/goal-setting strategies. Planning-conference presentations of the open-forum type dispense information that enables conference participants to avoid conflict and overlap and to discover opportunities for mutual support. The open presentation, when used to evaluate whether previous aims have been met or to define new targets, places the responsibility for establishing goals and strategies and assessing achievements on the shoulders of the person who will implement the project. The presentation is a timely and original lesson on innovation in strategic planning and on creativity in the organization of resources and control processes that offer learning opportunities to conference participants.

Strategy Management

Strategy management, defined in Chapter 12 under the heading "Synergizing Strategies," provides managerial training to task-force leaders whose programs support the broad business objectives defined during the long-range planning conference. A strategy manager's competence is a function of his or her ability to identify and influence resource personnel throughout the organization regardless of their functional ties. Perhaps the most developmental aspect of the strategy manager's assignment is the requirement that human commitment must be obtained without using official authority. Because strategy teams cut across departmental lines, the power of organizational authority is not available. Hence, successful attainment of strategy goals requires the exercise of leadership skills.

Attitude Surveys

Attitude surveys, when conducted along the lines described in Chapter 12, offer a multifaceted opportunity for employee development. Management development in its broadest sense results from employee involvement in suggesting questions for the survey, refining the questionnaire, administering the survey, completing the questionnaire, interpreting the results, and translating the conclusions into applications. Unlike the traditional approach, which restricts people to completing questionnaires and receiving survey feedback, the survey described here involves employees in the total creative, diagnostic, and managerial process, enabling them to think and act like managers. Although task-force membership directly involves only a small percentage of the work force, their informal impact on the grapevine evokes the involvement of many of their peers. Hence, this program broadens the management perspective of employees and develops a greater sense of responsibility at the lower levels. In short, the process of creating and applying the survey system has far more developmental influence than do the action plans spawned by the survey. Thus, companies that hire an outside consultant to provide, administer, and interpret a questionnaire fail to realize at least 90 percent of the potential developmental value of the survey. The role of an outside consultant in connection with an attitude survey would more appropriately be to guide an organization in learning how to develop and administer surveys through the use of the company's own internal resources.

Job Posting

Job posting, described in greater detail in Chapter 6, is another example of a system with developmental potential extending beyond its original or intended purpose. Properly administered, job posting gives people the information, freedom, and incentive to take charge of their own careers. Rather than waiting around for a mentor or other authority figure to discover them and prescribe an advancement plan, they learn to be on the lookout for opportunities that fit their own unique qualifications and aspirations. Feedback from the system alerts bidders to the knowledge, skill, and experience requirements for posted jobs and thus activates employee involvement in the tuition-refund program. The developmental value of the job-posting system is proportional to its availability to all members of the organization, under ground rules that satisfy the characteristics of an effective system, as described in Chapter 6.

Work Simplification

Work simplification, described in Chapter 12, is the downward extension of planning, organizing, and control functions that enable people at lower levels to apply their talents, individually and collectively, in managing their own jobs. It replaces traditional time-and-motion study on the assumptions that: (1) most people have the creative potential necessary for improving their own jobs; (2) improvements are best made by those who perform a job; (3) self-initiated change is positively motivational, but change imposed by authority is usually resented and opposed; and (4) people satisfy social and achievement needs through cooperative work-improvement activities.

Employees learn work simplification through standardized company programs, taught by professional trainers or their own supervisors. Classroom sessions, which usually total about twenty hours, provide lessons on the principles and techniques of time-and-motion economy, flow-process charting, cost analysis, human relations, and an on-the-job project for applying newly learned techniques. Development occurring through work simplification broadens the perspective of employees to enable them to exercise initiative in the management of change and thus to perceive their jobs and the organization as if through the eyes of a responsible manager.

Problem Solving/Goal Setting

Problem-solving and goal-setting through natural work groups or quality circles, defined in Chapter 12, are an evolutionary outgrowth of work simplification and, in many respects, resembles the corporate planning model. On the production line, for example, they are initiated for specific purposes, such as reducing costs, increasing quality, and shortening schedules. They involve teams of operators, engineers, inspectors, and supervisors, who gain a better understanding of their goals and problems and their interdependent relationships in solving problems and setting goals. The process fosters collaborative relationships and responsible behavior across horizontal and vertical boundaries.

After-Hours Training Opportunities

After-hours training opportunities offered through company education-assistance programs enable individuals to assume the initiative for their own development. Employees who are pursuing specific knowledge and skills, acquiring a general education, or working toward a college degree must define their own career goals and must make commitments of time, effort, and finances in order to attain their goals. Self-initiated after-hours activities, whether in the classroom or through correspondence courses, are reinforced in an environment of promotional opportunity, as offered by the internal staffing strategy defined in Chapter 11. Apart from the doors opened by improved educational credentials, the intellectual messages received from textbooks and lectures may ultimately have a profound impact on behavior, but usually by a process so subtle and delayed that cause-and-effect relationships are difficult to establish.

Pre-employment Training

Pre-employment training is becoming increasingly necessary for bridging the gap between the requirements of technology-based organizations and the qualifications of people entering the work force. The public-education systems in America have not adapted their curricula to the changing needs of modern organizations. Many industrial organizations, in collaboration with the U.S. Department of Labor, have undertaken projects for preparing the disadvantaged for responsible job roles. For example, four hundred participants in one of Texas Instruments' contracted pre-employment programs were exposed to varied experiences designed to enable them to overcome obstacles—social, psychological, and educational skill deficiencies—that had deprived them of meaningful employment. In addition to 280 hours of remedial academic instruction and world-of-work orientation, the training plan also offered socialization opportunities provided by the pre-employment-training environment. The educational curriculum included spelling and grammar; reading fluency, comprehension, and analysis; fundamental arithmetic skills; and application of math skills to work-related problems in measurement and decimal conversions. Reading assignments and discussions encompassed history, civics, basic science, and job-related materials. The goal was to raise the minimum academic achievement level to that of the eighth grade. The world-of-work orientation covered information on getting and holding a job and moving toward advancement; on the basic economics of family budgeting; on how to use credit intelligently; and on how to understand employee benefits, taxes, and payroll deductions. People entering the work force after completing this training program were, on the average, superior to those hired through the normal selection and placement process, particularly in regard to self-responsible behavior.

Job-Skill Training

Job-skill training on the job is also placing heavy demands on organizations to overcome the shortcomings of the public educational system. Training programs that attempt to provide skills training for the organization are limited because the staff trainer usually has neither the technical background to cope with diversifying technologies nor the resources to cope with the logistical problems stemming from the combination of increasing numbers of employees, changing technologies, and geographical dispersion. Increasingly, the professional trainer's role must be that of training line people to become trainers.

Earl Weed, a professional trainer at Texas Instruments, provided a good example of this new role when he was asked by the head of a drafting department to provide a training program for sixty drafters. Weed involved the department head and his supervisors in the training-needs analysis by asking them to define the drafting skills and knowledge in which the drafters were most deficient. When the line managers had completed this preliminary analysis, Weed taught them how to write multiple-choice test questions covering the areas of deficiency. A test of approximately a hundred multiple-choice questions was developed and administered to all the drafters in the department. An item analysis of test results showed the primary areas of deficiency for the total department and specific areas for each drafter. The curriculum for the training program was designed to emphasize areas of deficiency.

In planning the training program, the search for technically qualified trainers led back to the supervisors themselves, who after being briefed on training techniques, were the people best qualified to conduct the training programs within their own departments. Upon completion of the training program, the same multiple-choice test was used again, this time to measure the success of the program. Drafters who failed to meet standards, as measured by the test, were given additional training. Not only did this training program give the drafters more valid training, but more importantly, it familiarized the supervisors with the levels of competence and talent in their department and prepared them for future trainer roles. An even better strategy would be to allow qualified drafters in the drafting department assume this training role.

Laboratory Experiences

Laboratory experiences, particularly off-site, are sometimes desirable, if for no other reason than to disengage people from cultural entrapments within the organization. Laboratory experiences take many forms but always employ some aspect of sensitivity training. Training groups may be composed of members of separate organizations (strangers), members of the same organization who are not closely related in function or chain of command (cousins), or members of natural work groups (family). The sensitivity process is guided by ground rules against the use of criticism and places the emphasis on understanding and accepting oneself and others. The trainer's role is largely one of observing and of intervening when appropriate to sensitize members to group processes. A successful laboratory generates a climate conducive to interpersonal competence—an atmosphere in which candor and spontaneity have affirming rather than threatening impacts on participants. The assumptions underlying this process are that self-understanding and self-acceptance are keys to eliminating the protective facades that prevent authentic human interaction and that the results of laboratory experiences will be transferred to the work situation to improve organizational effectiveness. In industry, laboratory experiences become more relevant to the job situation when combined with intellectual messages and goal-oriented exercises, such as the team-improvement program described in Chapter 12 and the JIT/VAM processes described in Chapter 3. Although candor or leveling may occur more easily in labs made up of strangers because of the absence of established social or authority relationships, the ideal in terms of ultimate job success is the development of compatible relationships within and between natural work groups.

Supervisory Skills

Supervisory-skills training is becoming increasingly important as rapidly changing technology-based organizations promote technically trained personnel into leadership roles. Ideally, supervisors should have at least a basic orientation in the philosophy and techniques of supervision before assuming their new supervisory roles. However, in practice this orientation is usually not undertaken until after the supervisory appointment. If not delayed too long, learning while supervising can provide a more realistic training, particularly if the new supervisor does not pretend to know all the answers and is willing to ask the operators for help.

An innovative program for training new supervisors, described later, was instituted by Earl Gomersall, a department manager at Texas Instruments, who taught operators in various departments to train new supervisors who arrived in those departments. (Gomersall

& Myers, 1966). Some of the first-line supervisory positions were filled by promotion and transfer, but approximately 60 percent of them were filled by new college graduates. The pre-employment conditioning of new supervisors (in earlier parent-child, teacher-student, or hierarchical-military relationships) caused many of these employees to approach their first supervisory jobs with the traditional notion that leaders are people with authority who can do everything their subordinates can do, only better. Because of a desire to be the infallible leader, a new supervisor understandably feels inadequate supervising large numbers of individuals, most of whom know the operations better than any recently arrived administrator. Supervisors often do not realize that operators recognize and accept the limitations of new leaders and that it is self-defeating to try to conceal deficiencies.

To help new supervisors to gain early acceptance of their limitations and to better understand their supervisory role, a plan was developed for having operators train the supervisors. Working in pairs, operators (who had received trainer training) gave the new or transferred supervisors their first orientation at the assembly line, acquainting them with the pitfalls traditionally encountered by new administrators and defining supervisory roles as perceived by the operators. This innovative approach served three basic purposes:

1. It provided supervisors with valid information directly from the people who had the most detailed knowledge of the operations.

2. It provided assurance to the operators that the supervisors were properly qualified and acquainted with employee problems. Because the operators were personally involved in the training, they were more willing to help the new supervisors to become successful.

3. Most important, it reoriented the values of the supervisors and lessened the likelihood of their drifting into authority-oriented supervisory behavior. Supervisors who, during their first experiences as leaders, learn to expect and seek information from subordinates and who discover that operators are creative and responsible are favorably conditioned or "reprogramed" to look to, and rely on, members of the work teams for assistance in solving problems.

Job Orientation

Job orientation is becoming an increasingly critical requirement as people seek to adapt to the complex systems, restrictive legislation, and rapidly changing job requirements of large organizations. Because they have no realistic expectation of being able to exercise initiative and creativity in the overwhelming environment that characterizes the new world of work, many new employees unquestioningly accept conforming roles. For many, work is expected to be unpleasant and meaningless, having value only as a source of money for buying necessities. Therefore, to say the least, creativity and self-confidence cannot be expected from people conforming to the requirements of what they perceive as an alien and sometimes threatening environment.

A CASE STUDY IN JOB ORIENTATION

Earl Gomersall at TI recognized this problem of alienation and initiated an orientation process for reducing job stress. The study (Gomersall & Myers, 1966) involved more than fourteen hundred operators who collectively performed approximately 1,850 different operations on three shifts (the most frequently replicated of these operations involved only seventy operators per shift.) All jobs placed a premium on visual acuity, eye-hand coordination, and manual dexterity. Most of the jobs in the study have been displaced by the advancement of manufacturing technology, but the applications described here can apply to any type of job or organization.

The staffing of operations required continual training: training new people hired for expansion and replacement purposes and retraining transferees and the technologically displaced. The learning curve of ball bonders, as shown in Figure 13-2, was fairly typical for production operators in the department.

Ball bonders required approximately three months to reach the competence level, at which stage they could independently perform the operation but had not achieved the speed and accuracy ultimately expected of them according to performance standards established by industrial engineering. The *competence* level would be about 85 percent of labor standards; in this department about 115 percent of standard was termed the *mastery* level.

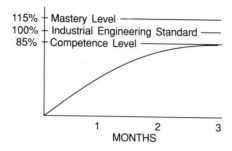

Figure 13-2. Learning Curve for Ball Bonders

In a process initially unrelated to the training effort described here, the department manager had, during the preceding year, followed a systematic schedule of interviewing individuals during the morning coffee break. The results of 135 interviews with 405 operators yielded the following facts:

- The first days on the job were anxiety provoking and disturbing;

- New-employee initiation practices by peers intensified anxiety;

- Anxiety interfered with the training process;

- Turnover of newly hired employees was caused primarily by anxiety; and

- New operators were reluctant to discuss problems with their supervisors.

Facts uncovered through these interviews underscored the impact of anxiety in inhibiting the job effectiveness of operators. It seemed obvious that anxiety dropped as competence was achieved. The relationship between the learning curve and what was believed to be the anxiety curve of operators is illustrated in Figure 13-3.

To supplement information obtained through personal interviews and to gain a better understanding of the characteristics of the anxiety to be reduced, a 92-item questionnaire was developed to measure the following possible causes of tension or anxiety: supervision; job knowledge and skill; social acceptance; physical condi-

tions; orientation; job pressure; regimentation; vocational adjustment; personal problems; financial worries; outside social factors;
and opportunities for the satisfaction of career-growth needs.

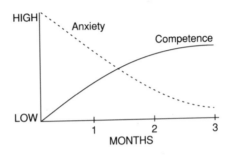

Figure 13-3. Relationship of Anxiety to Competence

Administration of this questionnaire to short-tenure and seasoned employees identified three types of tension in the job situation—the first two, harmful; and the third, potentially helpful:

1. The primary source of anxiety, mentioned previously,
   stemmed from the unpredictable, overwhelming and sometimes threatening new world of work. This anxiety was higher
   among new trainees and, according to the manager's interview results, appeared to diminish as competence was gained
   (see Figure 13-4).

2. Another type of tension, largely unrelated to job tenure, resulted from anxieties about nonjob factors such as personal
   finances, domestic problems, professional status, and outside
   social relationships.

3. The third type of tension was identified as a positive, inner-
   directed desire for constructive self-expression. This creative
   tension is the type observed in the job situation that finds
   expression after job competence is reached either in constructive job-improvement activities or counterproductive
   behavior.

Assuming the validity of the data in Figure 13-4, the manager
questioned the presumed cause-and-effect relationship between
competence and anxiety. Anxiety on the job is characteristically

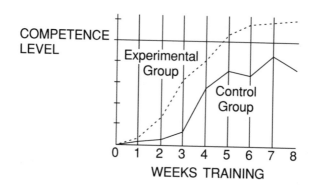

Figure 13-4. Learning Curves of Experimental and Control Groups: Ball Bonding

assumed to be the dependent variable, gradually dropping as competence is acquired. Might not the reverse be true? And if so, might it not be possible to accelerate achievement to the competence level by reducing anxiety at a faster rate? With this question in mind, he developed an orientation program to reduce the anxieties among experimental groups of new employees. Experimental groups were selected from the second shift and control groups from the first and third shifts. Precautions were taken to avoid what is called the *Hawthorne effect,* by which behavior is influenced through special attention.

Control groups went through the usual first-day orientation, which consisted of a two-hour briefing by members of the personnel department on hours of work, insurance, parking, work rules, and employee services. This session included warnings about the consequences of failing to conform to organizational expectations and, though not intended as a threat, tended to raise rather than reduce anxieties.

Following this orientation, it was customary to introduce new bonders to their friendly but very busy supervisors, who gave further orientation and job instruction. Unfortunately, the supervisors had such detailed familiarity with the operations that they often became desensitized to the lack of technical expertise among new operators. The following lecture might be typical of what the operator would hear the supervisor say:

Alice, I would like you to take the sixth yellow chair on this
assembly line, which is in front of bonding machine 14. On the left
side of your machine you will find a wiring diagram indicating
where you should bond your units. On the right-hand side of your
machine you will find a carrying tray full of 14-lead packages. Pick
up the headers, one at a time, using your 3-C tweezers and place
them on the substrate below the capillary head. Grasp the cam
actuator on the right-hand side of the machine and lower the hot
capillary over the first bonding pad indicated by the diagram. Ball
bond to the pad and, by moving the hot substrate, loop the wire to
the pin indicated by the diagram. Stitch bond to this lead, raise the
capillary, and check for pigtails. When you have completed all
leads, put the unit back in the carrying tray. Your training operator
will be around to help you with other details. Do you have any
questions?

Overwhelmed by these instructions, hoping not to offend a
polite and friendly supervisor, and afraid that they would look
stupid if they explained that they did not understand the instructions, the operators would go to their work stations and try to learn
by furtively observing nearby assemblers. However, the other operators, in pursuit of operating goals, had little time to assist the new
workers. Needless to say, the anxiety level among new employees
was increased and their learning ability was impaired. The longer
they remained unproductive, the more reluctant they were to dis-
close their wasted efforts to their supervisors and the more threatening the job situation became.

Experimental groups participated in a one-day program especially designed to overcome the anxieties not eliminated by the usual
process of job orientation. Following the two-hour orientation by the
personnel department, the new employees were isolated in a conference room before they could be initiated by their peers. They were
told that there would be no work the first day and that they should
relax, sit back, have a coke or cigarette, use the time to get acquainted
with the organization and with one another, and ask questions.
Throughout the one-day anxiety-reduction session, questions were
encouraged and answered. During this orientation the following
points were emphasized:

1. *Your opportunity to succeed is very good.* Company records
disclosed that 99.6 percent of all people hired or transferred into this

job were eventually successful at learning the necessary skills. Trainees were shown learning curves illustrating the gradual buildup of competence over the learning period. They were told five or six times during the day that all members of the group could expect to be successful on the job.

2. *Disregard "hall talk."* Trainees were told of the hazing game that old employees played—scaring newcomers with exaggerated allegations about work rules, standards, disciplinary actions, and other job factors—to make the job as frightening to the newcomers as it had been for them. To prevent these distortions by peers, the trainees were given facts about both the good and the bad aspects of the job and were told exactly what was expected of new employees. Furthermore, the basis for "hall-talk" rumors was explained. For example, rumor stated that more than one-half of the people who terminated were fired for poor performance. The interviews mentioned earlier disclosed the fact that supervisors themselves unintentionally caused this rumor by intimating to operators that voluntary terminations (those caused by marriage, pregnancy, or employees who left town) were really performance terminations. Many supervisors felt that this misinformation was a good negative incentive to pull up the low performers.

3. *Take the initiative in communication.* The new operators were told that many supervisors have a natural reluctance to be talkative and that it would be easier for the supervisors to perform well if the operators asked questions. Trainees were told that the supervisors realized that new employees would need continual instruction at first, that they would not understand technical terminology for a while, that they were expected to ask questions, and that supervisors would not consider them stupid for doing so.

4. *Get to know your supervisor.* The personality of the supervisor was described in detail. Candor was the rule. A supervisor might be described as follows:

- He is strict but friendly.
- His hobbies are fishing and ham-radio operation.

- He tends to be shy sometimes, but he really likes to talk to you if you want to talk.

- He would like you to check with him before you go on a personal break, just so he knows where you are.

Following this special day-long orientation session, members of experimental groups were introduced to their supervisors and their training operators in accordance with standard practice. Training commenced as usual, and eventually all operators were given regular production assignments.

A difference in attitude and learning rates between the two groups was apparent from the beginning of the training process. By the end of four weeks, experimental groups engaged in ball bonding were significantly outperforming control groups, as reflected in Figure 13-5.

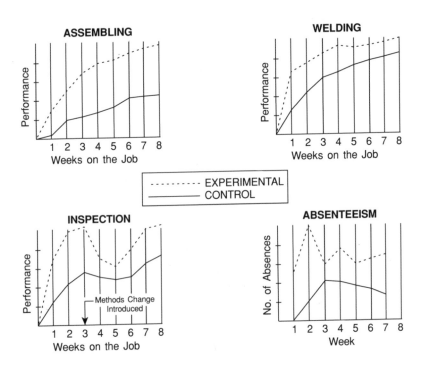

Figure 13-5. Further Comparisons of Experimental and Control Groups

Figure 13-5 shows performance curves reflecting results for over two hundred members of additional experimental and control groups for assembling, welding, and inspection, along with their absenteeism rates.

A significant effect of the new orientation program was the encouragement of upward communication. The sensitivity of the supervisors is a key ingredient of a climate conducive to natural and informal exchange of information. It was as a result of sensitizing supervisors to the importance of listening and maintaining fluid communication channels at all levels that the following incident took place:

> An operator approached a supervisor during a coffee break and casually struck up a conversation about the "units with little white specks on them that leaked after welding." The supervisor asked, "What little white specks?" The operator pointed out that almost all the units that leaked after welding had little specks on them, a fact unnoted by the supervisor before. Investigating and verifying this fact revealed that units were placed in plastic trays while still hot from a previous process; their heat caused many of them to fuse to the plastic container. Removing them from the container caused the units to pull away a small amount of plastic, thus insulating them during the welding process.

> Once this effect was discovered, the problem was solved simply by waiting until the units cooled sufficiently before placing them in the plastic trays. This single suggestion reduced rejects to less than one-fourth of their previous level for this product—a projected cost prevention of hundreds of thousands of dollars.

The point emphasized here is that casual questions and observations of the type described take place only in an atmosphere of approval and mutual respect, one in which open and fluid networking is the norm.

On the basis of increased production, reduced turnover, and decreased absenteeism and training time, annual departmental savings in excess of $50,000 were realized. Moreover, as trainees with less anxiety gradually became members of the regular work force, their attitudes began influencing the performance of the work groups they joined. The greater confidence of the new members seemed to inspire greater confidence among their peers. The higher performance of the new employees established new reference points for stimulating competitiveness, and more established employees were sometimes hard pressed to maintain a superiority margin between themselves and the newcomers. There were improvements in quality and quantity, not only among the immediate peers of the trainees but also among adjacent work groups who were influenced through the informal social system in the plant.

Operator control as a guiding principle is as important to the training of new employees as it is to the process of production. Operator control makes all employees the managers of their own jobs and the beneficiaries of a reward system that turns them into productive capitalists. These workers benefit the entire organization by taking charge of their own careers and by helping others to learn.

REFERENCES

Gomersall, E.R., & Myers, M.S. (1966, July-August). Breakthrough in on-the-job training. *Harvard Business Review*, pp. 62-72.

APPENDIX A

Theories of Human Effectiveness

Busy managers are understandably impatient with theory, expressing the view that practical matters leave little time or energy for theorizing. Few appreciate Kurt Lewin's (1969) viewpoint that there is nothing so practical as a good theory.

Theories are springboards to action and change. However, theories do not change a person's behavior unless they are translated into action. The intellectual understanding of management theory has about the same impact on a manager's supervisory style as the intellectual study of snow skiing has on teaching him or her how to ski. In either case, competence is developed primarily through application—through the acts of supervising or skiing. If people are satisfied with their styles of supervising or skiing, they have no incentive to learn new theories or to change their styles.

However, if people are dissatisfied with their performances to the point that their desire to improve exceeds their reluctance to accept assistance, they may approach the study of theory with a readiness to change. A theory will be useful to them if they can translate it into remedial action that will reward their efforts.

Some theories find immediate relevance when introduced in response to appeals for help in solving pressing problems (such as an anticipated union-organization drive, productivity improvement, or increased personnel turnover or absenteeism). Classroom experience is more relevant when actual problems are brought in for analysis and problem solving. Some theories serve a dual purpose: first as a process for identifying and diagnosing problems and then as a prescription for remedial actions. Such theories are illustrated under the Appendix-A heading "Commonality of Theories" in the descriptions of Likert's four systems, Blake's managerial grid, and Paré's power structures.

THE TRANSLATION PROCESS

A management theory is said to be translated when its application leads to desired changes in managerial behavior. The application of theory generally requires a four-step process: (1) awareness, (2) understanding, (3) commitment, and (4) new habits.

Step 1: Awareness. Awareness may result from a convincing speech, reading a book, viewing an educational film, attending a public seminar, or shoptalk. This first step may occur for managers when they gain at least a superficial insight into a new theory and recognize the implied deficiency in their present style of management.

Step 2: Understanding. Understanding is the stage beyond awareness and is reached after the manager has read books and articles on the theory and has attended training programs and lectures on the subject. This step may be thought of as an intellectual-conditioning process. The manager may talk a good line on this new theory and may be quite excited about it, but his or her managerial style usually still follows old habit patterns.

Step 3: Commitment. Commitment to change occurs when managers become aware of the discrepancy between the newly adopted theory and their own everyday behavior. However, this commitment develops only if the managers believe that they will benefit personally by changing their style of management. Initial attempts are often discouraging and, if not reinforced by some type of rewarding feedback, may gradually be discontinued. Commitment and reinforcement must be strong and continuous to overcome established patterns. Moreover, behavioral changes are often viewed with suspicion by people whose opinions of the manager were formed by long exposure to his or her previous style.

Step 4: New habits. New habits are established when sustained, deliberate applications of the new theory finally result in attitude changes and automatic and natural expressions of the desired changes in style of management. Attainment of the new habit-formation stage is a long and difficult process, requiring from five to ten years of sustained reinforcement. Some individuals never progress beyond Step 2, particularly when others in the organization are not good role models.

COMMONALITY OF THEORIES

Figure A-1 portrays twelve theories of human effectiveness, selected more to reflect variety than to be comprehensive. Each of these theories is presented on a linear scale, the left end representing conditions conducive to ineffectiveness, and the right end conditions for greater effectiveness. These scales do not reflect the full complexity of the theories or their application, nor are they intended to define the scope of their developers' professional competence. Rather, they are displayed as an aid in comprehending the commonality, as well as the uniqueness, of what might otherwise appear as a confusing and contradictory proliferation of theories. The top four theories place the focus on managerial styles or assumptions, the middle four are generally described as combinations of managerial style and management systems, and the lower four are predominantly descriptors of the impact of managerial styles and systems. The first four theories ultimately have as much impact as the middle four on systems, because managerial styles and values inevitably find expression in system design and administration.

Although the terminology and scope of these theories and their mechanisms for limiting or achieving effectiveness may differ, they have the common purpose of defining conditions that inhibit or enhance the expression of human talent. Applied in the business setting, these theories define conditions for improved goal orientation and for the reduced or more constructive use of authority. However, it should be noted that a descriptor on any given scale is not necessarily vertically aligned with synonymous terms on other scales. For example, Likert's System 1 refers to a style of management that employs exploitative use of authority, whereas Maslow's "lower-need fixation" represents a consequence of System 1 management or the environmental restrictions included in Bennis's "bureaucracy." Blake's 9,1 management style is similar to Likert's System 1 or Paré's "boss power" but is positioned to the right of these because Blake sees 1,1 as a condition of lesser effectiveness—

	INEFFECTIVENESS ◄- - - - - - - - - - - - - - - -► EFFECTIVENESS			
ROBERT BLAKE AND JANE MOUTON	**MANAGERIAL GRID**			
	1,1 Neutrality and indecision	1,9 Inadequate concern for production 5,5 Compromise, middle-of-the-road 9,1 Inadequate concern for people		9,9 Integration of resources
JAY HALL	**DECISION-MAKING GRID**			
	1,1 Decisions by default and precedent	1,9 Inadequate concern for quality decision 5,5 Decision through bargaining 9,1 Inadequate concern for commitment		9,9 Adequate concern for commitment and quality decisions
RENSIS LIKERT	SYSTEM 1 Exploitative authoritative	SYSTEM 2 Benevolent authoritative	SYSTEM 3 Consultative	SYSTEM 4 Participative group
DOUGLAS McGREGOR	THEORY X Reductive assumptions		THEORY Y Developmental assumptions	
CHRIS ARGYRIS	AUTOCRATIC RELATIONSHIPS Conflict and conformity; alienation		AUTHENTIC RELATIONSHIPS Interpersonal and technical competence; commitment	
WARREN BENNIS	BUREAUCRACY Authoritarian, restrictive management structure		DEMOCRACY Goal-oriented, adaptive management structure	
FREDERICK HERZBERG	◄- - - - - - ENVIRONMENTAL COMFORT Hygiene seeking -	MEANINGFUL WORK - Motivation seeking - - - -►		
JOHN PARÉ	BOSS POWER—Direction and control by authority SYSTEM POWER—Bureaucratic controls PEER POWER—Social pressure of group		GOAL POWER— Self-alignment with organizational goals	
ERICH FROMM	ESCAPE FROM FREEDOM Conformity, domination, destructiveness		FREEDOM Self-reliance, spontaneity, responsible behavior	
WILLIAM GLASSER	AVOIDANCE OF REALITY Maladjustment		COPING WITH REALITY Responsible behavior	
ABRAHAM MASLOW	LOWER-NEED FIXATION Halted growth		SELF-ACTUALIZATION Realizing potential	
DAVID McCLELLAND	LOW *n*ACH More interested in things like affiliation, security, money, possessions		HIGH *n*ACH Achievement its own primary reward, high challenges, moderate risks, independence	

Right-side vertical labels: MANAGERIAL STYLES · MANAGERIAL STYLES & SYSTEMS · RESULTS OF STYLES & SYSTEMS

Figure A-1. Theories of Human Effectiveness

something of a syndrome of disengagement or security seeking similar to that described in Fromm's *Escape from Freedom* (1941).

Robert Blake and Jane Mouton (1968) defined organizational effectiveness in terms of two coordinates of a grid, numbered from 1 to 9, showing the manager's concern for the human factor on the ordinate and his or her concern for production on the abscissa. Ideal 9,9 managers have strong and integrated concern for production and human needs. The 1,1 managers, at the other extreme, are disengaged from responsibility, and their behavior is typified by neutrality, conformity, and indecision. The 1,9 manager will subordinate organizational goals to human needs, while the 9,1 manager will drive for attainment of organizational goals at the expense of human resources. The 5,5 managers compromise their positions to balance the conflicting and fluctuating demands of commitment and authority.

Hall, O'Leary, and Williams (1964) described group effectiveness as a function of the decision maker's concern for the adequacy of the decision and his or her concern for the commitment of others to the decision. The mix of the group leader's concern is plotted on a grid, the ordinate denoting concern with commitment and the abscissa indicating concern with decision adequacy. Traditional decision making often presumes the pursuit of high commitment to be incompatible with decision excellence, requiring bargaining and compromise. Capitulation may take the form of a traditional 5,5 majority decision; a 1,9 good-neighbor decision; a 9,1 leader-knows-best decision; or (the worst result) a 1,1 acquiescence-to-a-default decision. The ideal 9,9 decision maker assumes that better decisions can be reached if all resources available in the group are utilized and strives to achieve both high commitment and the best decision.

Rensis Likert (1967) described managerial style in terms of four systems. System 1, *exploitative authoritative,* refers to a process that uses authority and coercion, with little concern for human needs. System 1 found common expression in the management-prerogative era of the nineteenth century and lingers as the dominant style of some managers today. System 2, *benevolent authoritative,* found accelerated acceptance with the Hawthorne studies (Mayo, 1933), which revealed, among other things, that people respond positively to attention and to expressions of interest in their welfare. Early human resource training efforts put a veneer over System 1, resulting in System 2, with its paternalism and increased benefits. System 3, *consultative*, evolved gradually as managers learned that people were more likely to support what they helped to create. Although participation sometimes emerged as manipulation and although management retained its prerogative of accepting or rejecting suggestions, at least people had increased opportunities to be heard. System 4, *participative group*, is presented as an ideal model, in which the influence of talent or competence, rather than the influence of authority, provides the basis for achieving organizational goals. System 4 is based on the assumption that people's initiative, creativity, and responsibility find constructive expression if they have access to information and the opportunity to solve problems and set goals.

Douglas McGregor's classic theory (1967) held that a manager's style of managing reflects his or her assumptions about people. The Theory X, or reductive, manager assumes that people need authority and coercion to motivate them, that satisfactory performance can be assured only through ordering and forbidding—that most people avoid work, shun responsibility, require definition of job goals, must be subjected to close control, and will misuse freedom. The Theory X manager thinks that employees should be rewarded for their successes and punished for their mistakes. The Theory Y, or developmental, manager assumes that people prefer to discipline themselves through self-direction and self-control. He or she believes that workers respond better to challenges than to authority, that people seek responsibility, and that under the right conditions they can enjoy work. These managers assume that if company officers have high expectations regarding their employees and at the same time allow job incumbents a broad range of goal-setting opportunities, the result will be higher aspirations and greater achievements. The Theory Y manager assumes that the freedom to exercise independence and to learn from mistakes is a necessary condition for responsible behavior and growth.

Chris Argyris (1964, 1965) defined *interpersonal and technical competence* and *internal commitment* as the key ingredients of organizational effectiveness. Technical and interpersonal competence are fostered by authentic relationships, high but realistic expectations, meaningful work, freedom to act, accountability, and goal-oriented team action. These conditions, in turn, can be significantly influenced by organizational relationships and administrative control systems.

Warren Bennis (1966) defined conditions for human effectiveness in terms of the organization's governing systems. *Bureaucracy* tends to quash initiative through its enmeshing network of complex, inflexible, and restrictive rules and systems. *Democracy* is inevitable for the successful organization, because it enables people to give expression to their talents in defining and achieving synergistic organizational-personal goals in a climate of goal-oriented supervision and adaptive and flexible systems.

Frederick Herzberg (1966) held that people's lower-order needs and higher-order needs do not operate on a single continuum. The satisfaction of *hygiene*, or lower-order needs, has only fleeting motivational value. However, motivational or self-actualization needs operate somewhat independently and have the potential for motivating people beyond the level attainable by hygiene satisfiers. Meaningless work that offers limited opportunity for the expression of talent may result in hygiene seeking. On the other hand, meaningful work that offers opportunities for growth, advancement, responsibility, achievement, and recognition inspires motivation and tends to desensitize people to their hygiene needs.

John Paré (1968) showed that the source of power is a key factor in limiting or enhancing human effectiveness. *Boss power* refers to the use of authority presumed to be associated with level or status in the organization, traditionally an expression of "management's prerogative." *System power* is expressed through controls imposed by management systems and procedures and, at its worst, represents networks of bureaucratic restrictions. *Peer power* is the influence of associates and springs largely from affiliation needs, which may emphasize the goals and needs of the group over the welfare of the organization. *Goal power* refers to the attraction of meaningful goals that offer an opportunity for simultaneously satisfying individual and organizational needs.

Erich Fromm (1941) described human effectiveness in terms of the ability of people to cope with freedom. If an individual during maturation is granted as much freedom, respect, and responsibility as he or she can handle, that person can emerge as a self-reliant, spontaneous, and responsible adult. If the severing of the apron string is coordinated with the individual's naturally unfolding growth and independence needs, that person is likely to attain autonomy and freedom. However, individuals who have been conditioned to dependency relationships and who have learned to associate security and love with the use of authority find freedom frightening after leaving home and seek substitute apron strings. The inability of these people to cope constructively with authority and autonomy attracts them to patterns of conformity, manipulation, and destructiveness.

William Glasser's *reality therapy* (1965) defined human effectiveness as a function of ability to get involved with others in responsible relationships and, through this involvement, to learn to cope effectively with reality. People in an environment in which their talents can be used and in which they are accountable for their conduct tend to develop patterns of responsible behavior. Maladjustment is a manifestation of escape from reality brought about by irresponsible social, authority, and work relationships. Unlike traditional psychoanalytic theory, reality therapy does not require the probing of the subconscious past. Rather, it helps the individual to face reality and to accept the responsibility for satisfying his or her own needs through responsible role relationships that do not deprive others of need fulfillment.

Abraham Maslow (1968) defined human effectiveness as a function of matching man's opportunities with the appropriate position on his *hierarchy of needs*, enabling humankind to progress upward. Primeval people, for example, were concerned with lower-order needs: survival, reproduction, finding food and shelter, and escaping the hazards of a dangerous environment. As early people were able to satisfy these physical needs, their status and social needs assumed relatively greater importance. In modern societies of increasing affluence, human beings are increasingly concerned with prepotent higher-order needs for growth, achievement, responsibility, and recognition. Thwarted self-actualization needs result in lower-need fixation and halted growth. However, people who have opportunities to utilize their talents are more likely to realize their potential—mentally, emotionally, and aesthetically.

David McClelland (1961) identified achievement motivation as a primary expression of human effectiveness. People who have a high need for achievement (*n* Ach) thrive on the freedom to pursue challenging goals involving manageable risks. The primary reward for these people is the satisfaction of a job well done. People with low *n* Ach are more interested in other things, such as peer acceptance, security, money, and material possessions and are more inclined to avoid all risks or to undertake unjustifiably high risks.

Although *n* Ach varies among individuals, it is situational in that a person's *n* Ach may differ with his or her various roles. Furthermore, *n* Ach can be developed and is often a function of cultural norms.

APPLICATION OF THEORIES

The application of management theory in a business organization generally begins with a Step 2 intellectual conditioning experience to prepare managers for the Step 3 translation process. Motivation seminars conducted at Texas Instruments in the 1960s and subsequently applied to other organizations are based on the motivation-maintenance theory in combination with other concepts and illustrate the intellectual conditioning process. Such seminars define media in the workplace for satisfying the needs illustrated in Figure A-2.

Maintenance needs are synonymous with Maslow's lower-order needs or Herzberg's hygiene needs. The term *maintenance* is used to denote the fact that people, like buildings and machines, must be maintained. Motivation needs, synonymous with Maslow's higher-order self-actualization needs, are being satisfied when people develop their potential through the pursuit of meaningful goals.

Maintenance Needs

The maintenance needs of people at work are similar whether the individual is a machine operator, a vice president, a middle manager, a technician, or a secretary. Although the maintenance of people is not the key to motivation in a business organization, it is usually a prerequisite for fuller motivation. The same needs apply to individuals outside of industrial organizations—people such as homemakers, police officers, members of the clergy, schoolteachers, and students. All require the satisfaction of their maintenance needs, defined here in terms of economic, social, and physical factors and issues of security, orientation, and status.

Economic. Economic maintenance needs involve wages, salaries, and benefits received almost automatically by virtue of simply being on the job. Economic maintenance needs are satisfied primarily through individual monetary systems that are not based on merit.

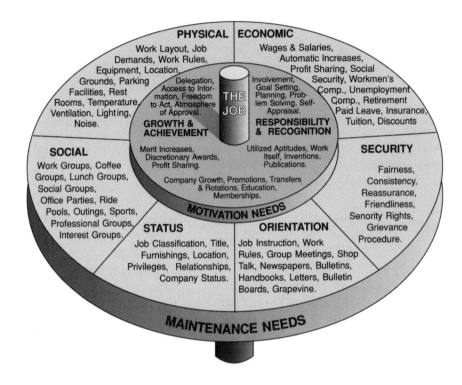

From M.S. Myers, "Who Are Your Motivated Workers?," *Harvard Business Review,* January-February, 1964, p. 86. Used by permission.

Figure A-2. Employee Needs: Maintenance and Motivational

Security. Security maintenance needs refer to the feelings evoked when people work in a managerial climate of impartiality, predictability, supportiveness and friendliness—a climate in which they believe that they will be treated fairly.

Orientation. Orientation maintenance needs are satisfied by having ready access to information about the company and the job. This information may come from supervision, printed media, or through the informal grapevine that exists in every organization.

Status. Status maintenance needs are generally satisfied through job classification, employee title, office location, furnishings, privileges, organizational relationships, and the company or product image. The process of acquiring status is related to the motivation factors of growth and achievement (discussed later), but the possession of status or symbols is largely a maintenance issue.

Social. Social maintenance needs are satisfied through formal or informal joint activities in work groups, lunch groups, coffee groups, and ride pools or during after-hours recreational activities.

Physical. Physical maintenance needs are satisfied through acceptable work layouts, parking facilities, air conditioning, lighting, rest rooms, eating facilities, noise levels, and other physical conditions.

When lower-order needs are maintained at adequate levels, dissatisfactions stemming from them are minimized. However, the maintenance factors in these six categories have only fleeting value as motivators. For example, when a manufacturing facility was newly air-conditioned, the enthusiastic response during the first week seemed like motivation. However, within two weeks, enthusiasm dwindled to a level that could only be called the absence of dissatisfaction with air conditioning. When the air-conditioning system failed, the response was immediate dissatisfaction, vociferous complaints, and lowered production. When the system was repaired, building occupants were not motivated; they merely returned to the state described as an absence of dissatisfaction. Their typical comments to the repairmen were "What took you so long?" and "Why did you let the air-conditioning go out?" Once employees have built air-conditioning into their expectations, their feelings about it can only go downward. Maintenance factors are characterized by their inability to inspire excitement when added but by their ability to incite strong negative reaction when removed.

Maintenance factors are usually peripheral to the job, because they are more directly related to the environment than to work itself. For the most part they are group-administered, customarily by staff personnel, and their success usually depends on their being applied uniformly and equitably throughout the organization.

Managers may find perplexing the ingratitude of employees toward maintenance factors such as the Christmas turkey, free coffee, and other expressions of well-intentioned paternalism. Company officers are particularly disillusioned when these "jelly beans," or unearned rewards, become the subject of collective bargaining and are then perpetuated as rights of labor (see Chapter 2). However, not all the items in the outer circle of Figure A-2 are jelly beans. Jelly beans are unearned rewards such as the Christmas turkey or free coffee and do not include earned rewards such as profit sharing or tuition refunds.

Since the turn of the century, benefits have increased in cost from less than 5 percent of the payroll budget to more than 30 percent. The greater their proliferation, the greater their potential for causing dissatisfaction. However, it would be an oversimplification to suggest that maintenance factors serve only to increase discontent or that they are the primary source of dissatisfaction.

Maintenance factors serve a necessary function that can be appreciated only in historical perspective. During the era ending in the early decades of the twentieth century, workers lived in a world of management prerogatives and could be hired and fired at whim. They lived and worked in substandard conditions and received substandard wages. However, over the years, four primary influences brought about what John Kenneth Galbraith (1958) called "the affluent society":

1. The intervention of labor unions, which forced the sharing of company success;

2. Labor legislation, which established standards for wages, hours, and working conditions;

3. Mass production technology, which priced automobiles, washing machines, refrigerators, and other consumer products within the reach of increasingly higher percentages of the population; and

4. Legislation creating free and mandatory education for children of all Americans, including immigrants.

Maintenance factors include wages, hours, and working conditions, all of which have been the focus of collective bargaining for many years. The emphasis on maintenance factors by unions raises a question about the future role of labor unions and their ability to survive through a continuing strategy based on satisfying lower-order needs. Life in an affluent society in which maintenance needs are satisfied would seem to preclude the need for unions that restrict their concerns to lower-order needs. Because people's requirements change, moving upward as lower needs are satisfied, employees in increasing numbers are failing to experience the satisfaction previously derived from improved maintenance factors and are aimlessly seeking, with mingled hope and despair, something more meaningful than comfortable working conditions and routine work. The union's role has gradually, subtly, and inadvertently shifted; the union is no longer a defender of the exploited but a medium for displacing the aggression stemming from thwarted motivation needs. In short, traditional union strategy tends to develop what might be called *maintenance seekers.*

Motivation Needs

The most constructive outlet for these frustrations in the business organization is upward through Maslow's hierarchy of needs to opportunities for self-actualization and for the satisfaction of motivation needs, providing growth, achievement, responsibility, and recognition (see the inner circle of Figure A-2).

Growth. Growth, in this context, refers to mental growth. Although physical growth generally levels off before age twenty, mental growth may continue throughout the life span of the individual. Factors associated with the continuing growth or obsolescence of managers are detailed in Chapter 9. One of the most effective antidotes to mental stagnation and vocational obsolescence is a challenging job.

Achievement. This term refers to the need for achievement (*n* Ach) that McClelland (1961) has shown to be a key motive when it can find expression. Individuals differ from one another in their need for achievement, and a given individual's level of achievement will vary with his or her opportunity to find expression for it. When jobs offer little opportunity for satisfying achievement needs, high achievers seek outlets for their talents within or outside the organization. Jobs rich in opportunities for growth and achievement attract and retain high achievers. Low *n* Ach people in such an environment may develop *n* Ach through the multiple influences of peer pressure, a challenging role, and image emulation. By the same token, jobs that are not challenging tend to attract and retain low achievers whose needs are satisfied largely through maintenance factors such as security, benefits, affiliation, and comfortable surroundings.

Responsibility. Responsibility refers to a sense of commitment to a worthwhile job. It has long been recognized that a sense of responsibility is a function of an employee's level in the organization; people high in management generally have a proportionally higher sense of responsibility than people at lower levels have. A study of factors relating to the motivation of managers at Texas Instruments (Myers, 1966) demonstrated this relationship, but it also revealed that the level of motivation was more strongly related to the style of supervision than it was to the employee's level in the organization. Figure A-3 shows the relationship between the level of motivation, the management level of the employee, and the boss's style of supervision. The levels of motivation were based on the scores by which 1,344 managers rated their jobs in terms of factors such as challenge, interest, utilization of talent, freedom to act, sense of achievement, and personal growth. Upper management consisted of the president and the two levels below him, lower management of first- and second-level supervision, and middle management of the levels in between. The boss's style was measured in terms of descriptions provided by subordinates—"developmental" and "reductive" being synonymous with McGregor's Theory Y and Theory X, respectively, and "traditional" representing a middle ground. Hence, a person's sense of commitment or responsibility is often a function of the style of supervision of his or her boss.

Recognition. Recognition, as a motivation need, refers to earned recognition stemming from meritorious performance. Unearned recognition or friendliness, defined in the outer circle of Figure A-2 as a condition of security, is for keeping communication channels open so that when vital issues arise, they can be surfaced and dealt with. However, as the inner circle of Figure A-2 illustrates, recognition as positive feedback for a job well done is a reinforcement of motivated behavior. Recognition is granted in the form of positive reinforcements such as praise, greater responsibility, advancements, respect, awards, pay increases, and other rewards. Many forms of recognition depend on the value judgments of managers, placing an often unjustified faith in the objectivity, reliability, sensitivity, attentiveness, and competence of the judges and fostering dependency relationships.

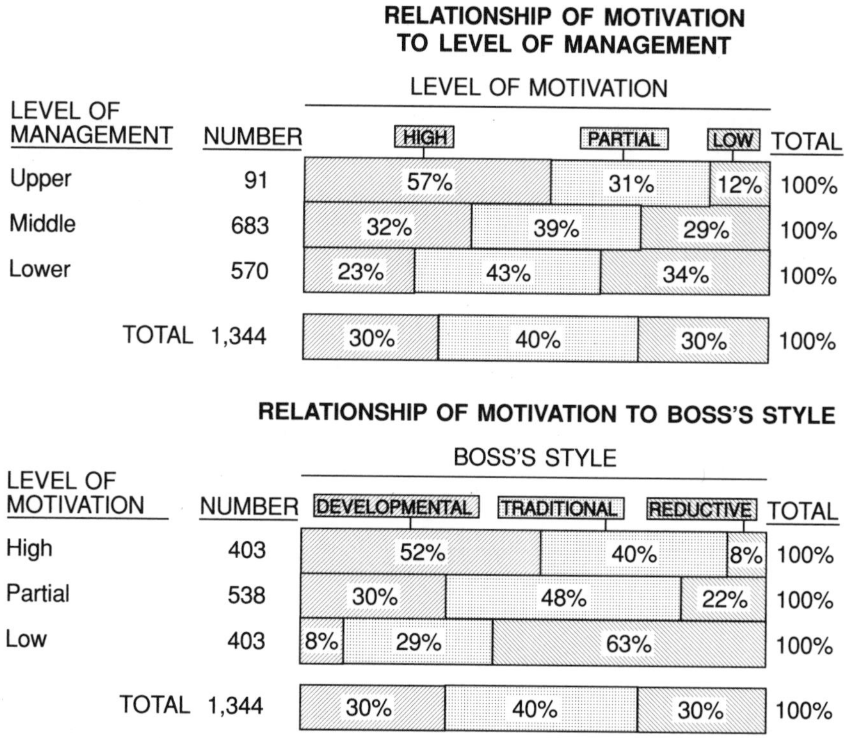

**RELATIONSHIP OF MOTIVATION
TO LEVEL OF MANAGEMENT**

LEVEL OF MOTIVATION

LEVEL OF MANAGEMENT	NUMBER	HIGH	PARTIAL	LOW	TOTAL
Upper	91	57%	31%	12%	100%
Middle	683	32%	39%	29%	100%
Lower	570	23%	43%	34%	100%
TOTAL	1,344	30%	40%	30%	100%

RELATIONSHIP OF MOTIVATION TO BOSS'S STYLE

BOSS'S STYLE

LEVEL OF MOTIVATION	NUMBER	DEVELOPMENTAL	TRADITIONAL	REDUCTIVE	TOTAL
High	403	52%	40%	8%	100%
Partial	538	30%	48%	22%	100%
Low	403	8% 29%	63%		100%
TOTAL	1,344	30%	40%	30%	100%

**Figure A-3. Motivation Related to Organizational
Level and Style of Supervision**

Ideally, recognition should not depend on an intermediary but should be a natural expression of feedback from achievement itself. When Olympic athletes compete or when scientists make medical breakthroughs, they do not need a supervisor to give them recognition. They receive feedback naturally and spontaneously, and the quality of this feedback is often reduced by the interpretation of an intermediary. Recognition at its best is primarily an expression of direct feedback.

Although achievement and responsibility may be their own rewards, they too are reinforced when recognition is granted by someone on whom the employee depends for continuing opportunities. If a supervisor's authority can provide those opportunities and if his or her judgment assures an equitable relationship between accomplishments and rewards, then the supervisor's expressed feelings are a constructive part of the feedback.

Figure A-2 suggests that only work itself offers motivational opportunities. Although the task for which the person was hired usually has the greatest potential for satisfying motivation needs, certain media in the outer circle, such as company newspapers, attitude surveys, and recreational activities, also provide outlets for the constructive expression of talent in the workplace. This observation is true, however, only if employees play an active role in administering these programs. Moreover, worker involvement in a variety of administrative matters narrows the perceptual gap that characteristically polarizes management and labor.

The Need for Balance

The relative importance of the six maintenance needs and the four motivation needs is situational, as can readily be seen in everyday situations. Poor air-conditioning, for example, as a physical maintenance factor, may loom as the most important problem if it is the main source of current dissatisfaction. However, once the air-conditioning or noise-level problem is solved, other factors may assume greater importance. If organizational stagnation stymies opportunities for development, growth needs assume greater importance. However, thwarted growth needs are often unwittingly expressed as an amplified concern for maintenance factors. Increasingly, the real problem of people at work is the lack of inner-circle opportunities, though outer-circle factors linger as the issue of conflict and collective bargaining. Both maintenance and motivational needs must be satisfied, not so that one can replace the other but in order to provide a better balance between the two.

People in the upper levels of management have relatively more opportunity to satisfy inner-circle needs than do lower-level employees, but upper-level managers devote much of their effort when coping with labor problems to addressing the frustration of lower-level people who want to get into the inner circle. Management's mission must be to move employees into that inner ring, not because managers are altruistic missionaries for participation, but because in the pursuit of organizational goals, practical business managers should provide outlets for human talent.

Further Examples of Theory Application

The application of a theory has the potential for changing a person in four ways: (1) an individual can discover and accept the fact that he or she has a problem; (2) attempting to apply a theory can provide insights and procedures for diagnosing the problem; (3) a theory can provide a frame of reference and a systematic approach for taking remedial actions; (4) the attempt at application can enable an individual to measure his or her progress. Innovative approaches for applying a theory are unlimited. The examples below serve simply to illustrate four separate and potentially successful processes.

Management Assumptions and Styles. Many training programs have based management-development efforts on McGregor's Theory X and Theory Y concepts (summarized in Chapter 4). Figures A-4 and A-5 are work sheets that enable individuals to define their own assumptions about people and to describe their supervisors' styles of managing. In completing the statements about his or her assumptions, the supervisor is able to determine where he or she falls on the Theory-X/Theory-Y continuum. The system is limited by its brevity and by the deliberate or subconscious desire of people to provide answers they think are correct rather than answers that describe their actual assumptions. The supervisory-style work sheet, particularly if completed by subordinates, can be used as a validity check on a supervisor's own self-defined assumptions. Use of these two work sheets helps to illustrate the interdependence of values and behavior as well as the distinction between them.

Organizational Profiles. Rensis Likert's four systems are translated into meaningful exercises by a profiling process illustrated in abbreviated form in Figure A-6. Individuals or groups may collaborate in completing this questionnaire by consensus or averages and by diagnosing the organization in terms of leadership, motivation, communication, decisions, goals, and control processes. Typically, the members of a group will profile both the actual pattern and the ideal pattern for their organization. The difference between the actual and the ideal represents the challenge or goal to be undertaken within the organization; the goal can be met through the appropriate mix of individuals, levels, and functions. Participation in the problem-solving task forces results in the development of remedial strategies and a commitment to their implementation. The comparison of current conditions and previous profiles provides the system user with feedback on the success of the remedial actions.

The statements below, arranged in pairs, represent assumptions about people. Assign a weight from 0 to 10 to each statement to show the relative strength of your belief in the statements in each pair. The points assigned for each pair must in each case total 10.

1. (a) It is only human nature for people to do as little work as they can get away with. ___
   (b) When people avoid work, it is usually because their work has been deprived of its meaning. ___
   10

2. (a) If employees have access to any information they want, they tend to have better attitudes and to behave more responsibly. ___
   (b) If employees have access to more information than they need to do their immediate tasks, they will usually misuse it. ___
   10

3. (a) One problem in asking for the ideas of employees is that their perspective is too limited for their suggestions to be of much practical value. ___
   (b) Asking employees for their ideas broadens the perspective of workers and results in the development of useful suggestions. ___
   10

4. (a) If people do not use much imagination and ingenuity on the job, it is probably because relatively few people have much of either. ___
   (b) Most people are imaginative and creative but may not show it because of limitations imposed by supervision and the job. ___
   10

5. (a) People tend to raise their standards if they are accountable for their own behavior and for correcting their own mistakes. ___
   (b) People tend to lower their standards if they are not punished for their misbehavior and mistakes. ___
   10

6. (a) It is better to give people both good and bad news, because most employees want the whole story, no matter how painful it is. ___
   (b) It is better to withhold unfavorable news about business, because most employees really want to hear only the good news. ___
   10

7. (a) Because supervisors are entitled to more respect than are those below them in the organization, it weakens the prestige of supervisors if they admit that a subordinate was right and that they were wrong. ___
   (b) Because people at all levels are entitled to equal respect, the prestige of supervisors is increased when they support this principle by admitting that a subordinate was right and that they were wrong. ___
   10

8. (a) If you give people enough money, they are less likely to be concerned with intangibles such as responsibility and recognition. ___
   (b) If you give people interesting and challenging work, they are less likely to complain about things such as pay and supplemental benefits. ___
   10

9. (a) If people are allowed to set their own goals and standards of performance, they tend to set them higher than the boss would. ___
   (b) If people are allowed to set their own goals and standards of performance, they tend to set them lower than the boss would. ___
   10

10. (a) When people have more knowledge and freedom regarding their jobs, more controls are needed to keep those employees in line. ___
    (b) When people have more knowledge and freedom regarding their jobs, fewer controls are needed to ensure satisfactory job performance. ___
    10

Figure A-4. Management-Style Work Sheet: My Assumptions

The statements below, arranged in pairs, represent supervisory style. Assign a weight from 0 to 10 to each statement to show the relative accuracy of the statements in each pair as descriptions of your supervisor's style. The points assigned for each pair must in each case total 10.

1. (a) Easy to talk to, even when under pressure.
   (b) You have to pick carefully the time when you talk to him or her. ____
                                                                          ____
                                                                           10

2. (a) He or she may ask for ideas but has usually already made a decision. ____
   (b) Tries to see merit in your ideas even if they conflict with his or hers. ____
                                                                              ____
                                                                               10

3. (a) Tries to help people to understand company objectives.
   (b) Lets people figure out for themselves how company objectives apply to them. ____
                                                                                   ____
                                                                                    10

4. (a) Tries to give people access to all the information they want.
   (b) Gives people the information he or she thinks they need. ____
                                                                  ____
                                                                   10

5. (a) Tends to set people's job goals and to tell them how to achieve those goals.
   (b) Involves people in solving problems and setting job goals. ____
                                                                    ____
                                                                     10

6. (a) Tends to discourage people from trying new approaches.
   (b) Tries to encourage people to reach out in new directions. ____
                                                                   ____
                                                                    10

7. (a) Takes your mistakes in stride, as long as you learn from them.
   (b) Allows little room for mistakes, especially those that might embarrass him or her. ____
                                                                                           ____
                                                                                            10

8. (a) Tries mainly to correct mistakes and to figure out how they can be prevented in the future.
   (b) When something goes wrong, tries primarily to find out who caused the problem. ____
                                                                                       ____
                                                                                        10

9. (a) His or her expectations of subordinates tend to fluctuate.
   (b) Has consistent, high expectations of subordinates. ____
                                                            ____
                                                             10

10. (a) Expects superior performance and gives credit when you meet expectations.
    (b) Expects you to do an adequate job; does not say much unless something goes wrong. ____
                                                                                           ____
                                                                                            10

Figure A-5. Management-Style Work Sheet: My Supervisor's Style

Organizational Variables	SYSTEM 1	SYSTEM 2	SYSTEM 3	SYSTEM 4	Item No.
LEADERSHIP					
How much confidence is shown in subordinates?	None	Condescending	Substantial	Complete	1
How free do they feel to talk to superiors about job?	Not at all	Not very	Rather free	Fully free	2
Are subordinates' ideas sought and used, if worthy?	Seldom	Sometimes	Usually	Always	3
MOTIVATION					
Is predominant use made of (1) fear, (2) threats, (3) punishment, (4) rewards, (5) involvement?	1, 2, 3, occasionally 4	4, some 3	4, some 3 and 5	5, 4, based on group	4
Where is responsibility felt for achieving organization's goals?	Mostly at top	Top and middle	Fairly general	At all levels	5
How much cooperative teamwork exists?	None	Little	Some	Great deal	6
COMMUNICATION					
What is the direction of information flow?	Downward	Mostly downward	Down and up	Down, up and sideways	7
How is downward communication accepted?	With suspicion	Possibly with suspicion	With caution	With a receptive mind	8
How accurate is upward communication?	Often wrong	Censored for the boss	Limited accuracy	Accurate	9
How well do superiors know problems faced by subordinates?	Know little	Some knowledge	Quite well	Very well	10
DECISIONS					
At what level are decisions made?	Mostly at top	Policy at top, some delegation	Broad policy at top, more delegation	Throughout but well integrated	11
Are subordinates involved in decisions related to their work?	Not at all	Occasionally consulted	Generally consulted	Fully involved	12
What does decision-making process contribute to motivation?	Nothing; often weakens it	Relatively little	Some contribution	Substantial contribution	13
GOALS					
How are organizational goals established?	Orders issued	Orders, some comments invited	After discussions, by orders	By group action (except in crisis)	14
How much covert resistance to goals is present?	Strong resistance	Moderate resistance	Some resistance at times	Little or none	15
CONTROL					
How concentrated are review and control functions?	Highly at top	Relatively highly at top	Moderate delegation to lower levels	Quite widely shared	16
Is there an informal organization resisting the formal one?	Yes	Usually	Sometimes	No—same goals as formal	17
What are cost, productivity, and other control data used for?	Policing, punishment	Reward and punishment	Reward, some self-guidance	Self-guidance, problem solving	18

Figure A-6. Profile of Organizational Characteristics

Managerial Grid. Blake and Mouton's (1968) two-factor Managerial Grid®, illustrated in figure A-7, allows individuals and groups to diagnose their own managerial styles and the styles of others in terms of concern for production and people. By completing questionnaires in which they describe actual behavior and define ideal styles, individuals become focused on developing a 9,9 managerial style and strategies for the organization.

Power Structure Seminar. John Paré developed a profiling system to enable individuals and groups to diagnose the power structure within retail-store operations in terms of the four sources of power

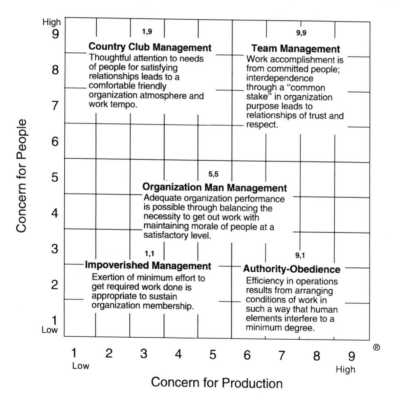

The Managerial Grid figure from *The Managerial Grid III: The Key to Leadership Excellence,* by Robert R. Blake and Jane Srygley Mouton. Houston: Gulf Publishing Company, Copyright © 1985, page 12. Reproduced by permission.

Figure A-7. The Managerial Grid

reflected in Figure A-8. After diagnosing the actual structure and concurring on optimal structure, the group then becomes involved in forming strategies for overcoming the gap between the actual and the optimal. The power-structure seminar has been highly successful in increasing organizational effectiveness in department stores, and its application illustrates a phenomenon noted in the discussion of management systems in Chapter 6. People's attitudes and perceptions are a primary cause of a system's successes and failures, and the success of the power-structure seminar in replacing other frameworks is probably as much a function of the attitudes of the users as it is of the intrinsic characteristics of the new system itself.

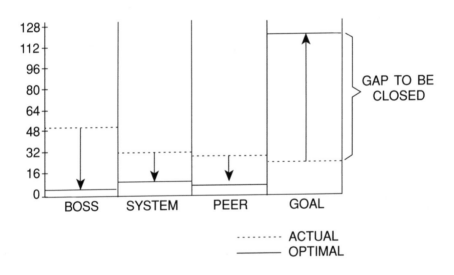

Figure A-8. Power-Structure Profile Sheet

CHANGING VALUES IN THE WORKPLACE

The foregoing discussion on relationships, goals, and systems does not recognize the rich variations in values in the workplace. Indeed, most discussions of people at work confer upon them a rather monolithic syndrome of personality characteristics that set them apart from accountants or engineers, for example, each of whom tend to be described in terms of unique personality traits. In reality, there are more similarities than there are differences among the various vocational groupings and a wide variety of differences within any given group.

Each person in the workplace has a built-in set of values that he or she uses subconsciously as a yardstick for judging himself or herself and other members of the organization. Informal relationships within peer groups are influenced by these differences. These real or imagined discrepancies have even greater impact on relationships among vocational groups. Thus, adversary relationships between management and labor may stem from a sense of social distance, which inhibits communication between the two classes. Workers may label managers as arbitrary, insensitive, and authoritarian; and managers may see workers as lazy, irresponsible, and incompetent. Managers commonly assume, for example, that one of the big differences between management and labor is that managers like their work and workers do not like theirs.

Managers sometimes marvel at the major shift in values that takes place when a worker is promoted into supervision. The promoted worker, in turn, is surprised to discover at this new level some heretofore unrecognized traits among former peers. Interpersonal conflict is a function of both value differences and class distinctions.

Progressive managers are learning to reduce the social distance created by traditional status symbols and protocol. However, these same managers have been less sensitive or responsive to the role of individual differences as the basis for conflict. Indeed, they are often intolerant of, and unable to understand, people whose values differ from their own. Supervisory problems are often symptoms of clashing value systems. A manufacturing manager expressed it this way:

> People here aren't the way they were when I was working my way up in the organization. We were here on time, put in a good day's work, and were pleased when the boss singled us out for a tough job. We seized every opportunity to work overtime and did everything we could to get ahead.

> We have very few of that type today. Their minds seem to be elsewhere and they're not as ambitious as we were. Some refuse transfers, even if the change would lead to a promotion. The other day I had to discipline one of these types for violating a safety

rule. I laid him off for three days without pay. You know what he said to me? He said, "May I have the other two days off, too?"

Most of them aren't troublemakers, exactly—they just don't seem to give a hoot for the company, their jobs, or their careers. Some of them *are* troublemakers. They are often tardy or absent and will lie, cheat, and steal. They know that we'll probably go easy on them.

This manager's lament is widely shared by peers who learned supervisory techniques through experience and through training programs strongly influenced by tradition. The problem is not restricted to business organizations but is encountered in all walks of life by parents, teachers, government officials, union leaders, athletic coaches, and others. Although some managers see these problems as symptoms of an illness in society, what the manifestations actually represent is a freer expression of disparate values.

John Gardner,[1] in recognizing the zeal with which traditional managers attempt to remold the values and life styles of nonconformists, writes:

A free society will not specify too closely the kinds of meaning different individuals will find or the things about which they should generate conviction. People differ in their goals and convictions and in the whole style of commitment. We must ask that their goals fall within the moral framework to which we all pay allegiance, but we cannot prescribe the things that will unlock their deepest motivations. Those earnest spirits who believe that a man cannot be counted worthy unless he burns with zeal for civic affairs could not be more misguided. And we are wrong when we follow the current fashion of identifying moral strength too exclusively with fighting for a cause. Nothing could be more admirable nor more appealing to a performance-minded people such as ourselves. But such an emphasis hardly does justice to the rich variety of moral excellences that man has sought and occasionally achieved in the course of history.

A good many of the most valuable people in any society will never burn with zeal for anything except the integrity and health and well-being of their own families—and if they achieve those

---

[1] From J. Gardner, *Self Renewal*. New York: Sterling Lord Literistic. Copyright 1964 by John Gardner. Used by permission of Sterling Lord Literistic.

goals, we need ask little more of them. There are other valuable members of a society who will never generate conviction about anything beyond the productive output of their hands or minds—and a sensible society will be grateful for their contributions.

Clare Graves (1970) believed that people evolve through stages of psychological existence, which are reflected in the personal values and lifestyles of the individual (Myers & Myers, 1973). Relatively independent of age and intelligence, a particular set of values can become arrested at a given level, can move to another stage, or can return to a previous level, depending on a person's cultural conditioning and on his or her responses to the opportunities and constraints in the environment. Graves referred to this framework as an open system in order to emphasize that the number of stages is not limited, though levels beyond Stage 7 have not been defined. Seven levels or stages of psychological existence are described below and illustrated in Figure A-9.

Stage 1: Reactive. The reactive stage of existence is most naturally observed in newborn babies or in people psychologically arrested in, or regressed to, infancy. Unaware of themselves or others as human beings, they simply react to hunger, thirst, fear of falling, and other basic physiological needs. Few people remain at this stage as they move through adolescence, and those few are rarely found on the payrolls of organizations.

Stage 2: Security Oriented. Most people, as a matter of course, move out of a reactive existence to a security-oriented stage. This level is characterized by concern with feelings of pain, temperature control, and safety and by a tribalistic submission to authority figures, such as supervisors, policemen, government officials, teachers, clergymen, parents, big brothers, or gang leaders. Security-oriented tribalism, in its purest form, is commonly observed in primitive cultures in which the tribal chieftain is boss and in which magic, witchcraft, ritual, superstition, and tradition play important roles.

Stage 3: Self-Oriented. Self-orientation is an overly assertive form of rugged individualism. The behavior of a self-oriented person reflects a philosophy that seems to say, "I don't care about the rest of the world; I'm for myself." He or she is characteristically unscrupulous, selfish, aggressive, restless, impulsive and, in general, not psychologically inclined to live within the constraints imposed by

Stage 7: REALITY. These employees like a job in which the goals and problems are more important than the money, prestige, or symbols of status. They prefer work of their own choosing that offers a continuing challenge and that requires imagination and initiative. To them, a good manager is one who gives them access to the information they need and who lets them do the job in their own way.

Stage 5: SUCCESS. The preferred job for this employee is varied, allows room for free choices and creativity, and offers pay and bonuses on the basis of results. These people feel responsible for their own success and are constantly on the lookout for new opportunities. A good manager for these employees understands the politics of getting the job done, knows how to bargain, and is willing to bend the rules.

Stage 3: SELF. The two major requirements of a job for this employee are that it pay well and that the manager not nag or interfere with the employee's work. People at this stage shun work that ties them down but will do it if they must in order to earn the money they want. They respond well to a tough manager but also respond to participative methods when subjected to peer pressure and the influence of respected leadership.

Stage 1: REACTIVE. This level of psychological development is restricted primarily to infants, people with serious brain deterioration, and certain psychopathic conditions. For all practical purposes, one can say that employees are not ordinarily found at Stage 1.

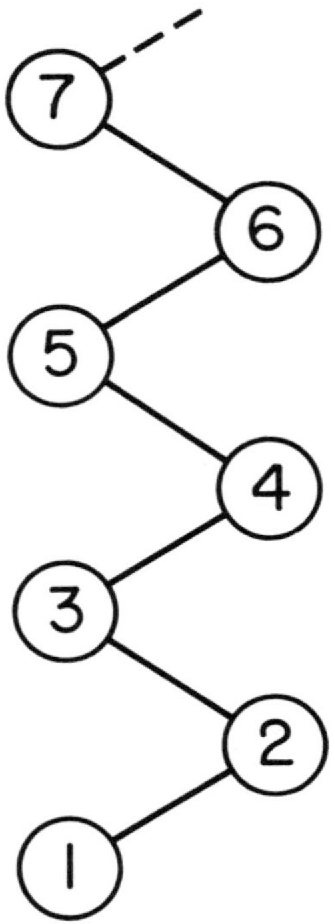

Stage 6: PEOPLE. A job that allows the development of friendly relationships within a work group appeals to these employees. Working with people toward a common goal is more important at this level than getting caught up in a materialistic rat race. These employees like a manager who fosters harmony by being more a friendly person than a boss.

Stage 4: TRADITION. These employees like job security, well-defined rules, and equal treatment. They feel entitled to rewards in exchange for loyalty. Their mode of dress and their subservience to protocol cause them to blend with the masses and to reflect a lack of individuality. They react strongly against value encroachments.

Stage 2: SECURITY. These employees require routine work, friendly co-workers, fair play, and, above all, a good manager. They like a manager who explains exactly what to do and how to do it and who encourages employees by demonstrations. Employees at this level may realize that their jobs lack status but may find them acceptable under conditions of peer solidarity and supervisory respect.

Figure A-9.   Values in the Workplace.

society's accepted moral framework. To this person, might makes right; authoritarian management seems necessary to keep him (or her) in line. Although group-management techniques may not at first seem successful with a self-oriented employee, structured participative management is sometimes effective for helping him or her to escape this egocentric mode.

Stage 4: Tradition Oriented. People at the tradition-oriented stage of existence have a low tolerance for ambiguity, difficulty in accepting people whose values differ from their own, and a need to persuade those people to change their values. The tradition-oriented individual conforms to the rules of a philosophy, cause, or religion and tends to be attracted to jobs for which the instructions are clear. Although normally docile, conformists will assert or sacrifice themselves with violence if their values are threatened. They prefer authoritarianism to autonomy but will respond to participation if it is prescribed by an accepted authority figure and if it does not violate deep-seated values. These people like specific job descriptions and procedures and have little tolerance for supervisory indecision or weakness. From the beginning of the Industrial Revolution until recently, people at this stage of psychological development have been the mainstay of the hourly work force. This value system is also frequently found in management ranks in bureaucratic organizations in which people are rewarded for perpetuating the status quo and for not "rocking the boat."

Stage 5: Success Oriented. Success orientation is the fifth stage of psychological existence. It is characterized by entrepreneurial, manipulative, or materialistic behavior. People at this stage are typically products of the Horatio Alger, rags-to-riches philosophy, striving to achieve their goals through the manipulation of people and systems. Individuals at this stage thrive on gamesmanship, politics, competition, and entrepreneurial effort. They measure their success in terms of materialistic gain and power and are inclined to prize self-earned (rather than inherited) status symbols. In the wage rolls, they may not blend well with peer groups, because success-oriented people are characterized by ambition and initiative, which tend to undermine group solidarity. In many organizations they are found at management levels, having earned promotions because of their demonstrated competence at manipulating resources.

Stage 6: People Oriented. People orientation characterizes the sixth, or sociocentric, stage of existence. These individuals have strong affiliation needs; being accepted or being perceived as a good person is often more important to them than getting ahead, the approval of peers being valued over individual fame. People-oriented individuals may be strongly religious, not because they necessarily crave ritual or dogma but because they value a spiritual attitude and are concerned with social issues. Many members of the so-called hippie movement during the 1960s and '70s were sociocentric—their shabby appearance being a symbolic rejection of the traditional company image expected by the establishment. A person at this level responds well to participative management methods but might revolt if an organizations's products or services do not serve humanitarian causes. People-oriented individuals tend to articulate their protests openly but characteristically dislike violence and counter authoritarianism with passive resistance. People at this stage are frequently perceived as "cop-outs" by people at Stages 4 and 5, and their nonconformist behavior is not generally rewarded, or even tolerated, in business organizations. As a result, individuals at this level who do not ultimately capitulate by adopting organizationally approved modes of manipulation and conformity may become organizational problems because of alcoholism, drug abuse, or other self-punitive behavior.

Stage 7: Reality Oriented. Reality-oriented or existential values characterize people at Stage 7. These individuals have a high tolerance for ambiguity and nonconformity and prefer to do jobs according to their own methods and without constraints of authority or bureaucracy. They have little tolerance for detailed job descriptions, written procedures, and the arbitrary use of power. They tend to be goal-oriented but focus on broader arenas and longer time perspectives than do people at other stages. Like employees at Level 5, they are interested in organizational profits, the quarterly review, and the annual plan; however, they are also concerned with the ten-year or fifty-year plan and with the impact of the organization on its members, on society, and on the environment. Like people in Stage 6, they are concerned with the dignity of their fellow human beings and are repelled by the use of violence. Their independent behavior, lack of interest in rank-oriented status symbols, and outspoken intolerance for constraints imposed by bureaucratic protocol are threatening to Level 4 and Level 5 managers. As a result, these individuals may be expelled from an organization because of issues of nonconformity or insubordination.

GUIDELINES FOR COMPATIBILITY

Managers often find themselves out of step with the people they supervise or the people to whom they report. Conformity behavior, once taken for granted, is no longer the norm. Not only are managers out of step but so are many of their systems. Because systems reflect the values of their designers and administrators, it is only natural to find people responding to systems as they do to the managers who created and administer them. Figure A-10 contains capsule descriptors of supervisory values, systems characteristics, and subordinate or systems-user values.

The three left columns of Figure A-10 show characteristic supervisory (S) attitudes toward subordinates at Stages 2 through 7 as they relate to the supervisory functions of performance review, communication, and career planning. Immediately beneath each supervisory value statement at each level is shown a characteristic value statement for the supervised employee (E) at that stage. Stage 1 responses are not included in the figure, because personalities at that level of development are rarely found in business organizations.

The right side of Figure A-10 contains descriptors and values relating to three personnel-management systems: compensation, attitude surveys, and job posting. At each stage is a capsule descriptor of the system as it might characteristically be conceived by a system designer (S) at that stage of psychological existence. Immediately beneath each system-designer viewpoint is summarized an attitude toward the system as it might characteristically be expressed by an employee (E) at that stage of existence.

This chart identifies conditions of compatibility and conflict within the organization. For example, under the category labeled *communication* relationships, the Level 7 supervisor's view ("We discuss things informally, and I give them access to any information they want") is compatible with the needs of the people he or she supervises who are in Levels 7, 6, and 5:

		SUPERVISION			SYSTEMS		
		PERFORMANCE REVIEW	COMMUNICATION	CAREER PLANNING	COMPENSATION	ATTITUDE SURVEY	JOB POSTING
7	S	We work together in setting goals and reviewing progress.	We discuss things informally, and I give them access to any information they want.	Self-development is the key; people should have the opportunity to plan their own careers.	A smorgasbord approach that rewards merit and adapts to individual needs.	A democratic process involving all people in analyzing problems and suggesting improvements.	A system for maximizing organizational effectiveness by encouraging the natural flow of talent.
	E	I like to have a major role in defining my goals and methods for achieving them.	I like to feel free to talk to anyone in order to get the information I want.	I am responsible for my own career and require the opportunity to develop my capabilities.	A good system rewards merit and doesn't tie you to the organization.	Greater commitment and solidarity are achieved when people have a hand in solving problems.	Now that I know what the openings and requirements are, I can run my own maze.
6	S	I try to review employees without hurting their feelings.	I want to be on good terms with them so they will feel they can discuss anything with me.	Every career should include the ingredients of social and civic responsibility.	Pay and benefits tailored to the needs of the people and their circumstances.	A vehicle for diagnosing and solving human problems.	A system providing opportunity for employees to find compatible work groups and supervisors.
	E	The manager should use this occasion to get better acquainted with us.	The manager is easy to talk to and is interested in us personally.	Our careers should be oriented toward bettering relationships among all people.	Money should serve all people and should be more equitably distributed.	Working with others in analyzing survey results is a good way to improve human relations.	I like being able to find a job where the people and work don't clash with my values.
5	S	I find that the carrot and stick work best.	I give them the information I think they need to get the job done.	I keep track of their progress and specify developmental programs and assignments.	Distribution of money according to amount of responsibility and level or performance.	A management tool for taking the pulse of an organization.	A controlled, competitive system to upgrade the best emloyees into company job openings.
	E	I like to set my own goals and get recognition for achieving them.	If I am to do a good job, I need to know everything my boss knows.	My career depends on my taking the initiative in finding opportunity for advancement.	Money is a measure of my success.	If what we learn from an attitude survey can make our employees more productive, I'm all for it.	It's one way to find advancement opportunities, but it helps to know the right people.

4	**S**	I define the goals and standards I expect them to follow.	I give them the information they should have and keep our relations businesslike.	I define their career paths and promotional opportunities and give them continuous guidance.	Compensation programs based on community and industry surveys and standard practice.	The systematic measurement of attitudes toward company goals, policies, and practices.	The orderly, systematic, and fair implementation of a promotion-from-within policy.
	E	We need to know the company goals and how we can support them.	The manager should tell us what we're supposed to know in order to do our jobs properly.	I will be promoted when I earn it through productiveness and loyalty.	Money is a reward for loyalty and hard work and should not be subject to favoritism.	Management is asking for our help, and it is our duty to answer all questions as honestly as possible.	I will be given the job I bid on if I deserve it.
3	**S**	I make clear what employees have to do if they want to keep their jobs.	I tell them whatever I feel like telling them.	Look out for yourself —don't look to me for your breaks.	Manipulative, arbitrary and secretive use of money.	Rigged questions and whitewashed reports.	Posting of jobs that cannot be filled more economically from the outside.
	E	I don't like anyone finding fault with me and telling me how to act.	The less I hear from my boss, the better.	I don't want anyone planning my life—I'll look after Number One myself.	I'll work for the highest bidder.	I don't want any part of a stool-pigeon system that can be used against me.	It's no use trying— the cards are stacked against you.
2	**S**	I tell them how I think they did and how they can improve.	I explain company rules to them and talk with them about their problems.	They expect me to tell them what to do and to take care of them.	A fair and uniform system administered by the boss.	A way of letting employees know the company is interested in their ideas.	A way of increasing job security by filling job openings from within.
	E	I want my manager to tell me whether I've done what he or she wanted me to do.	My manager tells us what to do in a friendly way and promises to help us.	What's most important is that I'll always have a steady job and a good boss.	I need steady pay to make ends meet.	My boss should know how we feel so he or she can help us.	I'll bid on a job if my supervisor tells me to.

Figure A-10. Values Reflected by People and Their Systems. S = supervisor system; E = employee.

- Level 7: "I like to feel free to talk to anyone to get the information I want."
- Level 6: "The manager is easy to talk to and is interested in us personally."
- Level 5: "If I'm to do a good job, I need to know everything my boss knows."

However, reading down the column, Levels 4, 3, and 2 are shown to have less compatible values:

- Level 4: The manager should tell us what we're supposed to know in order to do our jobs properly."
- Level 3: "The less I hear from my boss, the better."
- Level 2: "My manager tells us what to do in a friendly way and promises to help us."

Those at Levels 4 and 2 want more structure and those at Level 3 need more structure than a supervisor at Level 7 might naturally provide.

However, the actual situation in organizations is more serious than the picture of partial incompatibility reflected in the example above. Managers are typically oriented more toward Level 5 or 4 than they are to Level 7 and, consequently, encounter more conflict. For example, the Level 5 supervisor's communication philosophy ("I give them the information I think they need to get the job done") is not compatible with any level except 4 ("The manager should tell us what we're supposed to know in order to do our jobs properly"). This means that a manager at Level 5, a common type of leadership style, has little opportunity to succeed unless he or she is surrounded by conformists. This solution is ultimately self-defeating, of course, because the organization would, in the long run, be immobilized by excessive conformity.

The same phenomenon exists regarding the compatibility of people and management systems. Compensation plans, attitude surveys, and job-posting systems designed in terms of Stage 7 concepts are usually compatible with values at Stages 7, 6, and 5 and match equally well with values at Stages 4, 3, and 2. Because systems are customarily designed in terms of Stage 4 and 5 concepts, they tend to meet the requirements of Stages 2, 3, and 4 and to frustrate people at Stages 5, 6, and 7. In other words, systems in traditional organizations are more acceptable to people at the stages labeled *traditional, self,* and *security* than they are for the entrepreneurial self-starters in Stages 5, 6, and 7. Paradoxically, systems are usually designed by Level 4 conformists to curb the creative, nonconformist behavior of people at Levels 5, 6, and 7. This phenomenon stems in part from the fact that the job of systems and procedures writers is more likely to attract Level 4 conformists than any other type. Therefore, as a counterbalancing influence, a Stage 7 editor is needed to remove the unnecessary and inflexible constraints typically reflected in policy and procedure statements.

These realms of natural incompatibility can be overcome through understanding and deliberate adaptation. As mentioned earlier, psychological level is not correlated strongly with intelligence but, rather, determines the way in which intelligence is used. Hence, training programs can help supervisors and nonsupervisors at any level to understand the problem of potential incompatibility and to learn how to adapt to one another. The objective of such training programs should not be to teach supervisors to diagnose other individuals. Instead, supervisors should learn to anticipate, recognize, and understand the different value systems that they will encounter.

The new work ethic is not a new set of values; rather, it is a heterogeneity of values and a shift in the source of influence. The seven stages of psychological existence described above have existed for a long time, but for several centuries business organizations and most realms of society have been dominated by either entrepreneurs or conformists whose influence has been unchallenged until recently. For instance, the Level 4s and Level 5s of Iran, Russia, China, and South Africa are being challenged by Level 6 and Level 7 leaders.

Figure A-11 portrays the modern supervisor's challenge. Traditional supervisory training programs reflected assumptions that supervisors were Level 5 people charged with the responsibility for motivating Level 4 or Level 2 followers. The traditional supervisor performed the following duties:

- Set goals for subordinates and defined work methods;
- Trained subordinates in job skills;

- Established standards of performance;
- Evaluated and critiqued the performances of subordinates;
- Disciplined incorrect behavior and set examples;
- Motivated through strong leadership and persuasion;
- Developed and installed new methods;
- Gave career guidance to subordinates; and
- Praised achievements and punished failures.

Although people at Stages 2 and 4 tend to acquiesce to this traditional leadership style, people at Stages 3, 5, 6, and 7 rebel—openly or covertly. Moreover, because Stage 2 people are often identified with Stage 3 egocentrics, they often emulate Stage 3 behavior. As a result, the leadership repertoire of supervisors must be broadened to enable them to deal with the whole spectrum of value systems.

Value conflicts are not resolved simply by adopting the clothing and language of a cultural fad. Such conflicts can be ameliorated only by learning to operate with "people power" rather than "boss power." Traditional Level 4 or 5 managers who have used boss power must learn to apply systems and supervisory techniques that are compatible with all value systems. This means learning how to let talent find free and constructive expression.

CAN EVERY EMPLOYEE BE A MANAGER?

The question is sometimes raised, "Is it possible for a security or self-oriented person to become a manager of his or her job?" The answer is a qualified "yes," provided the definition of *manager* refers to the process of managing a job within the limitations established by the individual's capabilities and aspirations. In a real sense, each person manages his or her own life away from the workplace. The opportunity for self-management on the job is but an extension of this responsibility. Just as the individual in the home and community learns to manage within the legal, moral, financial, and social constraints imposed by society, he or she is potentially capable of performing within the constraints of the workplace.

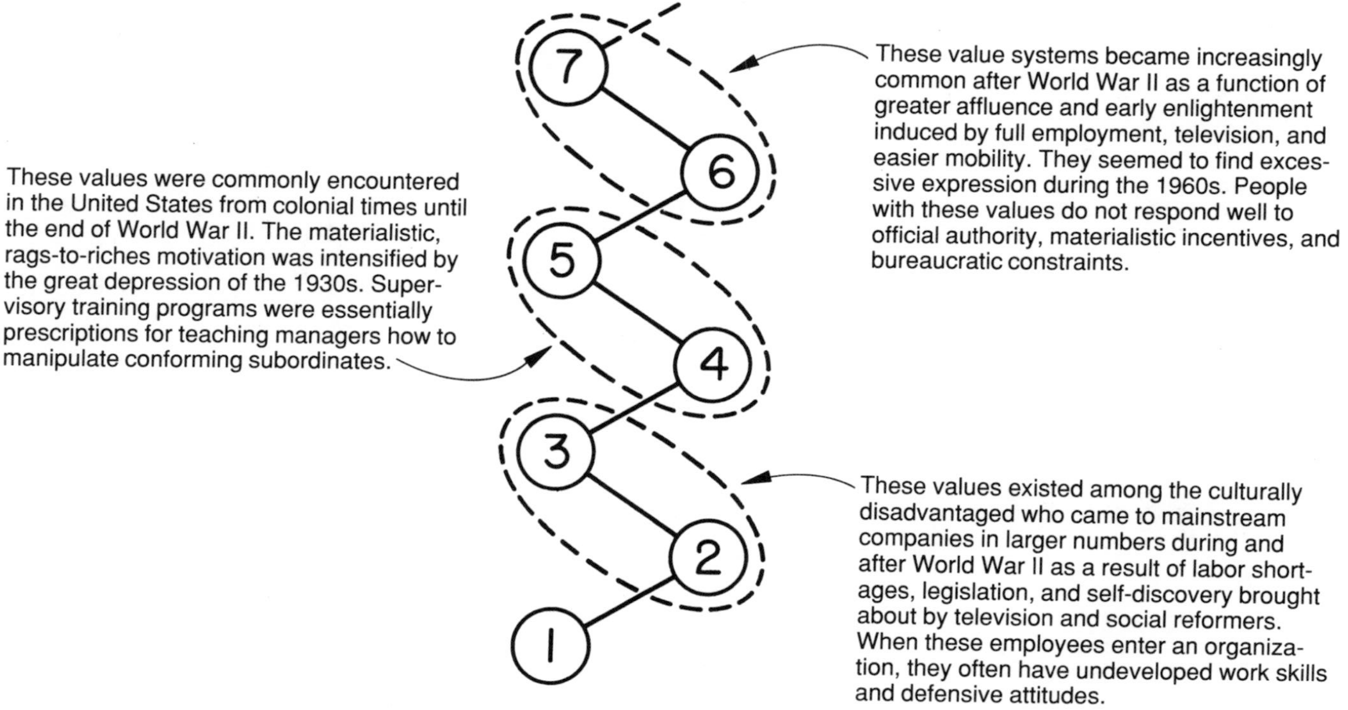

These value systems became increasingly common after World War II as a function of greater affluence and early enlightenment induced by full employment, television, and easier mobility. They seemed to find excessive expression during the 1960s. People with these values do not respond well to official authority, materialistic incentives, and bureaucratic constraints.

These values existed among the culturally disadvantaged who came to mainstream companies in larger numbers during and after World War II as a result of labor shortages, legislation, and self-discovery brought about by television and social reformers. When these employees enter an organization, they often have undeveloped work skills and defensive attitudes.

These values were commonly encountered in the United States from colonial times until the end of World War II. The materialistic, rags-to-riches motivation was intensified by the great depression of the 1930s. Supervisory training programs were essentially prescriptions for teaching managers how to manipulate conforming subordinates.

Figure A-11. The Supervisor's Challenge.

Some individuals do not manage their own lives successfully in the home and community and seem to require occasional rescue by friends, family, welfare agencies, and counselors. However, the help that they receive from these protectors is often dispensed in a paternalistic Parent-Child style that fosters and perpetuates dependency relationships and incompetence. By the same token, these same individuals, when in the workplace, cannot be made responsible through the Parent-Child use of permissiveness, coercion, paternalism, threats, persuasion, and manipulation. If ever these people are to become responsibly self-reliant, it will be through the influence of Adult-Adult leadership. Indeed, learning to be responsible in the workplace could influence their life styles away from the job.

However, just as some people choose complex or simple life styles away from the job, so do individuals differ in their preferred vocational roles on the job. At one extreme, some desire complex and continuously challenging jobs; at the other extreme, employees prefer simple, routine tasks. However complex or simple the job, the incumbents have one desire in common: the freedom to choose the kind of work they prefer and to relate to it in a way that is compatible with their personal values. Hence, the concept *every employee a manager* can have meaning for people at all psychological levels, though the preferred job-management roles of employees may differ significantly in terms of complexity and difficulty.

Differences among individuals regarding their preferred job roles become understandable when examined in terms of the levels of psychological existence described earlier. Such a framework helps to explain why and how people differ in their choice of vocational roles and in their life styles away from the job.

As humans grow out of the reactive stage of infancy, they develop peer relationships that tend to be characterized by ritual, common attitudes, solidarity, conformity in dress code, and subservience to "tribal chieftains." During childhood older siblings, dominant associates, parents, television personalities, clergymen, teachers, and police officers become the usual tribal chieftains. If this tribalistic value orientation carries over into adult life in the workplace, the supervisor or union leader becomes the authority figure looked up to for direction, protection, discipline, and affirmation. Being a manager of a job at this psychological level means pleasing the supervisor by carrying out duties that he or she has prescribed or by obeying a union leader. The delegation of planning and controlling functions to a person is a valued vote of confidence from the tribal chieftain. Having a whole job is intrinsically satisfying, but, more importantly, doing it well earns praise from the boss.

The self-oriented person is often expelled from the work force as a troublemaker, and sometimes the baby is thrown out with the bath water when the creative talent of such a person is not constructively harnessed. To the traditional supervisor the concept *every employee a manager* seems unattainable for people at this stage of development. However, self-management is an appealing concept to self-oriented people, and their defiant behavior is merely an irresponsible expression of their desire to escape regimentation and to be self-reliant. Adult-Adult supervision, peer pressure, and a joint stake in the success of the organization has the potential for giving constructive expression to such talent.

The traditional person often has a procedure-manual mentality—an attitude not associated with the initiative and self-reliance of a manager. However, extremes in conformity behavior are usually a function of extremes in suppressed talent. Paradoxically, the official prescription of a more creative role along with mechanisms for managing innovation (such as JIT/VAM, described in Chapter 3) may begin unfreezing conformist behavior. When these people feel an obligation to manage their own jobs (because they have been told to do so by an accepted authority figure), they will tackle their new roles with the zeal of crusaders, even to the extent of bending the rules a bit. Furthermore, managing a meaningful job may ultimately dissipate the bonds of tradition, in which case the individual may evolve to other stages of psychological existence.

Success-oriented personalities respond naturally and enthusiastically to the opportunity to manage their own responsibilities. These people desire and expect that they will manage their own jobs, resent supervisory intervention, and are intolerant of constraints imposed by policies and procedures. Perhaps the primary shortcoming of the success-oriented personality is a tendency to be excessively competitive and to be insensitive to the needs of other people who also wish to be responsible.

The people-oriented personality can also relate enthusiastically to the *every-employee-a-manager* concept. However, it is essential that sociocentrics who see themselves as part of a counterculture fully understand organizational goals and constraints. Although their informality and sometimes unkempt appearance may be disconcerting to a traditional manager, they are capable of productive effort in a climate of approval, provided they are not involved with the production of what they may see as harmful products, such as weapons, tobacco, or pesticides. Managing their own jobs is appealing to them, particularly when they can relate to supervisors on a first-name basis and are free to experience solidarity with other members of the work force.

Reality-oriented personality types are by definition already in charge of their lives, and the opportunity to manage their jobs is a natural extension of their life styles. They are goal-oriented people whose behavior seems to say, "O.K., I understand the job to be done; now leave me alone and let me do it in my way." Self-management is the only acceptable condition of employment for these workers. If deprived of this opportunity, they are likely to leave the organization or to become preoccupied with personal goals on company time.

In summary, *every employee a manager* is a universally applicable concept but one that depends on appropriate job conditions for its fullest implementation. Every individual has the potential for managing some jobs but not all jobs. However, every person has the potential for managing certain components of any job or combinations of several jobs. The realization of this potential depends on matching each employee's talents and aspirations with the appropriate job, particularly if the employee has an influential role in the matching process. The term *job* in this case refers not only to the work itself but also to procedural constraints, peer relationships, style of supervision, and other climate factors in the workplace.

REFERENCES

Argyris, C. (1964). *Integrating the individual and the organization*. New York: John Wiley.

Argyris, C. (1965). *Organization and innovation*. Homewood, IL: Richard D. Irwin.

Bennis, W. (1966). *Changing organizations*. New York: McGraw-Hill.

Blake, R., & Mouton, J. (1968). *Corporate excellence through grid organizational development*. Houston, TX: Gulf.

Fromm, E. (1941). *Escape from freedom*. Fort Worth, TX: Holt, Rinehart & Winston.

Galbraith, J.K. (1958). *The affluent society*. Boston, MA: Houghton Mifflin.

Gardner, J. (1964). *Self Renewal*. New York: Sterling Lord Literistic.

Glasser, W. (1965). *Reality therapy*. New York: Harper & Row.

Graves, C. (1970). Levels of existence: An open system theory of values. *Journal of Humanistic Psychology, 10*(2).

Hall, J., O'Leary, V., & Williams, M. (1964, Winter). The decision-making grid: A model of decision-making styles. *California Management Review*

Herzberg, F. (1966). *Work and the nature of man*. Cleveland, OH: World.

Lewin, K. (1969). Quasi-stationary social equilibria and the problem of permanent change. In W.G. Bennis, K.D. Benne, and R. Chin (Eds.), *The planning of change* (pp. 235-238). New York: Holt, Rinehart, Winston.

Likert, R. (1967). *The human organization*. New York: McGraw-Hill.

Maslow, A.H. (1968). *Toward a psychology of being* (2nd ed.). New York: Van Nostrand.

Mayo, E. (1933). *The human problems of an industrial civilization*. New York: Macmillan.

McClelland, D. (1961). *The achieving society*. New York: Van Nostrand.

McGregor, D. (1967). *The professional manager*. New York: McGraw-Hill.

Myers, M.S. (1966, January-February). Conditions for manager motivation. *Harvard Business Review*.

Myers, M.S. & Myers, S.S. (1973, Winter). Adapting to the new work ethic. *Business Quarterly*.

Paré, J. (1968, April). What's your power structure? *Canadian Business*.

APPENDIX B

Waste Analysis

Definitions of Waste

Waste is anything other than the minimum amount of equipment, materials, parts, space, and work time essential to add value to the product. What does not add value is waste.

1. Processing

Ineffective methods for doing a job, requiring excessive use of labor or operations unnecessary for meeting product or service requirements.

2. Overproduction

Producing goods or services over and above amounts required by consumers.

3. Delays

Unproductive time waiting for supplies, equipment, repairs, or other people.

4. Defects

Faulty product or service causing low quality, scrap, rework, repair, or customer dissatisfaction.

5. Motion

Activities, such as looking for or repairing tools, that do not add value to a product or service; activities resulting from poor methods or caused by inconvenient placement of tools, equipment, and supplies.

6. Inventory

Excessive raw materials, work in process, or finished goods that increase the cost of handling or that require extra space or paperwork, increased interest charges, or more employees or that lead to deterioration, obsolescence, inflexibility, delayed defect detection, or increased lead time.

7. Transportation

Unnecessarily distant, indirect, or redundant routes traveled by people, supplies, paperwork, and products.

8. Talent

Underutilization of people as a result of factors beyond the employee's control, such as work rules, poor job design, peer pressure, or failure of leaders to create opportunities for initiative and productivity.

Underutilization as a result of factors within the employee's control, such as the unwillingness of people to improve themselves and to assume greater responsibility; sometimes caused by low self-esteem, lack of initiative, or other overriding interests.

Waste Examples

Give an example of each of the eight kinds of waste in a shop and in an office.

	SHOP	OFFICE
1. Processing		
2. Overproduction		
3. Delays		
4. Defects		
5. Motion		
6. Inventory		
7. Transportation		
8. Talent		

Waste Profile

Rate your workplace in terms of the eight measures of waste. Circle a number on each scale; to obtain your score, add all the numbers that you have circled.

1. PROCESSING

0   1   2   3   4   5   6   7   8   9   10

Redundant, nonproductive operations

No unnecessary operations

2. OVERPRODUCTION

0   1   2   3   4   5   6   7   8   9   10

Production exceeds customer demand

Just-in-time production to customer demand

3. DELAYS

0   1   2   3   4   5   6   7   8   9   10

Much idle, nonproductive time

Productive effort synchronized with process flow

4. DEFECTS

0   1   2   3   4   5   6   7   8   9   10

Numerous errors, scrap, and rework

Zero defects through SPC or other measures

5. MOTION

0	1	2	3	4	5	6	7	8	9	10

Most motions add cost   Most motions add value

6. INVENTORY

0	1	2	3	4	5	6	7	8	9	10

Excessive inventory: RM,   Low Inventory: RM, WIP,
WIP, FG*   FG

7. TRANSPORTATION

0	1	2	3	4	5	6	7	8	9	10

Long distances and wasteful   Short distances and efficient
routing   routing

8. TALENT

0	1	2	3	4	5	6	7	8	9	10

People working far below   People utilizing their full
capabilities   potential

Total Score _____

---

*Raw materials, work in progress, and finished goods.

APPENDIX C ✗

JIT/VAM Learning Instrument

The following multiple-choice questions are based on various opinions and facts about JIT/VAM management philosophy and techniques. Answer these questions to the best of your ability, and be prepared to review and discuss your responses. Do not be discouraged if you do not know all the answers. No one has ever answered them all correctly. In fact, some questions do not have "correct" answers; the responses are simply a matter of opinion. You may complete the questionnaire individually or in groups. Your papers will not be collected nor will you be graded on your answers. The purpose of these questions is to identify topics to be clarified.

1. **SMED is an acronym for**
   a. Simulated Manufacturing with Electronic Data.
   b. Setup Maximization Empirically Derived.
   c. Single Minute Exchange of Die.
   d. Simplified Manufacturing through Employee Decisions.

2. **Setups apply to which of the following operations?**
   a. Processing
   b. Inspection
   c. Transporting
   d. Storage
   e. Cocktails

3. **External die change (OED) refers to setups**
   a. Engineered outside the organization.
   b. Prepared while operation is in process.
   c. That can be performed only when operation is stopped.
   d. Engineered by outside consultants.

e. Prepared outside normal working hours.

4. Internal die change (IED) refers to setups

a. That can be performed only when operation is stopped.

b. Engineered within the organization.

c. Performed by machine operator.

d. Conducted while operation is in process.

e. Conducted during regular working hours.

5. What is the impact of each of the following operations?

	Add Value	Add Cost
a. Counting it	( )	( )
b. Moving it	( )	( )
c. Improving it	( )	( )
d. Expediting it	( )	( )
e. Eliminating it	( )	( )
f. Searching for it	( )	( )
g. Storing it	( )	( )
h. Simplifying it	( )	( )
i. Inspecting it	( )	( )

6. Work Simplification espouses which of the following principles?

a. Every job is capable of being improved.

b. If it works, try to improve it.

c. If it works, don't try to change it.

d. The ultimate improvement is to eliminate the task altogether.

e. Work Simplification works best when it is tied to a paid suggestion system.

7. The five-step pattern in Work Simplification includes which of the following? (Number 1 through 5 in the order they are applied):

a. [ ] Locate your quality problems.

b. [ ] Select a job to improve.

c. [ ] Locate batches of excess inventory.

d. [ ] Get all the facts.

e. [ ] Check with your customers.

f. [ ] Develop the preferred method.

g. [ ] Challenge every detail.

h. [ ] Establish problem-solving teams.

i. [ ] Install it and check results.

8. **Match flow-process symbols (□ △ ○ D ⇦) with the processes below.**

a. Store   _____

b. Transport   _____

c. Delay   _____

d. Inspect   _____

e. Change   _____

9. **JIT/VAM production management includes**

a. Inventory-control system.

b. Quality and scrap control.

c. Streamlined plant layout to raise process yield.

d. Production-line balancing approach.

e. Employee involvement and motivation.

f. Gaining early commitment from suppliers.

10. **Which staff functions might require fewer people under JIT/VAM?**

a. Maintenance

b. Production Control

c. Materials Management

d. Quality Assurance

e. Design Engineering

11. **Which functions might require more involvement under JIT/VAM?**

a. Industrial Engineering

b. Purchasing

c. Accounting

d. Manufacturing Engineering

e. Design Engineering

12. **Invisible inventory refers to**

    a. Paperwork.
    b. Reprocessed waste.
    c. Inventory lost through shrinkage.
    d. Material in warehouse storage.
    e. Inventory en route from supplier.

13. **Which functions should be actively involved in JIT/VAM?**

    a. Personnel
    b. Manufacturing
    c. R & D
    d. Sales
    e. Purchasing
    f. Accounting
    g. Data Processing
    h. Maintenance

14. **The more informed operators are, the more likely they are to have ideas for**

    a. Controlling defects.
    b. Improving delivery performance.
    c. Increasing the levels of management.
    d. Cutting setup time.
    e. Reducing operating expenses.

15. **Legitimate excuses for not using JIT/VAM include**

    a. Uncooperative suppliers.
    b. Delay production.
    c. Unavailability of software.
    d. Lose control of inventory.
    e. Low-volume operation.
    f. Job-shop batch operations.
    g. Doing O.K. without it.
    h. Opposed by union contract.
    i. All of the above.
    j. None of the above.

16. **Which of the following SMED concepts are advanced by Shigeo Shingo?**

   a. The most important step in implementing SMED is distinguishing between internal and external setups.

   b. Normal setup times can usually be reduced from 30 to 50 percent by separating internal and external procedures.

   c. If new perspectives are adopted, operations performed on internal setups can often be converted to external setups.

   d. Once internal and external setups are clearly distinguished, each can usually be shortened by further streamlining.

   e. Setup changes should allow defect-free products to be produced from the very start.

   f. The ideal setup change is no change at all.

   g. It is important to cut setup times, to diminish lot sizes, and to even loads simultaneously.

   h. The SMED system is the most effective method for achieving just-in-time production.

   i. Setup is the key to moving toward future technologies— robotics and advanced automation.

   j. Machines can be idle; workers must not be.

   k. If you can't figure out how to do something, talk it over with your machines.

17. **The economic-lot concept lost its justification with the development of**

   a. SPC   b. MRP   c. SMED   d. FMS   e. SQC

18. **The goal of the company is to**

   a. Keep inventory low.
   b. Make money.
   c. Capture a larger share of the market.
   d. Make high-quality products.
   e. Reduce operating expenses.
   f. Keep as many people employed as possible.

19. Classify each of the constraining conditions

	Leadership	Logistical	Behavioral	Environmental
a. Limitations in material, time, space, equipment ....( )	( )	( )	( )
b. Careless or counter-productive behavior ....( )	( )	( )	( )
c. Outside factors such as govern-ment, union, weather, and economy ....( )	( )	( )	( )
d. Managerial attitudes, assumptions, policies, business strategies ....( )	( )	( )	( )

20. Before investing in new equipment

a. Consider alternative manufacturing methods.

b. Redesign product to off-load bottleneck.

c. Improve setup methods.

d. Improve yield.

e. Improve tools or gauges.

f. Train operators.

g. Reduce employees' wages.

h. Consider make vs. buy.

i. Incorporate special quality demands.

j. Improve preventive maintenance.

21. The manufacturing term *backflushing* means

a. Returning to the original manufacturing process.

b. Flushing out the rejects.

c. Subjecting the WIP to an acid wash.

d. Salvaging the unused work in process.

e. Deducting inventory in FG from the BOM.

22. *Burn-in* **is a manufacturing process to**

a. Test a product under stress conditions.

b. Cause a product to fail through simulated aging or stress conditions.

c. Stamp performance specs onto a product during manufacturing.

d. Accelerate the production rate to maximum capacity.

e. Crystallize a final production procedure.

23. Moving work stations closer together reduces several kinds of waste, including

a. Transit time.

b. Queue time.

c. Transit inventory.

d. Queuing inventory.

e. Space.

f. Defect detection.

g. Problem-solving barriers.

h. Communication and teamwork barriers.

24. JIT/VAM usually applies to

a. Product design.

b. Supplier development.

c. Raw-material receiving.

d. Production flow.

e. Preventive maintenance.

f. Space utilization.

g. Greater use of robots.

h. Inventory management.

i. Setup technology.

j. Eliminating time clocks.

k. Use of quality circles.

l. Bar coding.

m. Problem recognition.

n. Problem recording.

o. Problem solving.

p. Permissive management.

q. Reuseable containers.

r. FG distribution.

s. Goal setting.

t. Defect prevention.

u. Personal time off.

v. Operating expenses.

w. Teamwork.

x. Area management (housekeeping).

25. Area management (housekeeping) includes

a. Removal of everything from work area not immediately needed.

b. Removal of excess inventory and tools not in use.

c. Removal of personal effects and trash.

d. Removal of backup machines.

e. Keeping the floor and equipment free of dirt and dust.

f. Creating a special place for personal belongings.

g. Assigning specific work areas to individuals.

h. Painting a line around each person's area.

i. Following work rules.

j. Restricting operators to their areas.

k. Support shops such as tool rooms, die shops, and maintenance shops.

l. Maintaining production data.

26. Area management serves to

a. Improve quality.

b. Shorten setup times.

c. Streamline material flow.

d. Enhance morale.

e. Please customers.

f. Promote safety.

g. Keep track of tools.

h. Improve visibility of conditions.

27. **Shop-floor conditions and materials can be seen at a glance by visual controls such as**

a. Workplace organization.

b. Signal lights.

c. Dials and gauges.

d. Kanban systems.

e. Number of standard containers.

f. Halted conveyors.

g. Idle work stations.

h. Operator deployment.

28. **Lights can be used to signal**

a. Machine malfunctions.

b. Parts out of spec.

c. Out of parts.

d. Tool change needed.

e. Normal setup required.

f. Normal maintenance.

g. Supervisor required.

h. Coffee or lunch break.

i. Relief operator needed.

j. Anticipated problem.

29. **Methods for finding and eliminating problems include**

a. Ouija boards.

b. Pareto analysis.

c. Fishbone charts (CEDAC).

d. Identifying defect patterns in workpiece.

e. Identifying time patterns of defect occurrence.

f. Identifying malfunctioning tools or equipment.

g. Asking for advice from others.

30. **Cycle time refers to**

a. Amount of time material spends in house.

b. Time between units in repetitive manufacturing.

c. Amount of time an operator devotes to an operation.

d. Worker time plus idle time per operation.

e. The life cycle of a product.

31. **Compared with JIT/VAM processes now in widespread use, conventional manufacturing is wasteful in its approach to**

a. Quality.

b. Design.

c. Purchasing.

d. Job assignment.

e. Plant configuration.

f. Equipment selection.

g. Maintenance.

h. Scheduling.

i. Accounting.

j. Product-line development.

k. Material handling.

l. Material control.

m. Shop-floor control.

n. Employee motivation.

32. **Computer tracking of inventory under JIT/VAM conditions is unnecessary because**

a. The product spends less time in the plant.

b. Kanban batches constitute exact current inventory.

c. Lack of rework minimizes abnormal flow paths and times.

d. Counting of inventory is more efficiently done by operators.

e. Product flow is so short and disciplined that inventory is visible.

33. **Small job shops, which already resemble cellular manufacturing, usually gain little by rearranging equipment but can improve flexibility by**

a. Reducing setup times.

b. Becoming more rigorous in machine maintenance.

c. Splitting and overlapping lots.

d. Improving defect-detection techniques.

e. Chopping lead times through customer development.

f. Sharpening competitive-analysis capability.

g. Acquiring larger, more versatile equipment.

34. JIT/VAM and automation strategies are compatible, particularly if automation is in the form of piecemeal homemade devices, to

a. Measure.   g. Align.

b. Hold.   h. Orient.

c. Identify.   i. Pull forward.

d. Locate.   j. Protect.

e. Index.   k. Adjust.

f. Receive.   l. Record.

35. Smaller lots and inventories can lead to

a. Reduction of waste and rework.

b. Quality improvements.

c. Enhanced worker involvement.

d. Better process yield and productivity.

e. Operator anxiety about job security.

f. Increased awareness of causes of errors and delay.

g. Reduced operating expense.

36. The involvement of operators in setup reduction is encouraged by

a. Teaching them the simple principles of setup reduction.

b. Teaching them the techniques of motion & time charting and analysis.

c. Getting their ideas pertaining to procedures.

d. A climate of approval that allows them to apply new procedures.

e. Providing day-to-day guidance, coaching, & encouragement.

f. Recognizing individuals and groups for improvements.

g. Rewarding major contributors with a day off with pay.

37. MRP (Materials Requirements Planning) is a computer system with the following elements

a. A production schedule (what to make).
b. A bill of material (the parts required).
c. A routing plan (how to make it).
d. A shop schedule (production flow in the plant).
e. A capacity plan (how much capacity required).
f. A reliability index (estimated rejects).
g. On-hand inventory (what you have now).
h. New requirements (what you have to go out and get).

38. Lead time consists of which of the following elements? (Place an "M" in the bracket of the element that usually consumes the most time and an "L" after the element that takes the least time.)

a. Engineering design   [ ]
b. Production time   [ ]
c. Setup time   [ ]
d. Queue time   [ ]
e. Transit time   [ ]

39. A thoughtfully planned factory assures flexibility through a combination of

a. Increased use of MRP-type computer systems.
b. Simple, low-cost-dedicated machines.
c. Costly equipment capable of easy moving and rapid setup.
d. Versatile human effort.
e. Discouraging the decertification of labor unions.

40. Successful supplier development includes

a. Receiving deliveries on time.
b. Assuring high quality in purchasing material.
c. Having redundant suppliers.
d. Overcoming traditional adversary relationships.
e. Providing supplier training where necessary.

41. *Kanban,* a Japanese word meaning "card," is used to
    a. Signal the forward flow of inventory.
    b. Make a quick count of inventory.
    c. Prevent a pileup of WIPI.
    d. Signal a call for help.
    e. Facilitate defect detection.
    f. Help maintain an orderly workplace.

42. As lead times and buffer stocks are reduced, operations must move toward
    a. Shorter production runs.
    b. Fast changeovers.
    c. Tight process control.
    d. Total preventive maintenance.
    e. Frequent small deliveries.
    f. Synchronized scheduling.
    g. Smaller, more flexible equipment.
    h. Parallel equipment at bottlenecks.
    i. Arranging equipment into compact flow lines.

43. Which problems might be eliminated or reduced through JIT/VAM?
    a. Capacity constraints (bottlenecks)
    b. Too many models
    c. Improper parts transfers
    d. Quality problems
    e. Engineering changes
    f. Inventory shrinkage
    g. Labor problems
    h. Inaccurate bill of materials
    i. Inadequate training
    j. Poor vendor performance

44. If visiting a plant, what would you consider relevant to man- ufacturing excellence?

a. Flexible layout for flow of RM to FG

b. Evidence of cross-training

c. Balanced mix of people by gender, age, race, and so on

d. Evidence of operator initiative and influence

e. Visibility of problems and conditions

f. Evidence of quality-improvement efforts

g. Preventive maintenance

h. Producible product designs

i. Small lots or flexibility in process

j. Process capability

k. Clean and orderly work areas

l. Bottleneck management

m. Spirit or level of motivation

n. Fluid communication processes

o. System simplicity

45. Zero inventory is desired because of its direct or indirect impact on

a. Carrying costs—interest, storage, handling, and so on.

b. Identification of defects.

c. Facilitating engineering changes.

d. Due-date performance.

e. Investment per unit.

f. Margins.

g. Forecast validity.

h. Cash flow.

i. Return on investment.

j. Net profit.

Index

346 Every Employee a Manager

Training and development, 261
  pitfalls, 261
  through the management
    process, 262
Translation of theory to practice,
  286
Two-class system, 141

UAW (United Auto Workers), 66,
  133, 134
Union action, unwitting sabotage,
  190
Union rights, 188
United Steel Workers, 45
Uris, Auren, ix
U.S. Department of Labor, 272

Vaill, Peter B., 130, 152
Values, a supervisory challenge,
  319
  by psychological level, 314, 315
  guidelines for compatibility, 313,
    316, 317, 320, 321
  people and systems, 314, 315
VAM (value-adding-manage-
  ment), vii, 47
Versatility, 59
Visual controls, 59
Vroom, Victor H., 90, 97

Walker, Charles R., 129, 130, 152,
  191, 202
Waste, definitions of, 325, 326, 329
  eight kinds of, 47
  examples worksheet, 327
  profile worksheet, 328, 329
Weber, Max, 128
Weed, Earl, 273
When work is fun, 103
Why play is fun, 101, 102
Williams, Martha, 290, 322
Win-lose adversary, 133
Win-lose adversary relationships,
  132, 190, 192
Win-lose adversary (stage 1), 263
Work, historical perspective, 124,
  125
Work ethic, religious underpin-
  nings, 126, 127
Work improvement principles, 231
Work in America Institute, 68, 135,
  151
Work itself, 123
Work simplification, vii, 42, 227
  case study, 228-235
  five-step pattern, 231
  underlying assumptions, 229
World class manufacturing, 53

X-bar charts, 55